GREAT MARQUES OF GERMANY

conrero
RICAMBI ORIGINALI OPEL
MICHELIN
OPEL
1

WURTH Racing
JURID
31

39

JENS WINTHER
Castrol
Castrol

Great Marques Of Germany

Compiled and edited by Jonathan Wood
Foreword by Professor Dr. Ferdinand Porsche

Viscount Books

This edition published 1989 by
Viscount Books
an imprint of the Octopus Publishing Group
Michelin House
81 Fulham Road
London SW3 6RB

ISBN 1 600 56443 6

Produced by Mandarin Offset
22a Westlands Road
Quarry Bay, Hong Kong

Printed and Bound in Hong Kong

PAGE 1, TOP TO BOTTOM, LEFT TO RIGHT *The badges of Audi, Mercedes-Benz, BMW, Opel, Porsche and Volkswagen.*

PAGES 2–3 *Opel Ascona, Volkswagen Scirocco, Mercedes-Benz 230SL, Porsche 936, BMW M1, Audi Quattro.*

THIS PAGE *Audi Quattro, Porsche 924 Turbo, BMW 628 CSi, Mercedes-Benz W124 series, Opel Corsa, Volkswagen Golf GTI.*

The chapters on BMW, Mercedes-Benz and Porsche originally appeared in the Great Marques series published by Octopus Books Limited. These sections have been abridged and updated. The BMW section was written by Jeremy Walton, Mercedes-Benz by Roger Bell and Porsche by Chris Harvey. These have been edited by Jonathan Wood. All other sections were written by Jonathan Wood.

The publishers would like to thank Audi, Volkswagen and Opel for permission to reproduce their logos. The three-pointed star used in the Mercedes-Benz section is a registered trademark which is the property of Daimler-Benz AG of Stuttgart, Federal Republic of Germany, and has been reproduced with their permission. The BMW logo is the copyright of BMW AG of Munich, Federal Republic of Germany, and has also been reproduced with their permission.

This book is dedicated to my wife, Rosemary Wood.

CONTENTS

The German automobile industry is spread across the country, from Emden in the north to München in the south. The creation of East Germany in 1945 seriously affected the German manufacturers, particularly BMW and Auto Union.

FOREWORD

The name of Porsche is closely bound up with the history of the German car. Porsche has built up a worldwide reputation as a manufacturer of particularly fast and reliable sports cars and, of course, successful racers, and in so doing has contributed greatly to the excellent image of German automobiles. And in his creation of the Volkswagen – built in the largest numbers to date of any of the world's cars – my father, Professor Ferdinand Porsche, helped towards the unparallelled triumphant progress of the car in general.

Without the VW Beetle it would not have been possible to give the German public its new and hitherto unknown degree of mobility so quickly. The Beetle has made people more independent; it has also imprinted the concept 'Made in Germany' around the world and laid the foundations for the prestige German companies in general enjoy today.

Ferdinand Porsche was in fact involved in German automotive history at a much earlier date. As a designer with Auto Union he, with others, created successful racing cars; and during his time at Daimler-Benz, famous sports cars and world record breakers were brought into being. Today Porsche is again creating and constructing for other companies. As Germany's smallest car firm we turn out a specialist product that the others do not build. As we have no competition in any real sense, those other German manufacturers come to us as customers.

At our Development Centre at Weissach, near Stuttgart, we are therefore continuing the tradition begun many years ago by my father: a design office for everyone.

Ferdinand Porsche

INTRODUCTION

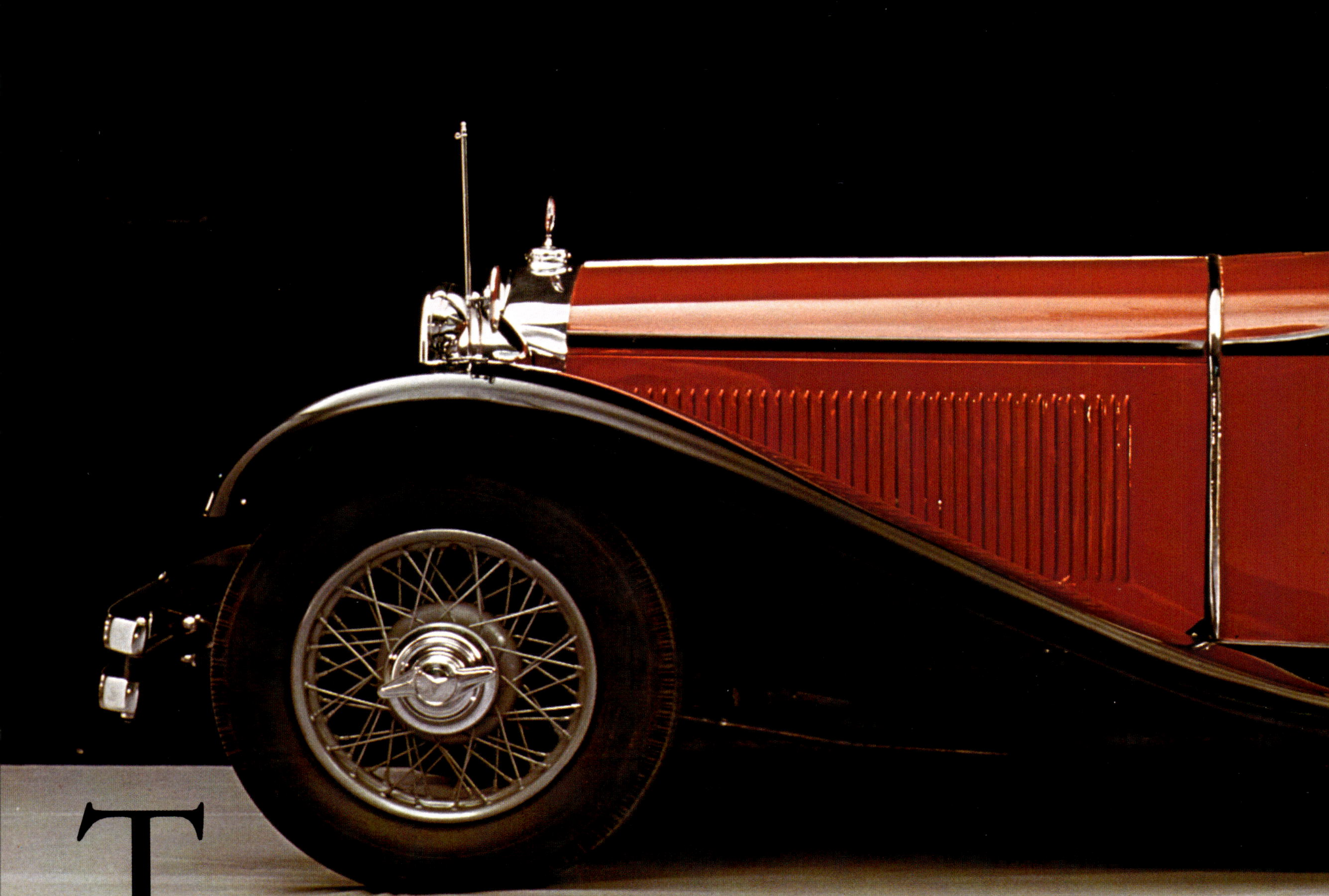

Today's German motor industry, the third largest in the world behind Japan and America, has an enviable reputation for quality, engineering refinement and innovation. Yet, as will emerge in this book, it has not always been so. There was a time in the 1920s when German cars were distinguished, with a few exceptions, by a universal dullness. But it was in the following decade that the country's pioneering enterprise was rekindled, providing a momentum that continues to this day.

The motor car, as is well known, was born in Germany, and the industry's foundations were laid on the pioneering efforts of Carl Benz and Gottlieb Daimler. Both were able to benefit from a carefully orchestrated programme of colleges and universities funded by the German States—unity did not come until 1871—specifically geared to the industrial needs of the day. By the end of the 19th century Germany would be able to boast the finest system of technical education in the world. It was the provision of such facilities that permitted Benz, whose engine-driver father had died of pneumonia when he was a child, to attend, in 1860, the Karlsruhe polytechnic.

Such a scientific rather than a purely empirical grounding, as was mostly the case in Britain, provided a buoyant technological environment in Germany in the 1880s which not only gave birth to the automobile but was also to see the country attain world leadership in the fields of chemistry and electrical engineering. Benz and Daimler's efforts for the motor car were to see established a lasting tradition for innovation within the German automobile industry based on the informed approach of its engineers, who also enjoyed a high social standing within their communities.

Benz was set on producing a self-propelled vehicle, and did so in 1886, while Daimler was intent on manufacturing a self-contained power unit, but the duo differed from their ingenious and often isolated predecessors who trod similar paths in that their efforts triggered the creation of the world's motor industry. But, while Benz obstinately stuck to his original single-cylinder belt-driven design—albeit with some commercial success—Daimler forged ahead with a new two-cylinder high-speed engine in 1892, fitted with a jet carburet-

ABOVE *Mercedes-Benz of the 1930s: The Mannheim 370S. It had a 3.7-litre six-cylinder engine.*

tor but with, ironically, archaic hot tube ignition. Further German refinements came in the shape of the low-tension magneto, conceived by Robert Bosch and used by Daimler in 1898, followed by a high-tension unit in 1902 which soon gained widespread popularity throughout the world.

Yet another landmark in the evolution of the Daimler company's designs was the arrival, in 1901, of the Mercedes model, named after the daughter of diplomat Emil Jellinek. The car stood head and shoulders above its contemporaries because of its effective use of design features which were not in themselves new but which combined to set the pattern for car design for many years to come. The 5.9-litre four-cylinder engine boasted mechanically operated rather than atmospheric inlet valves and jet carburettors actuated by a throttle control. Any cooling problems were alleviated by the fitment of a forward-mounted honeycomb radiator, while the gear lever operated within a visible gate and there was a coil spring clutch, although drive was still by chain. Daimler soon adopted the Mercedes name for all its models.

Birth of the Opel

Diametrically opposed in concept to the efforts of Benz and Daimler, yet destined to be immensely successful, was the Opel company's entry into the motor car business. The firm produced its first car in 1898 and, after a hesitant start, went on to become Germany's largest vehicle maker, and eventually Europe's; a position it was to hold until the outbreak of the Second World War. Where Opel—already a successful sewing-machine and bicycle manufacturer—differed from the famous pioneers was in that, from the very outset of its excursion into car production, the company showed little interest in original design but displayed talents in streamlining and improving the manufacturing process. Therefore the original Opels were based on the Lutzmann car and subsequently Darracq was the inspiration. And then Citroën's car design was surprisingly plagiarized, of which more later.

However, an exception to this rule was the racing cars that Opel produced in pre-First World War days although it was an era dominated by Mercedes, which among all the German manufacturers made most impact abroad. A Mercedes won the prestigious French Grand Prix in 1908 with Benz cars in second and third places. Another event was not held until 1912, and in this and the following year French Peugeots took the chequered flag. But the 1914 Grand Prix, held just a month before the outbreak of the First World War, saw Mercedes achieve its greatest victory with a one-two-three win for the cars from Stuttgart and a Peugeot relegated to fourth place. The engines of the winning cars reflected the Daimler company's growing expertise in the aero-engine field, echoed by the use of light, welded-on steel cylinder jackets, and valves actuated by a single overhead camshaft and rockers.

The First World War produced its terrible social convulsions and technological advances. But with Germany's defeat in 1918 this new engineering was not, in the main, passed on to the motorist. The exception was the supercharger, developed by Daimler for aviation and submarine engine use and offered for the first time on the 1922, rather clumsily titled, 10/40/65, the last two figures relating to the engine's horsepower output in blown and unblown form. It was the first car in the world to be offered with the facility, but it was very much the exception to the rule. Most German cars of the 1920s were dull, unadventurous designs that in many respects featured pre-war thinking. This was in part due to the financial and political upheavals that marked the Weimar Republic's early post-war years which were compounded by the 1923 inflation, when the mark's value plummeted to an astounding 18 billion to the pound. The stability which came with the creation of the Reichsmark in 1924 was to last until 1929. But even then the German industry was small by European standards, since the market was flooded by American imports and the country's car makers were forced to subjugate their undoubted talents and mirror Detroit styles in their own products.

One manufacturer—Opel—was to beat the Americans at their own game by aping Henry Ford's production methods and one-model policy to emerge in the 1920s as Germany's largest car maker. In the terrible 1923 inflation year Opel built just 910 cars, but such was its growth that, by 1927, the figure had spiralled to 42,771. The Rüsselsheim firm had found an ideal model by copying the 5 CV Citröen, almost nut for nut, but the straightforward, cheap car was well suited to the times and was soon to evolve into a popular range.

The first BMWs

It was in 1928 that another distinguished name joined the ranks of Germany's car makers. This was the Munich-based Bavarian Motor Works (BMW) that had rapidly expanded its aero-engine business during the First World War and in 1923, while temporarily prevented from manufacturing these products by the terms of the Versailles Treaty, had diversified into motorcycle production. In October 1928 it purchased the Eisenach Vehicle Factory, which had bought the manufacturing rights of the British Austin Seven. It was a timely buy, for in 1928 the Eisenach plant had built 4915 cars, its largest figure to date, and the 748 cc model was an ideal vehicle with which to weather the bleak Depression years. In 1930 no less than 6792 examples of the 3/15, as the Seven was known, were sold, and in 1932, the very worst of the economic crisis, 2886 were produced. But BMW soon turned its back on the archaic Seven and at the 1933 Berlin Motor Show revealed a new generation of cars. Of all the models produced by BMW at Eisenach in the 1930s, the 328 two-seater of 1936 was one of the finest sports cars of its day. The bodywork—with its integral headlights, cowled radiator and spatted rear wheels—reflected the growing aerodynamic awareness in the German motor industry of the day. The chassis was tubular with transverse leaf independent front suspension, brakes were hydraulic, and rack-and-pinion steering was employed. But the 328's *tour de force* was its 1971 cc six-cylinder engine, cheaply evolved from a touring unit. For to obtain the benefits of a hemispherical combustion chamber and inclined valves, but without the cost or complication of overhead camshafts, engineer Fritz Fiedler came up with an ingenious solution. The new aluminium cylinder head had its inlet valves directly operated by the existing side camshaft, but the exhaust ones opposite were actuated by rockers and short pushrods running *across* the head and all operated from the one camshaft. The engine developed 80 bhp and gave the 328 a very respectable top speed of 152 km/h (95 mph). Not only this, but the design was to endure until the 1960s.

If BMW managed to weather the Depression years successfully, then the same could not be said for the car companies that combined in 1932 to produce the Auto Union alliance. It had been in 1928 that the DKW motorcycle concern, which was about to enter the car market with a cheap two-stroke, took over the ailing Audi company of Zwickau. This had been founded in 1909 by August Horch, who only five years previously had moved the Horch car company to the same town and had left the firm following a disagreement with his co-directors. However, he left Audi in 1920 and thereafter the

RIGHT *BMW's classic 1936–40 328, from the company's collection.*

firm's fortunes declined, although Horch fared rather better with a line of well-engineered straight-eights. Despite this, in 1932 Horch joined the already allied DKW and Audi companies, while the fourth member of the automotive quartet was the Wanderer company which was also Saxony based. Auto Union was therefore able to offer a wide variety of models, following some modest rationalization. Most popular of the range were the two-stroke DKWs, which boasted front-wheel drive from 1931 and were destined to be strong sellers throughout the decade. By contrast, Audi also used this system but the 1933 Front was a poor seller. Wanderer looked after the middle ground, while the stately and commodious Horches continued to sell in small but consistent numbers. Although all these cars displayed the combine's *Vier Ringe* emblem on their radiators, the Auto Union name did not appear on any of the cars—with one glorious exception. This was the fabled mid-engined Grand Prix racing car, which was just one of the projects made possible by the arrival, on 30 January 1933, of Adolf Hitler as Germany's chancellor.

The Nazi party, which Hitler headed, had come to power in the wake of the country's economic collapse, triggered by the American Wall Street Crash. Unemployment soared and reached a staggering 7.5 million in 1932, and Hitler swept to power denouncing the Versailles peace treaty and blaming international communism and Jewry as the cause of the country's ills. With the reins of power in his hands, Hitler immediately implemented a programme of *Autobahn* (motorway) construction and supported Daimler-Benz and the new Auto Union combine with their racing car development.

The great racers

The racing era of 1934 to '37 has been rightly titled The Years of the Titans, with the silver cars from Germany displaying enormous advances in suspension, engine development and streamlining and, after a shaky start, sweeping all before them. It was much the same story in the succeeding 1938 to '40 3-litre formula, with the momentum cut short only by the outbreak of the Second World War.

Ferdinand Porsche had been responsible for the overall design of Auto Union's mid-engined racer, and he also has the Volkswagen, another Hitlerian preoccupation, to his credit. He was approached by the German chancellor to take on the project in late 1933 and began work on it the following year. Hitler had stipulated that the car's price should not exceed RM 1000 (£86) and that it should be air cooled. Fortunately, Porsche had already completed a rear-engined design for NSU and this represented a starting point for the project. Consequently, the body and chassis designs were resolved relatively speedily, but Porsche believed that the price constraint would demand a two-cylinder engine. Numerous variations proved unsatisfactory and it was not until 1936 that a cheap four-cylinder *boxermotor* (horizontally opposed engine) was standardized. Had it not been for this delay the Volkswagen could have been in production by 1939. The entire design was finalized by 1938 but the car did not reach fruition until the post-war years.

In 1932 Germany had produced a mere 44,232 cars, but by 1938 this figure had rocketed to 276,592 and the country was fast catching up Britain as Europe's largest automobile manu-

facturer. Much of the credit for this expansion can be placed with Opel, which by 1938 was the Continent's principal vehicle producer. The firm had been bought in 1929 by the mighty American General Motors Corporation and output had soared from 1933 onwards. The 1935 Olympia was a technological milestone, as it was Germany's first mass-produced unitary construction car and the Rüsselsheim plant was the country's most up-to-date car factory. Ford had also followed General Motors into Germany but, instead of buying an existing manufacturer, established its own plant, at Cologne, in 1931.

The outbreak of the Second World War, following Hitler's invasion of Poland in 1939, saw the car makers take up war work to a greater and lesser extent. Despite the outbreak of hostilities, a BMW 328 coupé won the 1940 Italian Mille Miglia and the first KdF-Wagen, as the Volkswagen had been renamed, left the production line of its purpose-built factory near Hanover, although none were to reach the general public during the following five years. Germany's 1945 defeat also saw its motor industry in ruins. The Daimler-Benz factories had been almost obliterated, and the same fate had overtaken Opel's Rüsselsheim plant. BMW's Munich aero-engine works was also suffering from war damage, and this also applied to the Volkswagen factory at the newly named Wolfsburg community. A number of car firms had disappeared behind the Iron Curtain: all Auto Union's factories were in East Germany and so was BMW's Eisenach works where automobile production had been concentrated before the war.

The post-war Beetle

It was the Volkswagen, tirelessly perfected in the 1930s and now ready for manufacture, that constituted Germany's only car production in 1945. Located in the British military zone, the works was run under the auspices of the Royal Electrical and Mechanical Engineers. The car and its factory could have been taken as reparations booty by any of the victorious Allies, and Britain even commissioned a report on the VW. But the appraisal failed to appreciate the ingenuity of the Porsche design. Then, in the autumn of 1947, REME appointed Heinz Nordhoff, a former Opel director, as Volkswagen's general manager and he took over the day-to-day running of the factory. The following year, in 1948, the by then worthless Reichsmark was replaced by the Deutschmark and the currency stabilized. Volkswagen was handed back to the German people and Nordhoff set about refining the model, but at the same time preserving its distinctive mechanics and appearance. The 100,000th Beetle, as the car was to become known, was built in 1950, and in 1955 the millionth example left the Wolfsburg production line. Germany, 'the spark plug of Europe' as Alfred Sloan Jnr, General Motors' famous president, had described the country, was firing again.

In the south, Daimler-Benz and Opel began car production in 1946 and 1947 respectively, and Ford was soon back in business at Cologne. The Allied powers had clearly defined the industry's terms of reference with Volkswagen producing the cheap cars, Ford and Opel the middle-class ones, and Daimler-Benz the most expensive vehicles. There was also a newcomer to the manufacturing ranks. The Porsche design bureau had moved to Austria during the war and it was there that the 356 Volkswagen-based sports car made its appearance in 1948. Following a return to its Stuttgart headquarters, Porsche has gone on to become Germany's most famous sporting marque, with the 356 evolving into the 911 in 1964, and the best-selling 924 and superlative 928 arriving in the 1970s.

Of all the car companies it was BMW that received the most severe mauling in the post-war years. Its aero-engine activities, which included pioneering jet developments, were confiscated by the Allied powers, while vital elements of the firm's pre-war cars had found their way to Britain. With BMW engineer Fritz Fiedler acting as consultant, the outcome was the Bristol 400 of 1947, effectively a BMW 326 chassis, 328 engine and 327-derived body. The 328 engine, in particular, was to remain in production until 1961 and was also used to power a wide variety of racing cars. All these activities were little comfort to BMW, back in Munich, who in 1952 had put its expensive 501 model into production. But the car and its derivatives were out of step with the times, and by the end of the decade there were rumours of a merger with Daimler-Benz. However, practically all the other car companies boomed, and in 1956 Germany overtook Britain as Europe's largest automobile producer, a position it holds to this day.

BMW renaissance

Growth was the theme of the 1960s and it was then, at last, that BMW, after ten years of building the wrong cars, finally produced a model that was ideally tailored for the use of the prosperous middle classes. From the 1500 of 1962 sprang the popular 1800 and 1600 saloons and a new generation of stylish coupés. The Bavarian Motor Works was, once again, on its way. In 1965 came a revival of the Audi name that had been in abeyance since 1940 and was derived from Auto Union's revived DKW marque, re-established in the West in 1948. Bought by Daimler-Benz in 1958, in 1965 DKW was sold to Volkswagen, which was celebrating its first million-Beetle year and wanted extra capacity. The two-stroke engines were dropped, four-strokes introduced and the front-wheel-drive theme perpetuated. The coming of the Audi 100 in 1968 gave Ingolstadt its first big seller and was followed in 1971 by the even more successful 80. In 1969 Audi merged with NSU, which had been devoting its energies to the rotary engine and in 1967 had produced its Ro 80 Wankel-powered saloon.

The 1970s were dominated by the outcome of the 1973 Arab/Israeli war and the soaring of oil prices. Of the German car companies, Volkswagen was in the deepest trouble as the downturn in the economy coincided with demand dropping for the ageing Beetle. Fortunately in 1974 Wolfsburg came up with the Golf with an Audi-designed engine under its bonnet, and from the model sprang a new generation of front-wheel-drive cars. The Beetle, which had overtaken the Model T Ford as the most popular car in the history of the automobile, was phased out in Germany in 1978, although it remains in production in VW's overseas subsidiaries: total production now stands at over 20 million. Audi, in the meantime, had developed its own distinctive character with the arrival of a five-cylinder engine, permanently engaged four-wheel drive and aerodynamically efficient bodywork with distinctive flush-fitting windows.

Such innovations show that Germany is maintaining its tradition for engineering excellence and executing it with competence and vigour. Porsche today offers an impressive and potent range, while Opel is spearheading General Motors' assault on the European market with some outstanding family cars. Volkswagen, having bidden farewell to the Beetle in Germany, is concentrating on its stylish front-wheel-drive models; BMW offers luxury for the upper middle classes and Daimler-Benz maintains a 100-year-old tradition for technical refinement and outstanding quality. After nearly 30 years at the top of Europe's car manufacturing ladder, Germany shows every sign of staying there.

RIGHT *The Porsche Speedster of 1955, provided by Ray Wright. These cars were so light they performed well despite the small engine. They were particularly popular in America.*

AUDI

In many respects the modern Audi represents an embodiment of the German automobile industry: ingeniously engineered, refined and reliable. Yet the marque has had a chequered career, having been founded by August Horch at Zwickau, Saxony, in 1909 after he had left the firm that bore his name. But in 1928 came a take-over by DKW and four years later, in 1932, at the depths of the economic depression, these two firms were joined by Horch and Wanderer to create the Auto Union combine, while the Auto Union name was made world famous by its Porsche-designed mid-engined racing cars. With the ending of the Second World War, all Auto Union's factories were lost to East Germany, but 1948 saw the firm re-established at Ingolstadt in the West, and DKW two-stroke car production resumed. In 1958 the firm was bought by Daimler-Benz but in 1965 was taken over by Volkswagen; there was a switch to four-stroke engines and, after 25 years, a re-introduction of the Audi name.

A146 WRP

NLOP
4

In 1932, in the very teeth of the worldwide economic depression, the Horch and Wanderer companies joined with the already allied Audi and DKW firms to create the Auto Union combine. Its badge was four interlocking rings which represented the constituent makes. Of these only Audi—founded in 1909—has survived and, although in abeyance from 1940 until 1965, was effectively re-born that year. Audi, which retains the Auto Union *Vier Ringe* (four rings) emblem, is once more a force within the German motor industry.

The fortunes of Audi are intertwined with those of Horch; both have a common ancestry as the two firms were established by August Horch. His father was a blacksmith and Horch was born in 1868 at Winningen. Although he began by working for his father, he soon progressed to wagon building at Heidelberg and subsequently the railway on the distant Serbian-Bulgarian border. Following a technical education at an engineering school at Mittweida, Horch worked for a Leipzig company making engines for torpedo boats, but by 1896 he was managing Carl Benz's Mannheim motor works, which at the time was the world's largest automobile manufacturing establishment. Any engineer of talent would have been frustrated by Benz's staid technical approach and, late in 1899, Horch received financial backing from a Rhenish cloth merchant to produce motor cars under his own name.

His first model, a 5/10 PS car with a two-cylinder horizontally opposed engine, was progressive for its use of shaft, rather than chain, drive but by 1902 August Horch had a new Reichenbach factory, fresh backers, and a more orthodox car with a 2.5-litre vertical two-cylinder engine. By 1903 the model was even available in London, although it was marketed under the Krupkar name as the great Essen steel and armaments firm was probably better known in the British capital than Horch's.

Birth of the Audi

In mid 1904 came a move from Reichenbach to Zwickau, in Saxony, which was destined from there on to be the firm's headquarters. Then came a new four-cylinder 2.7-litre 18/22, followed in 1905 by a similar but larger 5.8-litre 35/40. A six-cylinder 50/60 model of 8 litres arrived for 1907, while the following year saw some special Horches with aerodynamic bodies which were prepared for the 1908 Prince Henry Trials. Even though these cars did not attain great success, August Horch continued to produce vehicles specifically designed for trials and competitions. It was a costly business that generated hostility among his co-directors, and the six-cylinder 50/60 had been something of a flop. These factors conspired to produce discord which led, in the summer of 1909, to Horch leaving the company that bore his name. By July he had set up

LEFT *The first Horches were built at Reichenbach, but in 1904 came a move to Zwickau. One of the first cars to be produced there was the 18/22 PS model with a 2.7-litre four-cylinder engine and overhead inlet valves in the Mercedes manner. Ball bearings were used extensively, while oil circulation was maintained by exhaust pressure! Four- or three-speed gearboxes were offered. In 1905 came a similar but larger 5.8-litre 35/40 which boasted a camshaft-driven fan.*

ABOVE RIGHT *An Audi Type C 14/35 PS produced between 1912 and 1914 with a 3.5-litre overhead-inlet/side-exhaust-valve engine. It was while he was with the Horch company that August pioneered his* Torpedoform *aerodynamic body, and he perpetuated this feature, as can be seen, when he set up his Audi facility. From 1913 the model was known as Alpensieger in recognition of its successes in that year's Austrian Alpine Trial.*

his business virtually next door to the Horch works, under the name of August Horch Automobilwerk. Not unnaturally, his former associates were horrified at the creation of a rival make with the same name and a legal confrontation ensued. The matter was resolved when Horch translated his surname—which means 'listen'—into Latin, giving Audi.

With Horch's departure the firm slithered into decline, while the new Audi marque forged ahead. The first of the line was the 10/22 with a 2612 cc four-cylinder engine and overhead inlet valves, a progressive feature for the day. Designated the Type A, it was followed, in 1911, by the 10/28 Type B with the models lasting until 1912 and 1914 respectively. But the most enduring car was the 3.5-litre 14/35 Type C which continued until 1918. In 1913 it became the Alpensieger which was the result of Horch pursuing his competitive bent because, with the Prince Henry Cup having been discontinued, August looked to the Austrian Alpine Trials. Audis were entered in 1911, although it was not until 1913 that the make was awarded the coveted team prize with the cars of Lange, the firm's technical director, Graumüller and Obruba proving victorious. Other pre-war models included the 4.6-litre Type D of 1911/14, and the 5.7-litre 22/55 which lasted until 1914. The First World War of 1914–18 produced its upheavals and after hostilities, in 1920, August Horch resigned from the firm to work for the Berlin-based economics ministry, with technical director Lange thereafter directing car design. Like many other German makes, the Audis of the 1920s were mostly uninspiring boxy saloons which were technically unadventurous, although the 3.5-litre four-cylinder Model K of 1921–5 vintage boasted an aluminium cylinder block and pistons. More pedestrian was the 2-litre Type G carried over from the pre-war 8/22, and there was the 5.6-litre Type E, designated the 22/55, both of which were discontinued in 1926. Rather more advanced was the 18/70 having a six-cylinder power unit—Audi's first—of 4.6 litres and with overhead camshaft, while the servo-assisted four-wheel hydraulic brakes were a revol-

ABOVE *August Horch at the wheel of a 14/35 Audi in the 1914 Austrian Alpine Trial in a year when the Audi team shared the team prize with Hansa. The headlamps are no doubt turned inwards to prevent stone damage.*

RIGHT *August Horch (1868–1951), founder of both the Horch and Audi marques.*

utionary feature for 1923, its introductory year. Production lasted until 1928 although a mere 230 were built. In truth, the 1920s were disappointing years for Audi: annual production never exceeded the 309 mark, achieved in 1924 and 1929, and slumped to a low, in 1927, of 90.

Horch, conversely, was faring rather better. Initially its designs of the early 1920s were the work of Swiss engineer Arnold Zoller, but in 1923 the experienced Paul Daimler arrived at Zwickau and in 1926 he introduced the first of a generation of straight-eight models for which Horch soon became famous. Audi also adopted this cylinder configuration in 1927, producing the very American looking 19/100 with a 4.9-litre engine; it was expensive, however, and only 150 were produced before the model was discontinued in 1929.

Take-over by DKW

It was in 1928 that Audi was taken over by Jørgen Skäfte Rasmussen, whose DKW company had rapidly expanded during the 1920s, and who was attracted by the facilities offered by Audi's Zwickau factory. Rasmussen was a Dane who had entered the German market with an unlikely vehicle at a difficult time and, not surprisingly, little has been recorded about the original DKW steam-powered car, accordingly titled the *Dampkraftwagen*, which was introduced at the height of the First World War in 1916. With the arrival of peace, in 1919 Rasmussen, with a factory at Zschopau in Sachsen, entered the two-wheeled accessory market with the DKW, for *das kleine Wunder* (the little wonder), 119 cc two-stroke engine. Two-stroke single- and twin-cylinder motorcycles followed, ranging from 100 to 500 cc. Such was their popularity—40,000 machines were sold in 1928 alone—that, by the end of the decade and up until the outbreak of the Second World War in 1939, DKW was the world's largest motorcycle manufacturer. To cope with this phenomenal growth, Rasmussen was continually on the lookout for additional manufacturing facilities. There had been the Mollwerke car factory at Chemnitz and he also established the Frama concern, which from 1932 produced DKW-based three-wheelers at Hainichen which was also in Saxony. In addition, Rasmussen bought the manufacturing rights of the American Rickenbacker company, which had ceased trading in 1927, and offered that firm's six- and eight-cylinder engines as proprietary units.

With such growth, a progression to car production was almost inevitable, and the first DKW four-wheeler made its début at the Leipzig Trade Fair in 1928. It was powered by a water-cooled 585 cc vertical two-cylinder engine and was a two-stroke, a combustion cycle that was to be employed in every DKW car right up until 1966. Designed by Rudolph

LEFT *Audi brochure of 1922, displaying some artistic licence!*

BELOW *The V12 Horch arrived in 1931 and this is a 6-litre Type 670 model of circa 1933 with Spohn cabriolet coachwork. Horch offered the most expensive cars within the Auto Union range.*

Jørgen Skäfte Rasmussen (left) and his 1931 DKW Type FA 600 (above), with front-wheel drive and two-cylinder two-stroke engine.

Slaby, this first model was of a chassis-less wooden construction and there was also a popular sports version boasting 18 rather than the standard product's 16.5 bhp. The cars were produced in Berlin in a Spandau plant that had previously played host to the D-Wagen car, while the American Durant had also been assembled there for a short time.

Rasmussen used his newly acquired Zwickau works for DKW assembly, although Audi car production was also maintained. The straight-eight theme of the 19/100 was perpetuated with the arrival of the Rickenbacker-engined 4.3-litre 18/80 in 1929 and the 20/100 of 5.1 litres which, unlike the smaller capacity model, lasted until 1932. These eights were hardly suitable for the harsh economic climate then engulfing Germany and, in an attempt to offer a cheap, low capacity model, the 5/30 Audi was introduced in 1931 with a 1122 cc Peugeot engine under its bonnet. A total of 300 was produced at DKW's Spandau works until the model was discontinued, in 1932. This year was a disastrous one for Audi with only 22 cars sold.

DKW was, in the meantime, developing its two-stroke car with the resulting 1931 F1 effectively bringing front-wheel drive to Germany. The system had gained a momentum in Europe with the 1926 introduction in France of the Tracta car, although the 1926 Voran was an early German essay on the theme. This made little impact, but the F1 DKW and its derivatives were to become increasingly popular as the decade progressed. It had a 500 cc (68 × 68 mm) two-cylinder, transversely mounted two-stroke engine and narrow, ladder-type chassis with swinging half axles at the front and a transversely sprung dead axle at the rear.

AUTO UNION FORMED

The cheap, popular DKW was to form the corner-stone of the Auto Union combine, established in the worsening economic climate of 1932. The first steps were taken in August with the allied Audi and DKW firms forming the first two recruits. The Horch company closely followed Audi at Zwickau and was a natural third member. After a 23-year separation, the two makes were reunited under the Auto Union umbrella. As it happened, Horch had fared far better than its neighbour for, in 1926, Paul Daimler had come up with the 3.1-litre twin overhead camshaft straight-eight model which sold in modest but consistent quantities, though in variations of mind-numbing complexity. Then, in 1931, a new generation of single overhead camshaft eights appeared, the work of Fritz Fiedler, who had joined Horch from Stoewer and was to leave Zwickau in 1933 for BMW. August Horch was to return to the presidency of Horchwerke in 1933, a goodwill gesture by Auto Union, but he was to die in 1951, penniless and forgotten.

The fourth member of the automotive quartet was the Wanderer company, also Saxony-based and a mere 12 km (20 miles) from Audi and Horch at Chemnitz. This firm had followed a traditional route from bicycles, in 1885, via motorcycles in 1902, with cars arriving in 1911. The first Wanderer had an 1150 cc four-cylinder engine, though with rather formal tandem seating, when it was known as *Puppchen* (little doll). Fours and sixes followed after the First World War and examples of the latter, the 2.5-litre W11, were built under licence by Martini in Switzerland. In 1931 Wanderer had been the first customer at Ferdinand Porsche's design bureau, the diplomatically titled Type 7 having a 1.7-litre six-cylinder wet-liner overhead-valve engine, with alternative 2-litre size, which owed something to the Type 30 Steyr that Porsche had designed during his brief stay with that Austrian company in 1929–30. This entered production, though a 3.5-litre straight-eight model, with optional supercharger, titled Types 8 and 9 in Porsche's design register, was not produced, because by this time Wanderer had joined Auto Union and it was decided that the well-established eight-cylinder Horches would constitute the combine's large-car commitment.

Other constituent components were the DKW front-wheel-drive F1, while Wanderer could be depended upon to make unsensational but competent middle-class products. Horch would provide prestige, but if there was a weak point in Auto Union's four-link chain it was Audi.

As the emphasis was on integration, in 1934 Audi production was transferred to the Horch factory. By this time the Audi range had been simplified to just one model, the front-wheel drive appropriately titled Front, introduced in 1933. This was a much more progressive design than earlier offerings, and boasted a fashionable backbone chassis and all-independent suspension. The Porsche-designed 2-litre Wanderer six, mounted back to front in the chassis, was employed. The gearbox was consequently at the front of the car, while a transverse leaf spring and wishbone suspension system was used along with a swing axle rear. Although mechanical brakes were initially fitted these were soon replaced by hydraulics. Capacity was increased to 2257 cc for 1935, the model being re-designated the Front 225, and output continued until 1938.

LEFT *1936 W25K Wanderer sports car with 1936 cc supercharged six-cylinder engine and a reputed 150 km/h (93 mph).*

BELOW LEFT *1939 front-wheel-drive DKW Meisterklasse with 684 cc two-cylinder two-stroke engine and Horch-like radiator, suggesting an Auto Union corporate style.*

RIGHT *Audi Type UW built in 1933 and 1934 with 2-litre six-cylinder engine. 1255 examples were made by Audi and a further 680 by Horch.*

BELOW *A DKW in the thick of it, displaying the advantages of front-wheel drive during a cross-country event in the 1930s.*

Bodywork was of all too obvious Horch ancestry but despite their impressive mechanical specifications, the cars did not sell well. By all accounts they suffered from heavy steering, questionable handling and a poor gear change. This may account for the fact that a mere 1940 examples of the original 2-litre car were sold while its 225 successor did only marginally better with 2579 finding customers.

Increasing sales for DKW

By contrast, the little front-wheel-drive DKWs were going from strength to strength. In 1933 the original F1 twin was enlarged to 584 cc and named the Reichsklasse, while the 684 cc Meisterklasse was offered with four-seater bodywork but was still of wood and fabric construction. The Horch-like radiator was a reminder of in-house Auto Union associations. Sales were impressive with 16,991 cars sold in 1934, rising to 24,776 in 1935 and, by 1937, the figure had spiralled to 39,353, which was perhaps helped by more rounded and flowing body lines introduced in 1935.

A development of the vertical twin, a three-cylinder two-stroke, was undergoing tests in 1940, though the model was not destined to reach production status until after the war.

The success of the front-wheel-drive DKWs has tended to overshadow some more conventional rear-drive models introduced by 1933. These were also two-stroke, the Sonderklasse having a 1054 cc V4 engine, while the Schwebeklasse, which appeared in 1934, offered a synchromesh gearbox and hydraulic brakes. But the mere 2790 fours sold in 1937 tell their own story.

Horch, in the meantime, had strayed from its straight-eight commitment and introduced a side-valve 3-litre V8, consequently titled the Type 830. There were 3.25- and 3.5-litre variations in 1934, but overall production was relatively modest with 1270 cars sold in 1933. Although prospects improved with 2029 Horches built in 1935, ironically the firm's best ever performance came in 1939 with 2855 cars produced in the first ten months of the year; but by then the Second World War had begun.

Wanderer continued in its unsensational way. Up until 1936 all models were powered by the Porsche-designed six in capacities ranging from 1.7 to 2.3 litres. But the engineering was unadventurous, certainly when compared with its other Auto Union stable-mates. In 1933, independent front suspension put in an appearance, together with an uncharacteristic sports car—the 2-litre W25—complete with supercharger, but hardly a match for the BMW 328. Wanderer dispensed with overhead valves in 1937, reverting to side locations and a saloon range powered by 1767 cc four- and 2632 cc six-cylinder engines.

Rather more inspired was the new Audi, the 920, which went into production in December 1938 even though it looked more like a Wanderer than a Horch! Dispensing with front-wheel drive, the 920 used a 3281 cc (87 × 92 mm) Horch straight-eight engine, less two cylinders, and was accordingly an overhead camshaft unit. Suspension was all independent by transverse springs and, although more expensive than the Audi Front, it showed every sign of being more popular, with 1085 produced in 1939: the best ever Audi output figure of the inter-war years. Production continued until 1940. It is ironic, nevertheless, that Audi, the member of the Auto Union combine to make least impact in the 1930s, was the name destined to survive in the post-war years, albeit after a 25-year absence.

The famous Auto Union racer

Auto Union did not appear as a marque name on any of the cars within the group, although they all displayed the *Vier Ringe* badge on their radiators. There was a glorious exception, however, and that was the mid-engined Auto Union racing cars which appeared in 1934 and which, along with Mercedes-Benz, were to dominate Grand Prix competition until the outbreak of the Second World War.

The conception of these fabled racers dates from October 1932, when details of the new racing formula were released which required that racing cars should be limited to a weight of 750 kg (1650 lb) less fuel and tyres but, significantly, engine size was to be unlimited. Despite the Stuttgart-based Porsche design bureau being at a low ebb, it was decided to press ahead with a Grand Prix car for the new formula, although initially only the engine was designed, being allotted the type number 22. Then, in November 1932, a company was formed to produce a complete car. The *Hochleistungsfahrzeugbau* (High Performance Vehicle Development Company) was financed by Adolf Rosenberger, who had already backed Porsche in the establishment of his firm. Rosenberger had known Porsche during the latter's Daimler-Benz days and had also driven the mid-engined Benz Tropfen Auto, of Rumpler origins, and it was he who directed Porsche that the new car mirror this configuration. By 15 November the specifications of the P-Wagen (for Porsche) had been agreed. A 45-degree V16 engine of 4358 cc was ambitiously decided upon, and Josef Kales was responsible for its design—undertaken over the winter of 1932–3—while Karl Rabe, Porsche's chief engineer, looked after the suspension layout.

As Porsche had no resources to produce the car himself, it was essential that he interest a manufacturer who could take the design over, but, with record unemployment and national morale at a low ebb, he was unable to obtain any support. In the meantime, racing driver Hans Stuck, who had a financial interest in the P-Wagen, met with Nazi party leader Adolf

LEFT *The Auto Union team at Monza for the Italian Grand Prix, September 1934. The event was won by Mercedes-Benz, but Stuck in a P-Wagen Auto Union was second.*

RIGHT *French Grand Prix, July 1934. Stuck was the last Auto Union to retire, on lap 34, with fuel problems.*

AUTO UNION P-WAGEN
1934–7

ENGINE	
No. of cylinders	16
Bore/stroke mm	68 × 75; 1935 72 × 75; 1936–7 75 × 85
Displacement cc	4360, 4950, 6010
Valve operation	Single overhead camshaft, pushrod/rocker operated exhaust valves
Induction	Roots-type supercharger, twin Solex carburettors
BHP	295 at 4500 rpm, 375 at 4800 rpm, 520 at 5000 rpm
Transmission	Five-speed all-indirect gearbox, four-speed from 1935
CHASSIS	
Frame	Tubular
Wheelbase mm	2844, 2882, 2908
Track—front mm	1422
Track—rear mm	1422
Suspension—front	Independent, by trailing arms and transverse torsion bars
Suspension—rear	Swing axle with transverse leaf springs, longitudinal torque arms. From 1935, torsion bars replaced transverse springs
Brakes	Hydraulic; from 1937 twin leading shoe
PERFORMANCE	
Maximum speed	276 km/h to 313 km/h (172–195 mph) depending on drive ratios and tyres

Hitler, a regular attender at motor races and hill climbs. Stuck bewailed Germany's lack of prowess on the European motor racing circuits, which were then dominated by the blue and red cars from France and Italy.

However, Porsche, through his Wanderer connections, had begun talks with the newly founded Auto Union combine and in January 1933 von Wertzen, its sales manager, was presenting a case for the P-Wagen. News of Daimler-Benz's impending return to motor sport had already leaked out but, while the Auto Union board recognized the valuable publicity that a racing car would provide, the funds were not available to undertake such an ambitious project. It was agreed to approach the government for help and then, on 30 January 1933, Adolf Hitler became Germany's new chancellor.

Porsche, who already knew Hitler, met him in Berlin at the beginning of March and put forward a plan for government backing of the P-Wagen project. Hitler had already decided on an RM 500,000 (£42,918) grant for Daimler-Benz, but this was reduced to RM 450,000 (£38,629) and divided between Auto Union and the Stuttgart firm. This gave the green light for a contract between Porsche and Auto Union, and work on the construction of the racing cars began at the Horch works at Zwickau in May 1933, although it was not until July that the design was finally completed.

The project proceeded apace so that the first car was ready by October, with former Daimler-Benz driver and now Auto Union racing director Willy Waub at the wheel. He managed a few circuits of the Horch factory and then, no doubt to the consternation of other road users, took the single-seater on to the public highway. Later, on 13 November, the P-Wagen was taken to the Nürburgring for track testing and, although there were some teething troubles, on 12 January 1934, the car succeeded in averaging 200 km/h (124 mph) at the AVUS circuit, as stipulated in Porsche's contract. A second car was completed the same month, and there followed further high-speed testing at the Monza circuit, in Italy, while additional runs were undertaken on the Milan–Varese *autostrada*. These went sufficiently well for a long-tailed P-Wagen to make its public début at the AVUS on 6 March, when Hans Stuck broke a month-old one-hour world record by averaging 217 km/h (134.9 mph). The car was triumphantly displayed at the Berlin Motor Show, opened later by Adolf Hitler.

All too obviously unorthodox, the Auto Union, designated the A type, had its 295 bhp V16 engine located behind the driver. But, even though the P-Wagen was obviously unconventional in appearance, its engineering was remarkably simple and straightforward. The engine boasted two valves per cylinder with the inlets operated directly by a single overhead camshaft, while the exhausts were pushrod and rocker actuated from the same source. A vertically mounted Roots-type supercharger was employed. The chassis was of simple tubular construction and also carried the engine cooling water, with Porsche's patented transverse torsion bars and trailing links at the front, and a swing axle layout with twin transverse leaf springs at the rear. In the interests of weight saving, the 750 kg ceiling being an ever-present consideration, some of the body side panels were made of doped aircraft fabric, while the remainder were of light alloy.

At their first outing at the AVUS Grand Prix in March 1934 an Auto Union came second to an Alfa Romeo, then second at the Eifelrennen, although at the prestigious French Grand Prix the two Auto Unions retired. Here the rival sophisticated but conventionally engineered Mercedes-Benz W25 was equally unsuccessful, and Alfa Romeo took the chequered flag. The P-

Wagen redeemed itself for the German Grand Prix, when Hans Stuck gave Auto Union its first GP win with a Mercedes-Benz second and Alfa Romeo relegated to third place. Further successes for Auto Union and Stuck came with victories in the Swiss and Czech Grands Prix.

It had been a promising start and for 1935 the car's design was refined somewhat. The Type B had a 4950 cc engine, attained by increasing the bore size from 68 to 72.5 mm with stub exhausts replacing tail pipes, and the rear transverse leaf spring was dispensed with and torsion bars introduced. Bodywork was now all metal. Despite these modifications, the season was a patchy one for Auto Union with the rival Mercedes-Benz team forging ahead, although the *Vier Ringe* was triumphant at the Italian and Tunis Grands Prix and Bernd Rosemeyer, a new recruit to the team, who had graduated from Auto Union's DKW racing motorcycles, took a P-Wagen to victory in the Czech GP.

Even more modifications were made for 1936, the C type car seeing a leap in engine capacity to 6010 cc (75 × 85 mm) and a ZF limited slip differential was introduced to cope with the resulting 520 bhp. With Rosemeyer in fine fettle, Auto Union had an impressive year, its best ever, with victories in the Eifel, German, Pescara, Swiss and Italian Grands Prix and the European Championship. The following year saw Mercedes-Benz introduce the powerful W125, so that Auto Union and Rosemeyer had to content themselves with such second-string events as the Eifel, Pescara and Donington Grands Prix. With the ending of the 750 kg formula in 1937, the 4 seasons had produced 22 Mercedes victories and 18 Auto Union Formula race wins.

The new regulations for 1938 to 1940 saw the precondition of weight dispensed with and a 3-litre limit to engine capacity was introduced. Both Auto Union and Mercedes-Benz opted for V12 engines, but there the resemblance ended because, whereas Untertürkheim's W163 remained faithful to its front location, the Type D car from Zwickau represented a further refinement of the mid-engined position. As Ferdinand Porsche was at this time deeply involved with the Volkswagen and associated projects, the new Auto Union was largely the work of Professor Eberan von Eberhorst. The new engine boasted three rather than a single camshaft, with one operating the inlet valves and the remaining two located in each cylinder bank actuating the exhaust ones. Again a Roots-type supercharger was employed and the power unit developed 420 bhp. The D type's chassis was similar though 228 mm (9 in) shorter than its predecessor's and, while the torsion-bar front suspension remained the same, Auto Union followed the Mercedes-Benz W125 rear de Dion layout. Torsion bars, contained within the chassis tubes, were again the suspension medium with radius arms and Panhard rod also employed. As the fuel tanks were relegated from behind to either side of the driver and because of the shorter engine, he now sat in the centre

rather than at the front of the car, which was destined to improve the D type's weight distribution and, therefore, roadholding.

Unfortunately Auto Union's 1938 season was overshadowed by the death, in January, of Bernd Rosemeyer during a record attempt. From 1934 onwards Auto Union participated in record-breaking with high-performance versions of its Grand Prix car clothed in aerodynamic, all-enveloping bodywork. Late in 1937, Rosemeyer in such a machine averaged 408.3 km/h (253.7 mph) for the flying kilometre on the Frankfurt–Darmstadt *Autobahn*. Mercedes-Benz responded with 430 km/h (267.2 mph) and, on a blusterous day in early 1938, Auto Union came back with Rosemeyer at the wheel of one of these streamlined cars. It was while the car was running at top speed that it suddenly lurched, off came a tyre, and the vehicle crashed into a nearby bridge. Rosemeyer was thrown clear of the car but died immediately, and Auto Union never undertook any further record attempts.

ABOVE *Restored to its former glory, a 1938 D type (chassis number 2) which was on display at the Auto Union showrooms in Prague at the end of the Second World War. It was brought back to Germany by Hubertus Count Dornhoff in 1973. He then sold it and later an original V12 engine was found and the car was restored in Britain by Antique Automobiles.*

ABOVE RIGHT *Auto Union GP cars were fitted with streamlined bodywork and used for record-breaking attempts. This is a V16 C type car of 1937 shown on the Frankfurt/Darmstadt* Autobahn. *It was on this stretch of motorway that Bernd Rosemeyer was killed in January 1938.*

RIGHT *Tazio Nuvolari in the 1938 Swiss Grand Prix at Berne driving a D type Auto Union. However, the event was dominated by Mercedes-Benz.*

In addition to this catastrophe, the new cars were suffering from teething troubles and consequently Auto Union, still reeling from Rosemeyer's death, missed the first three major races of 1938. Their début at the French Grand Prix proved disastrous with both cars retiring during the first lap, so making a Mercedes-Benz one-two victory inevitable. It was then that engineering director Werner approached Tazio Nuvolari, the greatest driver of his day, and until then faithful to his native but increasingly uncompetitive Alfa Romeo, to sign to drive for Auto Union. The maestro agreed, although it took him three races to challenge and overhaul Mercedes-Benz successfully at the Italian Grand Prix and the British Donington event.

Two-stage supercharging was adopted for both Auto Union and Mercedes-Benz for 1939, and this boosted the Zwickau car's output to 485 bhp. Auto Union won the French Grand Prix, but thereafter their rivals had the upper hand, although Nuvolari beat the opposition at the Belgrade-staged Yugoslav Grand Prix held on 3 September, the day that Britain and France declared war on Germany. This put an end to Auto Union's racing activities, even though work was well advanced on a 1.5-litre V12 car intended for the post-1940 formula.

Post-war production

During the Second World War, firms within Auto Union made their individual contributions to the German war effort. V8-engined Horches, both in two- and four-wheel-drive forms, saw plenty of action, while six-cylinder Wanderers also saw combat service in car and truck variants. But the ending of hostilities in 1945 saw the partition of Germany, and a Russian-dominated Eastern Zone. This resulted in the end of Auto Union's Saxony-based activities which were all located in the south-east of Germany and thus under Soviet influence.

Horches, Wanderers and Audis had been produced in relatively small numbers, but there were plenty of DKWs in the West, the reliable little front-wheel-drive two-stroke models having made plenty of friends in pre-war days. It was estimated that there were around 150,000 of them and, with the demand for four-wheeled transport of any description in post-war Germany, there was an associated need for spare parts. In 1948, in response to this demand, two former Auto Union executives, Messrs Bruhn and Hahn, borrowed money from a local bank and set up a parts depot in Ingolstadt, and the following year, in 1949, Auto Union was registered as a new company. The first vehicle to enter production that year was the Schnell-Laster, a light delivery van, with the inevitable front-wheel drive and two-cylinder two-stroke power unit: it remained in production until 1954. By this time a bombed-out factory at Düsseldorf had been renovated, with the first DKW cars leaving the production line in 1950.

This was the pre-war Meisterklasse with 684 cc two-cylinder engine, although the hydraulic brakes were a welcome improvement and the bodywork was new. It was not until 1953 that the 896 cc three-cylinder Sonderklasse arrived which had been waiting in the wings since 1940. The power unit was mounted in the conventional longitudinal, rather than the transverse, position of its forebears, while the chassis frame and transverse leaf spring suspension, independent at the front with a dead rear axle, was retained along with a three-speed gearbox for the home market. In 1956 DKW developed a four-wheel-drive Jeep-type vehicle called the Munga and powered by the Meisterklasse's 896 cc three-cylinder engine. Not only was it used by NATO but it also proved popular with farmers as an ideal cross-country machine. The Munga remained in production until 1968, by which time 46,750 had been built.

Across the Iron Curtain in East Germany, what was to all intents and purposes the DKW Meisterklasse made its appearance in 1948. This was manufactured at the former Audi factory at Zwickau under the IFA name and production continued until 1955. In 1950 came IFA's F9 model with three-cylinder 894 cc DKW two-stroke engine, four years ahead of the West's DKW Sonderklasse. Production lasted until 1956, by which time output had been transferred to the former BMW works at Eisenach. It was replaced by the new Wartburg marque; the car was initially 894 cc powered, although capacity was increased to 991 cc in 1962. This two-stroke, front-wheel-drive DKW descendant is still in production at the time of writing.

RIGHT *The DKW F12, introduced in 1963, was produced until 1965. Like all DKWs from 1931, it had front-wheel drive, and a three-cylinder 889 cc two-stroke engine was fitted. Suspension was by wishbones and torsion bars at the front with a dead rear axle, trailing links and transverse torsion bars.*

BELOW LEFT *The DKW Sonderklasse for 1954, with 896 cc three-cylinder engine which had been perfected in 1940. Top speed was about 113 km/h (70 mph).*

BELOW RIGHT *The four-wheel-drive DKW Munga, introduced in 1956 and powered by the long-running 896 cc three-cylinder two-stroke engine. Produced until 1968 it was thus the last DKW two-stroke, a total of 46,750 having been built.*

Meanwhile, the two-cylinder F8 car was replaced in 1956 by the Zwickau, using the same 684 cc twin but with glass-fibre bodywork, probably the first mass-produced German car to feature the material. This continued until 1959, when it was replaced by the Trabant marque with 500 cc engine, enlarged to 594 cc in 1962, and the model, complete with its noteworthy bodywork, remains in production. The DKW front-wheel-drive twin was also the inspiration for Sweden's new Saab make that appeared in 1950, the firm producing the later three-cylinder two-stroke until 1968. Other imitators were the Polish Syrena of 1955 and the Argentine built IAME, manufactured between 1954 and '55, this Justicialista model re-appearing as the Graciela in 1960.

The Daimler-Benz take-over

Back in West Germany, DKW production was holding up well during the booming 1950s. Output had stood at a modest 8253 in 1950 and had progressively increased throughout the decade, so that by 1960 it stood at 126,237. The firm's corporate status changed from 1 January 1958, however, when Daimler-Benz took over the company. Another new factory was built at Ingolstadt for the production of a new model: this was the DKW Junior which remained faithful to the 750 cc three-cylinder front-wheel-drive two-stroke layout but had new bodywork. The first example left the new plant in August 1959. The new car was to sell well, with 350,859 produced before output ceased in 1965. There was also the DKW 1000 of 981 cc, introduced in 1958, although this was sold under the Auto Union name and remained available until 1962.

But, from the 1960 highpoint of 126,000 plus, DKW production thereafter declined so that by 1964 it had slumped to 78,790. The company had been wedded to the two-stroke formula for too long although, with the arrival of a new F102 car in 1964, the firm tried to rid itself of its small car image. This medium-sized saloon was powered by the established three-cylinder engine but capacity had been increased to 1175 cc. The model was to last only until 1966, with production having totalled 53,053.

In truth DKW was in trouble and, in 1965, Volkswagen bought the company from Daimler-Benz. At Wolfsburg, Heinz Nordhoff had been looking for additional capacity to cope with the seemingly insatiable demand for Beetles, and DKW's factories had their attractions. Nordhoff was not to know it, but the purchase, in the long term, was also to prove to be Volkswagen's salvation. On the face of it, however, VW could not have taken over the firm at a worse time, as DKW output was down again to 52,207 cars. Behind the scenes, work had been progressing at breakneck speed to dispense with the two-stroke—it was to survive on the Munga cross-country car until 1968—and introduce a new four-cylinder, four-stroke model. The architect of this transformation was Ludwig Kraus, who had joined Daimler-Benz in 1937 and in the 1950s was responsible for the chassis design of the W196 Grand Prix car that the firm had employed to return to the motor racing circuits in 1954. With the Mercedes-Benz retirement from Formula 1 in 1955, Kraus took over responsibility for saloon car developments and, when he arrived at Ingolstadt in 1963, he brought with him a so-called 'middle pressure' engine that had been developed under his auspices. This was an overhead-valve four, designed to run at higher compression ratios than usual, which offered economy though at the expense of weight.

RETURN OF THE AUDI NAME

As time was of the essence and money tight, it was decided to use the F102 bodywork as the basis of the new model, which was to be powered by the high compression engine. This 1696 cc unit ran at 11.2:1, and developed 72 bhp at 5000 rpm. Also, significantly, it was decided to discontinue the DKW two-stroke-related name although front-wheel drive was perpetuated, and re-introduce the Audi marque that had been dormant since 1940. This first new post-war Audi was offered in two- and four-door forms, and in 1966 came the L version with improved interior trim. That same year the Audi 80L was introduced, with the 1696 cc engine developing 80 bhp, along with the larger capacity 1770 cc (90 bhp at 5200 rpm) Super 90. Nineteen sixty-eight saw the arrival of the 60 with smaller 55 bhp 1496 cc engine, while the 75 of the same year was a perpetuation of the original 1696 cc, but with 9:1 compression ratio. All these models shared the same body, as well as wishbone and longitudinal torsion bar independent front suspension, with dead rear axle, radius arms and longitudinal torsion bars.

The German economy took a downturn in the late 1960s, and this was reflected in Audi's production slipping badly in 1967 to 39,062 cars, the lowest output figure since 1952. However, it recovered to close on 70,000 in 1968, and in 1969 120,499 Audis were sold.

These improvements in Audi's fortunes were, in part, due to the arrival, in 1968, of a new 100 model; the flagship of the revived marque and destined at the time to be its most popular product. When the series was discontinued in 1976 a total of 827,474 had been produced. The new model used the 1760 cc version of the former Mercedes-Benz four but developing 80 bhp. The 100 was a larger car than its predecessors, while the independent front suspension was a wishbone layout, although the intrusive drive shafts meant that the coil springs and telescopic dampers had to be mounted above the upper wishbones. The dead rear axle layout was similar to that used on the earlier Audi cars. The model was also available in 90 bhp S form, and there was a stylish 1871 cc 115 bhp coupé version of 1970–6 vintage.

It was in August 1969 that Volkswagen's Kurt Lotz, who had taken over as the firm's chairman, following Nordhoff's death, was able to achieve his objective of merging Audi with the Neckarsulm-based NSU company. The attractions were not only NSU's Wankel rotary engine, which was looked upon as a possible successor to the reciprocating power unit, but there was the added advantage of a front-wheel-drive, conventional-engined model as a possible Beetle successor.

RIGHT *1971 Audi 100, introduced in 1968 and produced until 1976. It was powered by a development of the four-cylinder high-compression pushrod engine of the 1965 Audi increased to 1790 cc. This is the LS version.*

BELOW *The first post-war Audi was the 1.7-litre 72 hp model of 1965 and this was the Super 90 derivative, visually similar but with 1770 cc engine and 93 hp. It was built between 1966 and 1971.*

AUDI SUPER 90
1966–71

ENGINE	
No. of cylinders	4
Bore/stroke mm	81 × 84
Displacement cc	1770
Valve operation	Pushrod
Compression ratio	10.6:1
Induction	Single carburettor
BHP	93 at 5200 rpm
Transmission	Four-speed
CHASSIS	
Frame	Unitary construction
Wheelbase mm	2490
Track—front mm	1335
Track—rear mm	1326
Suspension—front	Independent, wishbone, longitudinal torsion bar
Suspension—rear	Dead axle, trailing radius arms
Brakes	Hydraulic, front disc
PERFORMANCE	
Maximum speed	163 km/h (101 mph)

The NSU story

NSU had begun life in 1873, when Christian Schmidt and Heinrich Stoll, two enterprising Swabians, took over a knitting-machine factory at Riedlingen on the Danube. One of the partners transferred these activities to Neckarsulm, thereafter to be NSU's headquarters. In 1886 bicycle production began, which in 1900 developed into motorcycles, and cars followed in 1905. In the 1920s motorcycle production forged ahead, with cars playing second fiddle to two-wheeled output, and in 1929 NSU ceded its new Heilbronn car factory to Fiat.

Motorcycle and, later, moped production remained NSU's principal products for the next 28 years until 1957 following a decline in the firm's traditional market. The first effects of the Japanese offensive were felt in Europe, and the firm re-entered the car market with the air-cooled 600 cc rear-engined two-stroke Prinz. There was also the Sport Prinz, and it was a derivative—the convertible Spider of 1964—that was the first production car in the world to be powered by a Wankel rotary engine. This rotary system offered a compact, light power unit with around a third of the parts of a reciprocating engine. NSU became associated with its designer—Felix Wankel—in 1951, and took up the rotary engine idea which it embodied as a supercharger for a 1954 record-breaking motorcycle. In April 1954 NSU decided to press ahead with a four-stroke engine based on the rotary principle, and the resulting Wankel engine ran for the first time on 1 February 1957.

ABOVE *The NSU Prinz appeared in 1957 as a twin, with this 1100 cc four following in 1961.*

RIGHT *Felix Wankel and, below, the world's first rotary-engined car, the 1965 NSU Spider with single-rotor 1.5-litre engine.*

NSU's Dr Walter Froede introduced an eccentric motion to the rotor, and a 1.5-litre single unit was used to power the two-seater Spider, announced at the Frankfurt Motor Show in September 1963, just a month ahead of the Mazda Cosmo, which was the product of another Wankel licence. The Spider remained in production until 1967, but NSU's next Wankel-powered car, the Ro 80, was a far more ambitious project. Introduced for 1968, this front-wheel-drive model was voted Car of the Year. It had a stylish wind-cheating body powered by a 2-litre twin-rotor Wankel engine, and was a car worthy of the new power source. It was unfortunate that the Ro 80 did not live up to its good looks, even though NSU offered extremely generous warranty terms with engines replaced free of charge. Also, although the model was an impressive performer on the German *Autobahnen*, it did not fare so well in traffic jams when the engine was inclined to stall, a state of affairs exacerbated by the employment of an energy-absorbing torque converter and power-steering pump. It was at such times that the vital ferrous alloy rotor apex seals suffered from excessive wear, which accelerated the already high petrol and oil consumption.

The Wankel commitment stretched NSU's finances to the limit, making the firm vulnerable to a take-over, which was what Volkswagen achieved in 1969. NSU was also on the point of introducing a conventional-engined front-wheel-drive model, but it was shelved until late 1970 when, under the Volkswagen K70 name, it entered production at a new VW factory at Salzgitter. Sadly, it did not materialize as the hoped-for Beetle replacement, and was discontinued in 1975. The NSU name had continued on the rear-engined Prinz range that had progressively evolved since its 1957 arrival, but the model was dropped in 1972. This left the Ro 80 as the only NSU car but the Wankel engine, which had come so close to universal acceptance, particularly when General Motors began to consider the system seriously, suffered from the post-1973 energy crisis. Its high fuel and oil consumption, coupled with a poor exhaust emission record, outweighed the undoubted manufacturing advantages and, in March 1977, NSU discontinued its pioneering Ro 80 after 37,204 examples had been built. With it went the NSU name. It was a sad end for such a striking and innovative car.

ABOVE *The highly acclaimed NSU Ro 80, announced in 1967, with a 2-litre twin rotor Wankel engine. Front-wheel drive, power steering and semi-automatic transmission featured, along with stylish, windcheating bodywork. Unfortunately, there were problems with the revolutionary power unit and Volkswagen took the firm over in 1969. NSU persevered with the car for a further eight years, but production ceased in 1977 and with it went the NSU name.*

NSU Ro 80
1967–77

ENGINE	
Type	Twin-rotor Wankel
Capacity	495.2 × 2 cc
Displacement cc	1990
Compression ratio	9:1
Induction	Twin carburettor
BHP	115 at 5500 rpm
Transmission	Three-speed semi-automatic
CHASSIS	
Frame	Unitary construction
Wheelbase mm	2860
Track—front mm	1480
Track—rear mm	1434
Suspension—front	Independent, MacPherson strut
Suspension—rear	Independent, semi-trailing arms
Brakes	Hydraulic disc
PERFORMANCE	
Maximum speed	175 km/h (109 mph)

Audi Car of the Year

Audi, by contrast, was building on the reputation it had established in the 1960s. In 1972 the 80 came on the scene; a completely new model and the first to use Audi's own four-cylinder overhead camshaft engine. This was a 55 bhp 1297 cc (75 × 73 mm) unit, while front suspension was by MacPherson struts and there was the familiar dead axle and radius arms at the rear. In addition, there was the 80S and the 80LS in 1471 cc (76 × 80 mm) form, as well as a GT equipped with a 1588 cc (79 × 80 mm) power unit. Not only was the 80 to be hailed as Car of the Year on its announcement but, in 1973, its first production year, no less than 238,696 examples were produced—a record Audi output.

There were added bonuses for the parent Volkswagen company. The first came in 1973 with the arrival of the VW Passat, basically the Audi 80 with a fastback tail. When the Golf, the long-awaited Beetle replacement, finally arrived in 1974, under its bonnet was the Audi overhead camshaft engine in 1093 and 1471 cc transversely mounted forms. Thus the corporate parent was helped at a crucial time by its young, upstart adopted child. Yet another Audi, the small two-door

RIGHT *The Audi 100S coupé with 1871 cc engine and 115 bhp. Introduced in 1970, it remained in production until 1976, and had a top speed of 185 km/h (115 mph). For the last year of production, new larger wrap-around bumpers were introduced along with a maintenance-free gearbox.*

BELOW *Audi's top-selling 80 model; 1.1 million were built between 1972 and 1978. It marked the début of a new generation of four-cylinder engines with belt-driven single overhead camshafts, later shared with Volkswagen. The 80 was offered with three different engine sizes of 1.2, 1.5 and 1.6 litres. It was also hailed as Car of the Year.*

AUDI 80 (L)
1972–5

ENGINE	
No. of cylinders	4
Bore/stroke mm	75 × 73
Displacement cc	1297
Valve operation	Overhead camshaft
Compression ratio	8.5:1
Induction	Single carburettor
BHP	55 at 5500 rpm
Transmission	Four-speed

CHASSIS	
Frame	Unitary construction
Wheelbase mm	2470
Track—front mm	1340
Track—rear mm	1335
Suspension—front	Independent, MacPherson strut
Suspension—rear	Dead axle, trailing radius arms
Brakes	Hydraulic

PERFORMANCE	
Maximum speed	145 km/h (90 mph)

hatchback 50 with 1093 cc (69 × 72 mm) overhead camshaft engine, arrived in 1974, but the 50 was made only in Audi form until 1978. In 1975 the Volkswagen version, the Polo, was announced and is still in production.

Audi had now gained an impressive momentum and, in 1976, the firm introduced a new 100 with front MacPherson struts and a dead rear axle with trailing arms and coil springs. The 100 went overhead camshaft with 1588 cc (79 × 80 mm) and 1984 cc (86 × 84 mm) four-cylinder engines. But the really significant aspect of the 100 was that it was also offered in 2144 cc (79 × 86 mm) five-cylinder fuel-injected form, along with a 1986 cc (76 × 86 mm) diesel version. A carburettored 2144 cc arrived in 1978.

The name Audi and the five-cylinder power unit are now synonymous, but the concept was not brought to the firm until the arrival of Ferdinand Piëch, who took over from Ludwig Kraus as head of research and development in 1972. Piëch, grandson of Ferdinand Porsche, who has the fabled 917 sports racer to his credit, is Vienna-born and received his technical education at the Zurich technical university. Although he had joined Porsche in 1963, he subsequently left in 1972 to take up his Audi appointment. It had been during a consultancy with Daimler-Benz that Piëch had become interested in the five-cylinder engine which combines the smoothness of a six and the fuel economy of a four. The main difficulty that Audi experienced with the configuration was that of noise, which reached an unacceptable level at 4700 rpm. For production purposes Audi succeeded in moving this cacophony beyond the normal rev range. The five-cylinder engine was further extended in 1979 with the arrival of the Audi 200, the 5E version being available with fuel injection, while the 200 5T was offered in 170 bhp turbocharged form. It was this latter power unit that was to become the basis of one of the most celebrated Audis of recent years: the Quattro.

ABOVE *The Audi 50 of 1974 lasted until 1978, though the design was perpetuated as the VW Polo. 1093 and 1272 cc engines featured.*

The spectacular Quattro

The Quattro story really begins with the Volkswagen Iltris, successor to the DKW Munga and designed and manufactured at Ingolstadt. Its four-wheel-drive layout fired the imagination of Jorg Bensinger, Audi's chief chassis engineer, who, after testing the Iltris in Scandinavia in the winter of 1977, believed that the layout might be successfully transferred to a road car. He first approached Ferdinand Piëch and, although Bensinger felt that the facility might be offered as an option on the 100, it was Piëch who felt that it might be better employed on a high-performance model in its own right.

Work on the project began in March 1977. A hybrid Audi 80 with Iltris-based internals and coded A1 was exhaustively tested and, by November, it had a five-cylinder turbocharged Audi 100 engine under its bonnet. The project was officially approved by Audi management the same month and work on the project proceeded apace, with the Quattro making its début at the Geneva Motor Show in March 1980.

It was the undoubted star of the show, but what the public did not know was that the stylish Quattro was based on the then unannounced GT coupé due for unveiling later in the year. At the heart of the Quattro is the 2144 cc five-cylinder turbocharged engine, but developing 200 rather than 170 bhp with output boosted by the use of an intercooler which lowers the temperature of the air fed into the induction system.

The drive itself is permanently engaged and avoids the use of the heavy transfer box usually associated with a four-wheel-drive layout. This is achieved by the ingenious use of a hollow transfer shaft which transmits power to a centrally located differential, the size of a grapefruit. There are two further conventionally sized differentials, one positioned between the gearbox and flywheel and the other in the rear axle. One of the appeals of the project was that a high proportion of existing Audi components was employed. Many of the transmission and suspension parts came from the 100 and 200 models; an Audi 80 floorpan was utilized while the rear

RIGHT *The Volkswagen Iltris, successor to the DKW Munga, was designed and built by Audi at Ingolstadt, and its four-wheel-drive system forms the basis of that used in the Quattro. In March 1982 the Iltris world manufacturing and distribution rights were sold to Canadian Bombardier Inc.*

LEFT *The Audi 100 of 1976 was offered with 1588, 1984 and 2144 cc engines, (the latter had five cylinders).*

BELOW *The 1980 Audi Quattro, based on the 80 coupé which appeared afterwards. Note the all-independent suspension; effectively the front MacPherson struts were also employed at the rear.*

differential was courtesy of the Iltris, although the alloy casing is peculiar to the Quattro. Suspension is all independent; the front MacPherson strut layout being duplicated at the rear, along with its attendant sub-frame, while the four-wheel disc brakes were borrowed from the 1979 200 Turbo.

Audi thought that it might sell 400 Quattros, which would be sufficient for motor sport homologation and to gauge public response. However, by 1983 Audi would have produced 4851 Quattros and more than 5000 Quattro 80s—a pleasing but drastic under-estimate of the model's impact. A host of rival manufacturers have subsequently announced plans to follow in the Quattro's four-wheel-drive tracks.

Although the Quattro was a desirable and impressive road car it really came into its own in the rally field and was the first model from Ingolstadt to make a significant impression in that highly competitive sector. The European Rally Championship dated back only to 1953, and in the following year it was a DKW that won the competition. However, thereafter successive DKW and Audi activities were low-key affairs, and it was not until 1978 that fuel-injected works 80s began to appear in rally events, but they made no great impression.

However, with the Quattro, Audi recognized that it had a potential world-beater and, in 1979, champion rally driver Hannu Mikkola was invited to try a prototype and was sufficiently impressed to decide that, although he was contracted to drive for Ford in 1980, he would sign an option for Audi in the following year. This he took up and Audi succeeded in securing the services of top woman rally driver Michèle Mouton. With the as yet unblooded Quattro, 1981 was going to be a very interesting year.

In fact it proved to be one of mixed fortunes for the new car. Neither Quattro finished in the Monte Carlo Rally, although Mikkola was able to display the model's potential by winning the Swedish event. Then there followed a succession of failures with Quattros not finishing in the Portugal and Tour de Corse events. However, Mikkola raised Audi morale with a third place in the Finnish 1000 Lakes rally, and Michèle Mouton achieved her first victory in the Sanremo event. With Mikkola also victorious in the Lombard RAC Rally, the cars were clearly becoming more reliable and Audi was placed fifth in the World Championship of Makes.

Nineteen eighty-two at least began better, with Mikkola managing a second place in the Monte Carlo Rally. A locally entered Quattro won the Swedish competition, and Michèle Mouton took the chequered flag in the Portugal: she also won the tough Acropolis event and the Brazil. The 1000 Lakes again fell to the Quattro and the cars finished first and second in the Sanremo, while Mikkola won the RAC. Audi therefore achieved its objective by winning the 1982 World Championship of Makes, and Michèle Mouton was placed second in the Drivers' Championship ahead of team mates Hannu Mikkola and Stig Blomqvist. In 1983 Mikkola won the drivers' accolade although, in the World Championship of Makes, Audi was pipped to the winning post by Lancia.

AUDI QUATTRO
1980 to date

ENGINE	
No. of cylinders	5
Bore/stroke mm	79 × 86
Displacement cc	2144
Valve operation	Overhead camshaft
Compression ratio	7:1
Induction	Fuel injection, intercooler and turbocharger
BHP	200 at 5500 rpm
Transmission	Five-speed, to all four wheels

CHASSIS	
Frame	Unitary construction
Wheelbase mm	2520
Track—front mm	1420
Track—rear mm	1460
Suspension—front	Independent, MacPherson strut
Suspension—rear	Independent, MacPherson strut
Brakes	Hydraulic disc

PERFORMANCE	
Maximum speed	220 km/h (137 mph)

ABOVE *The Harald Demuth/ Arwed Fischer Quattro shown in the 1982 Lombard RAC Rally. It finished in fifth position.*

LEFT *The Audi Quattro Treser, developed by Walter Treser, who was competitions manager of Audi Sport during the Quattro's first year. He was replaced in mid-1981 by Reinhard Rode and subsequently left the firm to pursue such projects as the 209 km/h (130 mph) 80 Quattro.*

RIGHT *The winning Quattro of Hannu Mikkola and Arne Hertz in the 1982 Lombard RAC Rally. Another works Quattro with Michèle Mouton and Fabrizia Pons was second.*

ABOVE *Mikkola and Hertz again in action in the 1982 Sanremo Rally where they were second behind Blomqvist and Cederberg in another Quattro.*

TOP RIGHT *Quattro in 1983 form.*

RIGHT *The short-wheelbase 300 bhp Quattro Sport.*

← LEG
IN-NK 99

Back on the road

So much for the Audi in competition, but what of the development of the mainstream Audi road cars? The Audi GT coupé, which was foreshadowed by the Quattro, arrived for 1981 with a 1921 cc version of the five-cylinder engine, while a fuel-injected GTI model with a 2.2-litre version incorporating a five-speed gearbox appeared for 1983. Later, for the 1984 season, the GT's 1.9-litre engine was enlarged to 1994 cc and the five-speed gearbox standardized.

A new version of the 100 arrived for 1983 and was promptly acclaimed Car of the Year. It was an aerodynamically impressive four-door saloon with 0.30 drag coefficient and distinctive flush-fitting windows. The only four was the 1781 cc unit while there were no less than three five-cylinder engine options: a 1986 cc diesel, a 1921 cc with carburation and a fuel-injected 2144 cc.

Flagship of the Audi range and introduced for 1984 was the 200, essentially a more luxurious version of the 100 but exclusively five-cylinder-engined. There are two 2144 cc variants; one in 136 bhp fuel-injected form, while the other, the 200 Turbo, has a 182 bhp five. All-round disc brakes and power steering are standard fitments. Also established by 1984 was a Quattro version of the 80 with 2.2-litre turbocharged engine, and the range was offered with a new sloping radiator grille and headlight arrangement to echo 100 practice.

Nineteen eighty-five also sees the introduction of a new model, the 90. With its arrival the 80 has been limited to four cylinders, with capacities ranging from 1595 to 1781 cc, while the 90, which uses the same body, offers greater five-cylinder performance and refinement with luxurious trim. By the end of the year every Audi model will be available with the four-wheel-drive option. The Quattro, the car that started it all, continues virtually unchanged for 1985, together with the coveted 306 bhp Quattro Sport, a short-wheelbase coupé with 251 km/h (156 mph) top speed and 306 bhp.

With such a formidable model line-up, it is difficult to believe that it is only 20 years since Audi's rebirth. In recent years the marque has decisively scored in that it can now be regarded as demonstrably different from its Mercedes-Benz, BMW and Porsche contemporaries. This has been achieved by the tripartite package of a five-cylinder engine—which is unique to the make—four-wheel drive and obviously aerodynamically efficient 100 and 200 models. Production has now outgrown Ingolstadt and has expanded to the former NSU plant at Neckarsulm, where the 924 and 944 Porsches are also built, as well as Volkswagen's Emden factory. The cars are also produced overseas by VW's South African subsidiary.

Such progress is impressive, and it seems likely that Audi has more technological trumps up its sleeve. Since 1979 the firm has been under the direction of Dr Wolfgang Habbel. He originally joined Auto Union as a management assistant in 1951 and, although he left in 1957, he returned to the Audi NSU Auto Union board in 1971, having worked for a time for Ford. He was in charge of personnel until he took over from Gottlieb Strobl as board chairman eight years later.

If the past 20 years now appear momentous ones for the Ingolstadt company, then the next two decades look fascinating indeed.

ABOVE *The 1984 Audi Coupé GT which is available with a choice of two five-cylinder engines, either of 1994 or 2144 cc, and producing 115 and 130 bhp respectively. This is the 5E version powered by the larger capacity engine.*

LEFT *The Audi 80 Quattro, introduced in 1983, was the first of the firm's saloons to be offered with four-wheel drive. This is the 1984 model with 2.2-litre fuel-injected five-cylinder engine giving 136 bhp. A five-speed gearbox is a standard fitment. By the end of 1985 every Audi model will be available with the option of permanently engaged four-wheel drive.*

RIGHT *The Audi 100, introduced for 1983. It is offered with a range of no less than three-engine options. There is a 1781 cc four, a 2144 cc five and a 1986 cc five-cylinder diesel with turbocharger. But the really striking feature of the 100 is its outstanding aerodynamic bodywork with 0.30 drag coefficient. The windows are accordingly flush fitting, a feature which is now synonymous with the make.*

BELOW *Flagship of the Audi range is the 200, which arrived for 1984. Based on the 100, it is available only in five-cylinder 2144 cc fuel-injected form. There is a turbocharged version which develops 182 bhp, while the unblown car produces 136 bhp.*

AUDI 200

1983 to date

ENGINE	
No. of cylinders	5
Bore/stroke mm	79 × 86
Displacement cc	2144
Valve operation	Single overhead camshaft
Compression ratio	9.3:1, 7:1
Induction	Bosch fuel injection; turbocharger
BHP	136 at 5700 rpm; 170 at 5300 rpm
Transmission	Five-speed, four-wheel-drive option

CHASSIS	
Frame	Unitary construction
Wheelbase mm	2680
Track—front mm	1470
Track—rear mm	1450
Suspension—front	Independent, MacPherson strut
Suspension—rear	Dead rear axle, trailing arms, coil springs
Brakes	Disc

PERFORMANCE	
Maximum speed	186 km/h (116 mph); 199 km/h (124 mph)

BMW

The Munich-based Bavarian Motor Works came to cars in 1928 via aero engines and motorcycles. It took over the Eisenach-built Dixi which made a German version of the Austin Seven but soon developed an impressive, advanced vehicle range of its own, of which the 328 sports car of 1936 is the outstanding example. The Second World War resulted in the firm losing its car factory to the East and it was not until 1952 that output began at Munich, although the expensive 501 and its derivatives were out of step with the times while, at the other extreme, bubble car production underlined a massive gap in the BMW middle ground. It was filled by the 1500 model of 1962 from which sprang the successful 1800 and 1600 saloons, a fast-selling range of coupés and, from 1968, the 2500 six-cylinder line. Today's range is sophisticated, stylish and fast: a reminder that BMW has also pursued a successful racing programme in tandem with its astounding renaissance.

BMW D

WGC 6F

100
PORSCHE-KREMER
SCHNITZER
FALTZ-ALPINA
30
LUMITAS
LEUCHTTASTER
DUNLOP

When the Bayerische Motoren Werke (BMW) began car manufacture in 1928 there were 25 marques of German origin on the home market. Today only seven survive. Yet among these seven marques are some of the world's most successful and prestigious car makers, a testament to a tenacious industry that has emerged successfully from two world wars and their economic aftermath. How BMW survived at various stages in its history through such diverse activities as aircraft engine manufacture and the production of aluminium cooking utensils is a story worth telling in its own right.

BMW's first involvement in automobile manufacture can be dated to 3 December 1896. This date marks the foundation of the Eisenach Vehicle Factory. Now in the German Democratic Republic, Eisenach was the original headquarters for all BMW car-building activity between 1928 and 1939; the inevitable wartime production then occupied the period until 1945 and the Allied invasion.

Wartburg cars were sold from 1898 though from 1904 vehicles were made under the Dixi name. Before the First World War there was a variety of Dixi products to choose from, with truck production becoming the mainstay of the business until 1921. That year the company was taken over by Gothaer Waggonfabrik AG, but this famous manufacturer of railway coaches and military aircraft was not in the best of health after the post-war ban on German warplane production, so it was no surprise that the business steadily deteriorated through the 1920s. Part of the Gothaer business belonged to a well-known motor industry speculator, Jacob Schapiro, and he soon acquired majority control over the Eisenach/Dixi concern. As part of his plan to fight the deepening recession in the German market, Schapiro incorporated the Cyklon six-cylinder car range, from another of his factories, with the Dixi models of 1926. Still sales sagged and by 1927 even cycle manufacture was abandoned in favour of an exciting and highly successful small-car project.

By 1927 a minor miracle was necessary to keep the 1200 employees gainfully at work. However, Schapiro had found just what was needed, even though it was a design rejected for manufacture under licence by other German makers of the period. In Britain it was simply called the Austin Seven and Schapiro's direct negotiations with Sir Herbert Austin brought the British baby two-seater to Germany—and a mass production line to Eisenach at about the same time as Daimler-Benz was also introducing assembly line production.

The first 100 Austins went to Germany in right-hand drive form, similar to the model that had been such a success in Britain since its announcement in 1922. The 750 cc Sevens had the Dixi radiator mascots attached and were on sale in 1927 as Dixi 3/15 Typ Da 1s. Acceptance of the 75 km/h (47 mph) licensed Austin, with its fuel consumption of 6 litres/100 km (47 mpg), was immediate. Although only some 250 Wartburg-badged cars had been sold between 1899 and 1903, Dixi production amounted to over 15,000 units, of which more than 9000 were licensed versions of the Austin. Yet even this was not enough to prevent a BMW take-over of the factory in 1928 (see page 44).

LEFT *An Austin Seven in everything but name; the 3/15 Dixi introduced in 1927 was BMW's first car following the firm's take-over of the Eisenach Vehicle Factory in 1928. It remained in production until 1932. This is a 1929 DA 1* (Deutsche Ausfuhrung, *German version) of the design, with the similar DA 2 arriving in July 1929. Like its British equivalent, the diminutive four-cylinder engine was of 748 cc, but arranged in a reverse image of its Longbridge counterpart. Suspension was therefore by transverse leaf spring at the front with rear quarter-elliptics. The car sold well, with BMW making some 9000 DA 1s and 12,000 DA 2s, tiding the firm over the worst of the Depression years.*

ABOVE *The DA 4 version of the 3/15 Dixi, introduced in 1931, lasted until 1932. Around 3500 were built. Like the British version, it now boasted coupled brakes rather than the foot brake operating the rear and the handbrake the front!*

LEFT *One of the longest-running Dixis was the 3/16 built between 1911 and 1925, although only 710 examples of this four-cylinder 3.3-litre model were built.*

The origins of BMW

While it is easy to trace the links between Wartburg, Dixi, Cyklon and eventual BMW control, describing some of the dealing that went on before BMW was able to acquire that Eisenach car factory is more complex. The story begins with aero engines and the establishment of the Bayerische Flugzeugwerke AG (Bavarian Aircraft Works) in March 1916. This company was itself the result of a merger between the Karl Rapp Motorenwerke and the Gustav Otto Flugmotorenfabrik, a liaison that had come about in 1913. The name Bayerische Motoren Werke (BMW) was first used in July 1917 and reflected the diversification of the company born of that merger.

At the end of the First World War in November 1918 the Bavarian aero-engine company emerged fit and strong under the managerial and engineering influence of Max Friz. Less than a year after the war ended, a Friz-designed six-cylinder engine installed in a DFW biplane established an astonishing altitude record of 9700 m (31,826 ft). This was achieved from an airfield on what is now Munich's Olympiapark, opposite BMW's modern four-cylinder shaped headquarters building. At the time there were aircraft production facilities there that included part of the present factory area, so local pride was assured when aviation records were set in the immediate post-war period. But in 1919 aero-engine manufacture was banned under the terms of the Versailles peace treaty. However, the BMW name had been sold to Knorr Bremse AG: the intention was to turn the concern into a mere production facility concentrating on braking equipment for railway carriages and the like! It was 1922 before one of BMW's original trustees and principal investors, Viennese financier Camillo Castiglioni, managed to buy back again both the BMW name and the assets

of Bayerische Flugzeugwerke AG; to pay for these he used German currency that was by then becoming worthless. It was this reborn concern that used the round blue-and-white trademark in advertising designed to sell its engines for many purposes outside aviation, including boating and agriculture.

Friz had designed a flat-twin motorcycle engine of just under 500 cc and this was offered to other motorcycle manufacturers in Germany, and then installed by BMW itself in a frame marketed as the Helios. Finally BMW was drawn into the bike business with the 1923 R32 design which used the company's own running gear and frames. This featured two key parts of the present-day BMW motorcycle: the air-cooled flat twin *boxer* engine and the shaft drive to the rear wheel (the engine was called *boxer* because the cylinders 'boxed' each other). The same year brought the resumption of aero-engine manufacture, and BMW was also taking part in two-wheel competition by 1924, just a year after motorcycle production was resumed.

By 1925 BMW was becoming so interested in the possibilities of producing its own cars that negotiations were started with the famous aerodynamicist and engineer Wunibald Kamm. Based near Stuttgart, Kamm had produced an advanced two-cylinder *boxer*-engined car with front-wheel drive and all-independent suspension. BMW investigated this 1030 cc vehicle to the extent of having a small number of running prototypes made between 1925 and 1927, but it was apparent that it would not proceed with its own design, a decision ratified by the company board in July 1928.

The entrepreneur Castiglioni was influential in persuading BMW senior management and large shareholders that, while it might run against some of their interests to produce a rival to the Daimler-Benz cars of the period (that former BMW luminary, Schapiro, was the leading D-B shareholder!), a small car would be perfectly feasible. It was through Castiglioni that BMW started to talk seriously to Eisenach's Dixi representatives, even though BMW itself was in debt, thanks to the poor trading conditions in Germany at the time.

The agreement

An increase in shareholding capital from 10 to 16 million Reichsmarks enabled BMW to change the name of the Eisenach Dixi factory to that of Bayerische Motoren Werke for the sum of RM 10 million. It was not a particularly good deal as Eisenach turned out to have RM 7.8 million in hidden debts and these had to be taken on too, but the agreement was ratified by 16 November 1928. From January 1929 onwards the Dixi symbol disappeared from the 3/15 models and Britain's transplanted Austin Seven became the first BMW car: BMW 3/15 Typ DA 2. The 'DA' stood for *Deutsche Ausführung*, or German version. There was also a DA 3 sports variant.

On 1 March 1932 BMW struck out on its own, prematurely withdrawing from the agreement to build the Austin Seven, which the company had further developed with an independent front suspension layout (DA 4) that was not very well received. It is not clear whether this was the fault of the talented Friz, as some German sources imply, or because he did not enjoy a good enough working relationship with his design office for them to produce exactly what he had in mind. What is known is that the car was somewhat unpredictable in its steering and handling and that BMW quickly produced a more thoroughly engineered replacement.

The Austin contract was cancelled at less than a month's notice, and the launch of the new BMW (the body was produced by Daimler-Benz) was planned for 1 April 1932. Because of the continuing recession, the new BMW 3/20 AM 1 did not enjoy quite the sales success that the motoring press had forecast, yet it was a very important BMW because it combined the company's engineering and the larger body style to such a degree that it was taken more seriously than the Austin Seven-derived Dixis and BMWs. Most features were new, from the backbone chassis to the overhead-valve version of the Austin engine which was enlarged from 748.5 to 782 cc by a 2.2 mm increase in stroke.

The first six-cylinder

Despite the inevitable build-up on the military side, BMW's reputation for producing quality cars grew throughout the 1930s, and the 303, introduced in February 1933, was the starting point. Designed in Eisenach while Max Friz was absent, the 303 was externally significant for carrying the first of the traditional *Nieren* (kidney) shaped radiator grilles that are retained to this day. Underneath there was a stout tubular steel chassis with 90 mm (3½ in) primary tubing and a much improved independent front suspension, together with a live sprung rear axle via leaf springs. The steering was very direct—almost like a racing car's—at two turns lock to lock, and similar in construction to many sports cars in its use of rack-and-pinion principles.

The 303's six-cylinder engine, and the base from which increasingly powerful units would be built throughout the 1930s, was essentially the overhead-valve four with the same 56 × 80 mm bore and stroke, plus two extra cylinders. The result was a four-bearing (instead of two), six-cylinder engine of 1173 cc that produced 30 bhp. Running on large 16-inch steel disc wheels, the 303 suited the new *Autobahnen* that were being so rapidly constructed.

The four-cylinder 309, which came on the market in 1934,

LEFT *The Austin influence is still apparent on the 3/20 BMW of 1932–4 vintage. But beneath the surface is a new fashionable backbone chassis and swing axle. The 782 cc engine was a development of the Seven's unit but with its stroke increased from 76 to 80 mm and overhead rather than side valves. The AM 1 and AM 3 versions were produced between 1932 and 1933, while the AM 4 took over in the latter year, lasting until 1934. However, the 3/20 was rather less successful than the earlier 3/15 with 7215 sold, although it was launched in 1932 at the very nadir of the German economic depression.*

RIGHT *The BMW 303, introduced in 1933, was the first Eisenach car to embody the famous 'kidney style' radiator grille which has been a BMW feature ever since. The 1173 cc engine shared the 3/20's 56 × 80 mm bore and stroke. The chassis was tubular, the front axle transversely sprung, and there was rack-and-pinion steering. There were 2300 examples built in 1933–4.*

brought the same style at a lower price. The 845 cc engine was an enlarged version of the unit previously used in the 3/20, giving 22 bhp and a maximum speed of 80 km/h (50 mph). It was produced in five body styles, all with two doors. BMW sold 2300 of the six-cylinder 303s in 1933–4 and an impressive 6000 of its four-cylinder 309 brother during its 1934–6 production run (the basic two-door saloon was the most popular), but the best seller was to come.

The foundation of BMW's sporting prowess on four wheels had been laid with some of the Austin Seven derivatives but, strictly speaking, the 315—with 9765 sold it was the second most popular car in the pre-war range—really started the sporting reputation. In the summer of 1934 BMW decided to add to the five body styles already offered on the 315 (the saloon bodywork was by far the most popular choice, as it had been with the 303 and 309). The latest model not only looked good, but also received a power boost. It was also to pave the way to the fabled 328.

This two-seater was the BMW 315/1. From its two-tone colour scheme to its flowing tail, the 315/1 had all that was needed to encourage enthusiasts to seek out the 242 examples made from 1935 to 1936. The engine received triple Solex carburettors to replace the normal twin-carburettor 315 arrangement, and the compression ratio was raised from 5.6 to 6.8:1. The result was another 6 bhp (40 bhp at 4300 rpm) and a BMW guarantee that 120 km/h (75 mph) could be exceeded.

Both the 309 and its larger capacity successor, the 315, which was produced between 1934 and 1937, brought a logic to BMW's designations and initiated a system still in use today after an intermission in the 1950s and '60s of often bewildering badgework. For example, the 3 in the 309 designation indicated the type of model, and 09 the size of engine, in this case 0.9 litres. By the 1980s the complete range followed the same logical system, so that the four current series numbers—3, 5, 6, and 7—precede the capacity in litres, e.g. a 518 is a 5 series 1.8-litre car, and so on.

The 315 of 1934 continued the basic 303 six-cylinder theme and was mechanically very similar, except for the larger bore and longer stroke of the engine, which now provided 34 bhp from its 1490 cc. The BMW six-cylinder engine continued to progress under the engineering direction of former Horch employee Fritz Fiedler, and a 2-litre 319/1 development also appeared in 1934 and was phased out with the 315/1 in 1936. At first the 1911 cc in-line six of the 319/1 was made with the triple carburettors and raised compression ratio for sporting use in 55 bhp form, when 130 km/h (81 mph) was within reach in ex-factory, unmodified form. This was a useful competition car too, weighing little more than the 315/1, but the point was that the engine proved so adaptable. BMW took the unusual

RIGHT *The BMW 327 had a 2-litre overhead valve six-cylinder engine under its handsome bonnet. Production ran from 1937 until 1941, and totalled nearly 1400 cars. Provided by BMW, owner Henry Ingster.*

BELOW *BMW's first sports car was the 315/1 with 1.5-litre six-cylinder engine. Built between 1935 and 1936, a total of 242 was produced. Top speed was 120 km/h (75 mph).*

BOTTOM *Marketed in Britain by AFN Ltd, the Frazer Nash BMW 319/55 of 1937 made its British contemporaries look decidedly old fashioned. Owner Mark Garfitt.*

step of reducing power for a series of mechanically similar but visually different BMWs. These were the 1935–7 saloons, convertibles and tourers with 45 bhp twin-carburettor engines that were designated just 319 and 329. These were relatively popular; some 6646 of the 319 were sold, but only 1179 of the 329 (mostly four-window convertibles). However, there was a dramatically better and much more successful BMW motor car in production by then.

The 326 was a tremendously appealing car; its flowing lines made it a major attraction at the 1936 Berlin motor show, and stood the test of time by appearing in a number of designs of the 1950s. It was not a sporty machine: the four-door bodywork was entirely new to BMW and designed to appeal to the potential Mercedes customer as well as BMW's traditional clientele. New features included hydraulics for the four-wheel drum brakes, torsion bar springing for the live rear axle, a new design of independent front suspension, and a stout box frame to replace the previous tubular chassis; the rack-and-pinion steering system of the 315 and 319 survived. The engine was basically the same in-line six as before, but a slight increase in cylinder bore gave 1971 cc and an unstressed 50 bhp at a peaceful 3750 engine crankshaft rpm.

The 326 was the most popular pre-war BMW, selling 15,936 examples; more than 10,000 of these were the four-door saloon with its Ambi Budd steel body. Performance of this 1125 kg (2480 lb) saloon amounted to a fine 115 km/h (71 mph) top speed and an average fuel consumption of 12.5 litres/100 km (22.6 mpg).

The 326 was in production from 1936 and survived the early war years, finally being withdrawn in 1941. It was joined in July

BMW 328 1936–40	
ENGINE	
No. of cylinders	6
Bore/stroke mm	66 × 96
Displacement cc	1971
Valve operation	Side camshaft, pushrod, rocker and cross pushrod
Compression ratio	7.5:1
Induction	Triple Solex carburettors
BHP	80 at 4500 rpm
Transmission	Four-speed manual
CHASSIS	
Frame	Tubular
Wheelbase mm	2400
Track—front mm	1153
Track—rear mm	1220
Suspension—front	Independent, transverse leaf spring, lower wishbone
Suspension—rear	Live axle
Brakes	Hydraulic
PERFORMANCE	
Maximum speed	150 km/h (93 mph)

TOP *One of the most outstanding sports cars of all time: the BMW 328 of 1936–40. It was to dominate the 2-litre class in competition; Paul Heinemann is seen in one such event in the late 1930s.*

ABOVE *The 328's faired-in headlamps reflected German aerodynamic awareness.*

LEFT *Built in 1936 and 1937, the BMW 329 had a 1.9-litre six-cylinder engine. This is a 1937 Frazer Nash BMW. Capable of 110 km/h (68 mph), a total of 1179 was produced. Provided by Sytner of Nottingham.*

RIGHT *The 335 saloon was launched in 1938 and phased out in 1941. By then just over 400 had been made.*

1937 by an eseentially shorter and lighter two-door cousin called the 320 (which had the old 319 suspension at the front). The first 640 of these had the older 1911 cc six, but this was replaced by the 1971 cc unit. Also related in a typically BMW cross-pollination process was the 321, which was similar to but smaller than the 326, and actually adopted that car's front suspension and rear hinged doors.

The BMW sports car

The next logical step would have been the appearance of sporting versions of the 326, but it was 1937 before BMW presented these outstanding developments (the 327 and 327/28), for the company had decided to introduce a true classic into the range a year before. In June 1936 Ernst Henne, the renowned BMW motorcycle racer, demonstrated the latest and so far the most classic BMW design of all: the 328 two-seater sports car. With a combinuation of the developed 315/319 sports tubular chassis (with box-section crossmembers) and the new Fiedler-inspired aluminium cylinder head for the 1971 cc engine, BMW managed to produce a magical moment in sports car engineering (it made an impact rather like the original Jaguar E-type in the 1960s). It had flowing lines that complemented a well-balanced chassis and had adequate engine power. The suspension was the familiar BMW independent at the front and leaf spring at the rear, with that rack-and-pinion steering of excellent response, but there was the added braking capability of a hydraulic system. There was a choice of gearboxes from Hirth and ZF, both four-speed (the ZF was more suitable for competition). It was possible to have other competition-inspired features like doubling the fuel tank capacity, or wheels with one centre lock instead of five-bolt fixing, making wheel changes much quicker.

The bulk of 328s was manufactured in 1937–9, when production ran at over 100 examples a year. Only a couple were made for competition in 1936, the year of the 328's début, and fewer than ten in 1940. Most of the 462 produced had the flowing Eisenach two-seater open body, but specialist coachbuilders like Gläser, Wendler, Drauz and Weinberger also completed 328s.

From 1938 to 1940 BMW offered the 80 hp triple Solex carburettor power unit for the 327 in 327/28 form. The car was reckoned to reach 140 km/h (87 mph) compared with the 328's advertised 150 km/h (93 mph) in standard trim. Fuel consumption for both models was estimated at 14.5 litres/100 km (19.48 mpg). Some 569 BMW 327/28s were made, nearly 500 of them sports convertibles.

The final important pre-war BMW model was the 335, a four-door extension to the 326 theme, with a single-carburettor engine of 3.5 litres that was of initial interest to the British importers. No firm orders materialized in time to beat the imposition of wartime restrictions on materials, so a little over 400 of these long 4840 mm (190½ in) cars were made in 1938–41. The 335s proved popular with senior military officers and were really large-scale versions of the 326.

DIFFICULT YEARS

For much of the war BMW was a large business with factories not only in Munich (mainly aero engines) and Eisenach, but also in Berlin-Spandau, where there was another plant devoted to aero engines. In all, more than 42,000 people were employed in 1942. For the makers of military radial engines—powering such effective single-seater fighter aircraft as the original Focke Wulf Fw 190—and the 1943 series production BMW 109-003 jet engine, there were bound to be post-war repercussions. Not surprisingly, Allied bombing took its toll, particularly at the Milbertshofen plant in Munich, but the main post-war problem was that Eisenach came in the Russian zone and so BMW's car production plant was lost completely. Then the Americans supervised the confiscation of all useful BMW assets as war reparations: it is said that no fewer than 16 nations participated in the BMW spoils of war. In Britain a tangible result was the emergence of 328 technology within the Bristol Cars division of the famous aircraft maker.

It could so easily have been the end of the story, but former employees around the two Munich plants did not give up. There was only one answer in the immediate post-war years and that was to work at anything in the hope of getting both your country and yourself back to some semblance of peacetime prosperity. So it is not surprising that BMW came back into car manufacturing via any sort of metalwork production that could be managed. There was plenty of aluminium left around the Munich plant at Milbertshofen (the other factory was taken over by the Americans as an enormous military depot) and the first evidence that workers had cleared the debris and had started production again came in 1946 with the output of pots and pans, followed by bicycles and some agricultural machinery. Behind the scenes the Deutsche Bank arranged the necessary financing; it was the bank's Dr Hans Karl von Mangoldt-Reiboldt, who became BMW's chairman, a post he held until 1958.

The Western road back

Meanwhile, in Munich, the car-building dream persisted despite an initial absence of materials and a factory! A number of BMW *aficionados* made what they could of the BMW 328 technology that had not gone to Bristol in England. These included Alexander Freiherr von Falkenhausen, who was behind the AFM (this was a BMW derivative; another example was Veritas), and was a most influential figure in later BMW history: he became the company's power unit engineering director.

Inside BMW there was immediate confusion as to the type of car the firm wanted to make; a two-seater prototype of 600 cc had been produced but some of the directors felt this did not measure up to BMW's pre-war image and so they decided on a luxury car. It was unfortunate that BMW chose this course as, in these years of post-war austerity, there was no immediate demand for such a vehicle.

In April 1951 BMW displayed the first prototype of this car: the six-cylinder 501. It had generous flowing lines over its 4724 mm (186 in) length and was powered by a 65 bhp version of the 1971 cc engine that had also led the post-war revival in the East. There the engine was used in the EMW car built at Eisenach until 1955; thereafter the revived Wartburg marque was produced there. The steel body sat over a rugged separate chassis of mixed rectangular box sections and tubular construction.

When that first 501 was shown, BMW really had no means of mass-producing it. The company had decided to invest all its available capital in its own pressed-steel stamping plant, but that would not be fully operational before the mid-1950s. The temporary answer was to go to the coachwork specialists Baur in Stuttgart and have the bodies made. Even then it was November 1952 before the patient BMW customers began to receive their cars: in 1952 only 49 of BMW's first post-war cars reached the public; a more satisfactory 1592 were made in 1953, and 3410 in 1954.

LEFT *1957 BMW 502 with 3.2-litre V8 engine. Provided by TT Workshops.*

BELOW LEFT *501 of 1952–5.*

BMW 502 3.2-LITRE
1955–61

ENGINE	
No. of cylinders	8
Bore/stroke mm	82 × 75
Displacement cc	3168
Valve operation	Pushrod
Compression ratio	7.2:1
Induction	Single carburettor
BHP	120 at 2500 rpm
Transmission	Four-speed manual
CHASSIS	
Frame	Box section
Wheelbase mm	2835
Track—front mm	1330
Track—rear mm	1416
Suspension—front	Independent, wishbone, torsion bar
Suspension—rear	Live axle, torsion bar
Brakes	Hydraulic; 1959 front disc option
PERFORMANCE	
Maximum speed	170 km/h (106 mph)

ABOVE *The BMW 503 with 3.2-litre V8 engine was built for four years only, between 1956 and 1959, with just 412 examples made. Top speed was around 190 km/h (118 mph).*

RIGHT *The even rarer 507 of 1955–9 with similar 3.2-litre V8 but developing 150 bhp. Top speed was 190–220 km/h (118–137 mph) depending on the rear axle ratio. A mere 253 cars were built.*

From the beginning BMW knew that the 2-litre six-cylinder engine was not really powerful enough to pull such a hefty four-door saloon. In fact the 135 km/h (84 mph) top speed was certainly no disgrace, but the 0–100 km/h (62 mph) acceleration figure of nearly half a minute reflected the considerable task the engine faced. By way of comparison, the six-cylinder BMW took rather longer to reach a 100 km/h cruising speed than some late 1950s saloons of less than 1 litre.

BMW acted positively to regain its former prestige as suppliers of performance-oriented quality cars: the factory put the long-planned eight-cylinder engine into production. It was Germany's first post-war V8. Of 2580 cc, and made with all its major components in aluminium, BMW's V8 immediately overcame the power problem. Some 95 bhp was provided at the beginning of production in 1954, and 100 bhp by the time this long-lived 2.6-litre entered the 1960s. Few changes were made to the 501 design when the V8 was installed and this was reflected in the designation 502. Externally there was a chrome side strip added to the existing lower sill, and mechanically the first gear had a different ratio to suit the V8's extra pulling power. The 502, and from 1955 a V8-equipped 501, performed well, taking 10 seconds less to reach 100 km/h and having a top speed of 160 km/h (100 mph). Of course there was a fuel consumption penalty to pay, but this did not seem to worry BMW management as it took only until 1955 for the company to make a bigger version of the V8. Sold as the 502 3.2-litre, and subsequently the basis for much more sporting applications, the later V8 had a longer crankshaft stroke to provide 3168 cc and 120 bhp in its mildest form.

The large BMWs—and their subsequent sporting derivatives: the 503, made from 1956 to 1959, and the glorious 507 of the same period—certainly brought back a measure of the company's previous prestige. However, their low volume sales could not offset the increasing losses being incurred in motorcycle manufacture. By 1953 the German economic boom had propelled BMW to its 100,000th bike of the post-war period. However, motorcycle sales were now declining as the market seemed to want the better weather-protection of small and cheap cars.

The Frankfurt show of 1955 neatly demonstrated the BMW dilemma. The company exhibited the Count Albrecht Goertz-designed 503 and 507 coupé and cabriolet and the Italian-designed Isetta two-seater 'bubble car', for which the Munich company had acquired the manufacturing rights. There could not have been a bigger contrast. The 503 and 507 both echoed the large luxury sports car theme and carried a 3.2-litre V8 punch; the 507 was rated at 150 bhp and was said to be capable of anywhere between 190 and 220 km/h (118 and 137 mph), according to the ratio within the rear axle. Both these sports cars were based on the saloon car running gear, but the 507 had a shorter wheelbase, which contributed much to making it one of the great sports car styling triumphs of the 1950s.

Recipe for survival

In autumn 1958 the acquisition or demise of BMW because of financial losses looked all too real. BMW had lost DM 12 million that year, paying off 6.5 million by exhausting the capital reserves and leaving DM 5.5-million loss to be carried into 1959. That year there was a DM 9.2-million adverse balance and nearly half the shareholders' capital had to be depleted in preserving the company's existence. Throughout 1959 the management threshed ineffectively against its increasing liabilities, seeking further bank credits and even support from the Bavarian state.

It was against this background, and a drop in motorcycle sales from nearly 30,000 a year in 1954 to little over 5400 in 1957, that BMW was struggling to fill the obvious gap in its car model range. At the top end there were the fast and rapidly ageing big V8 saloons and sports cars. Then there was a huge model gap until the 600, introduced in 1957, and the Isettas. The 600, however, was not just another loss maker that was neither car nor bubble car proper, for the independent rear suspension was of the semi-trailing type that has since become standard on all BMWs. The advantage of the BMW system at the time—and it has since been modified to keep pace with modern tyres and roadholding demands—was simply the combination of a comfortable ride with good cornering capability.

BMW began its attempt to bridge that gap with the 700 of 1959. Mechanically it amounted to much the same recipe as the 600, with trailing arms and rear motorcycle-type engine, but it was clothed in a rakish two-door coupé body by Michelotti of Turin. Ready for sale by August 1959, the coupé rather unusually preceded the saloon version, also of 30 bhp and 697 cc, which was put on the market in December the same year. Both went on to become great successes in the 1960s and were also produced in a later long-wheelbase version until September 1965, when 188,121 had been constructed, around 150,000 of them in the 120 km/h (75 mph) saloon guise. The coupé was reckoned to be slightly faster, but they were both attractive propositions, combining good road manners with perky performance and 7.06 litres/100 km (40 mpg) economy.

However, a new middle-class car was still needed. While it could be planned by a team that included Alex von Falkenhausen at the head of the engine design department, putting it into production against a background of ever-worsening BMW financial results looked impossible. Indeed the annual general meeting held on 9 December 1959 was a dramatic occasion, for the chairman of the board of trustees, Dr Hans Feith, demonstrated just how the Deutsche Bank saw the future. He proposed a redevelopment plan that really amounted to a relatively low-priced Mercedes-Benz take-over bid. The bank was also a large shareholder in the Mercedes company. Further meetings showed that the board had little to offer as an alternative to the Mercedes acquisition, except bankruptcy, although there were said to be plenty of other companies outside Germany interested in buying BMW, particularly in Britain and America.

Nevertheless the smaller BMW shareholders and the dealerships across Germany stuck out for an independent BMW. Grouped together against the Mercedes, or any other take-over plan, the opposition appointed the Frankfurt lawyer and accountant Dr Friedrich Mathern. He succeeded in revealing some anomalies in the way the 700 had been financed and this, together with other points raised regarding the future ownership of the company, provided the BMW action group with a lot of muscle. Shortly afterwards Dr Richter-Brohm resigned from the chairmanship of BMW.

Now all that was needed was some money to make that new middle-class car that was to save BMW.

ABOVE *The 1961 250 BMW Isetta, made by the Munich company from 1955 until 1962 . The 250 had a 247 cc engine.*

BMW 1500 1962–4	
ENGINE	
No. of cylinders	4
Bore/stroke mm	82 × 71
Displacement cc	1499
Valve operation	Single overhead camshaft
Compression ratio	8.8:1
Induction	Single carburettor
BHP	80 at 5700 rpm
Transmission	Four-speed manual
CHASSIS	
Frame	Unitary construction
Wheelbase mm	2550
Track—front mm	1320
Track—rear mm	1366
Suspension—front	Independent, MacPherson strut
Suspension—rear	Independent, semi-trailing arms
Brakes	Hydraulic, front disc
PERFORMANCE	
Maximum speed	148 km/h (92 mph)

ABOVE *The BMW 700 with rear-mounted air-cooled 697 cc engine and Michelotti styling. Built between 1959 and 1964, it was available in coupé and saloon forms. A 1964 example of the latter is shown.*

RIGHT *The first of a new generation of BMWs for the middle ground: the 1500, which represented a turning point in the firm's fortunes. Built between 1962 and 1964, it was powered by a new 1.5-litre four-cylinder overhead camshaft engine and 23,807 examples were made.*

BMW'S SAVIOUR: THE 1500

During the early 1960s BMW's prospects were uncertain. The meetings between the creditors and the company ensured that a start was made with resettling debts. But how quickly the deficits could be made good and what kind of future BMW really had as a top car manufacturer demanded much more attention. In the event, BMW recovered quickly, simply through the sales success of new models; but getting them into production was a saga in itself.

In addition to the personalities already mentioned, Herbert and Harald Quandt, the German financiers, became increasingly important in the early 1960s. They acquired stock—the kind of shareholding that saw them so well represented at Mercedes-Benz—but Herbert Quandt's involvement went much further. This hard-headed businessman became convinced, like many of the BMW staff, that the company's future lay in manufacturing a car for the increasingly important West German middle class.

Just to produce a car for the Frankfurt Show of autumn 1961 was problem enough. However, the company engineers realized the car's importance and allowed themselves to be pushed through the development period of the 1500 at an abnormally fast pace. This haste was reflected at Frankfurt, for the 1500 was clearly not ready for production—yet BMW felt the car had to be shown in order to interest potential customers. Another clear indication that the BMW sales department, now headed by former Auto Union marketing director Paul Hahneman, was prevailing over the development engineers was the look of the new 1500. During the countdown period to that public début, the Italian stylists Michelotti were asked to incorporate the traditional BMW kidney grille within the front sheet metal.

However, the power unit was one area where all the development 'bugs' appeared to have been eliminated with a thoroughness that was unfortunately not matched in the 1500 chassis and bodywork. The five-bearing four-cylinder engine, complete with chain-driven overhead camshaft, was designed by a six-man team working on a minimal budget under the direction of Alexander von Falkenhausen.

To BMW's delight, the 1500 had attracted thousands of Deutschmarks in deposits from customers who had ordered the car either at the show, or in the wake of the attendant publicity. The principles of the 1500, and thus those of every succeeding mass-production BMW to this day, were established. Among the minor surprises was the use of MacPherson strut front suspension, a type made popular through its use by Ford. The semi-trailing arm rear suspension of the 1500 proved so effective that it has become a feature of luxurious family cars today. That BMW had problems getting the 1500 into genuine mass production is shown by the fact that, although a preliminary series was made in February 1962, full production did not begin until October that year! Some sources report that there were 20,000 orders for the new 1500 by the end of 1961, so BMW's embarrassment during 1962 can well be imagined as fewer than 2000 of the new 1500s were made in that first production year. Even by the end of production, when it was succeeded by the much better quality 1600 of similar design and appearance, BMW had manufactured 'only' 23,807 of the 1500 model.

Descendants of the 1500

BMW spent much of the early 1960s dispensing with models that proved less and less profitable following the sales success of the 1500 and subsequent variants. The Isettas were dropped in 1962. The large 501 and 502 V8 saloons ceased production the following year, although similar large cars (the 2600L, 3200L and 3200S) limped on a little longer. The 2600L, basically a 501/502 shape with minor styling and mechanical refinements, proved the most durable and stayed in production until 1964.

However, large V8-engined cars were not entirely forgotten at BMW in the 1960s. Introduced in 1962, the 3200CS coupé succeeded the 503 sports cars and indicated the direction BMW was taking with coupés. Only 603 were made before production stopped in 1965. Combining a 200km/h (124mph) top speed with harmonious styling—the Italian Bertone design team then included Giorgetto Giugiaro, who has earned such a fine reputation for his work on projects as diverse as the VW Golf and Lotus Esprit—the 3200CS was significant for more than merely being the last V8 BMW has produced to date.

In September 1963, the company introduced an 1800 model which was simply a 1773cc version of the 1500 with an additional chrome strip so that status seekers, or the merely curious, could tell the difference between the two cars. Already the 1500 had enhanced the company's reputation as well as putting new vigour into its marketing, and a lot more money into the once depleted bank reserves.

For the 1800, bore and stroke were increased from 82 × 71 to 84 × 80mm to provide 90 instead of 80bhp. Thus the normal 1800 (which was later fitted with a smoother but no more powerful engine) was capable of 162km/h (100mph) instead of the original 1500's 148km/h (92mph). Since the 1500 had already attracted the attention of small engineering companies that derive a living from improving the performance of mass-produced cars, it was no surprise that Munich anticipated any such moves. BMW announced its own 1800TI, a faster version of the 1800. The 110bhp TI was put on sale from March 1964, providing 177km/h (110mph) *Autobahn* motoring. The twin Solex carburettor version of the engine had its compression increased from 8.6:1 to 9.5:1, but there were few external changes apart from bigger 5in wide wheels (instead of 4½in).

By 1965 BMW could make some satisfying comparisons with the crisis year of 1959: turnover was five times as great; the labour force had doubled to approximately 12,000; and production was 58,524 vehicles, far above the company's previous records and especially gratifying because of the continuing growth in car sales. BMW has continued this success ever since.

The 1800TI stayed in production until 1966, but by then both it and the 1800 were overshadowed by the development of a 2-litre engine for much the same square-rigged four-door body. The 2-litre engine first appeared in coupé coachwork, for BMW took the distinctively large window area, with no centre pillar, first seen on the 3200CS, and grafted it on to lower bodywork mainly derived from the 1500/1800 saloons.

ABOVE *There were only about 140 right-hand-drive versions of the BMW 2000 CS of 1965–9. Provided by John Giles.*

BELOW LEFT *The Bertone-styled 3200 CS of 1962–5. A 3.2-litre V8 engine was employed. Top speed was 200 km/h (124 mph), but only 603 were built.*

RIGHT *Early hatchback. Introduced in 1971 as the 2000 Touring, from 1973 it became the 2002 and the 1802. A mere 18,966 were made.*

In June 1965, some seven months before the introduction of a 2000 saloon, BMW announced the 2-litre coupés. Constructed by Karmann at Osnabrück, the BMW 2000 C and 2000 CS (Coupé and Coupé Sport) kept the wheelbase and track of the saloon models but were slightly longer overall, almost 51 mm (2 in) narrower and over 102 mm (4 in) lower. When the 2-litre saloon models were announced in 1966 it became apparent that the sporting coupés were a little heavier than their four-door brethren.

The 2000 C and CS looked the same, but under the bonnet the former had a single carburettor engine of 100 bhp rather than the twin Solex carburettors, raised compression ratio, and 120 bhp of the CS.

Between 1965 and 1969 just 2837 of the 2000 C, and 8883 examples of the 2000 CS, were made: a healthy trade but nothing compared with the astonishing 43,431 of the BMW 2000 saloon in its first full production year, in 1966. The 2000 used the same 89 × 80 mm 1990 cc engine that the 2000 C had pioneered in 1965, right down to the 100 bhp rating. Also introduced in January 1966 was the 2000 TI saloon which had the twin-carburettor, 120 bhp unit that was also used in the 2000 CS. Performance and fuel consumption were obviously similar to the coupés; the coupé shape gave a marginal top-speed advantage of 6.5 km/h (4 mph). However, the 2000, with its improved carrying capacity and the delightful all-round response of the 2-litre engine, seemed to be everyone's period favourite. The 2000 single-carburettor saloon, with a number of cosmetic changes to front and rear lamps, remained in production until 1972. The TI developed a more luxurious character and was designated the 2000 tilux (the process of changing BMW designations from capital letters to lower case, as here, was begun in 1968) and lasted until 1970. Both models were a little overshadowed by the first fuel-injected BMW road car. This was the 2000 tii of 1969–72, which had the Kugelfischer mechanical system, of racing fame, tamed to provide 130 bhp. These cars were refined in performance and quite fast at 185 km/h (115 mph), but the 1500 to 2000 series had begun to show its age and weight by then. These cars were losing their appeal to a 1966 series that forms the next part of the story. Altogether, more than 350,000 *Neue Klasse* BMWs were made, some at the BMW-owned assembly plant in South Africa. It had been an astonishing turnabout.

LEFT *The BMW 2000, produced between 1966 and 1972. Provided by G.W. Jennings.*

BELOW *A rare cabriolet version of the 2002, produced by Baur of Stuttgart. Provided by Peter Rust.*

BMW 2002 1968–76	
ENGINE	
No. of cylinders	4
Bore/stroke mm	89 × 80
Displacement cc	1990
Valve operation	Single overhead camshaft
Compression ratio	8.5:1
Induction	Single carburettor
BHP	100 at 5500 rpm
Transmission	Four-speed manual
CHASSIS	
Frame	Unitary construction
Wheelbase mm	2500
Track—front mm	1330; from 1973: 1342
Track—rear mm	1330; from 1973: 1342
Suspension—front	Independent, MacPherson strut
Suspension—rear	Independent, semi-trailing arms
Brakes	Hydraulic, front disc
PERFORMANCE	
Maximum speed	173 km/h (107 mph)

Two-door versatility

The products that probably gave BMW its present fine reputation were the 02 series: the 1602, 1802, 2002 and the 1970s fuel-economy special, the 1502. When the new series was first introduced at the Geneva Motor Show of March 1966, the vehicle was simply known as the 1600-2 to indicate the number of doors the body carried compared to the earlier four-door series. The basic idea was to use the 1573 cc engine, the successor to the original 1500 installed in the BMW 1600 of 1964–6, in a much lighter body. The two-door 1600-2 weighed only 940 kg (2072 lb), compared with 1070 kg (2360 lb) for the equivalent four-door. This meant the 1600-2 could perform better at reduced fuel consumption. BMW reported a half-second improvement in the 0–100 km/h figures, an increase of 8 km/h (5 mph) in top speed, and 11.5 litres/100 km (24.57 mpg), which was nearly as good as the original 1500 and marginally better than the 1600.

These improvements were also coupled with a lower price; this welcome reduction was particularly important in BMW's expanding exports to Britain and the United States. In 1975 the 1600-2 became the 1602 to accord with the designation of its stablemates, particularly the 2002 of 1968 which combined a two-door body with a 2-litre engine. Until the 2002 arrived, the twin-carburettor version of the 1600, introduced in September 1967 and known simply as 1600 TI, and manufactured for one year only, was intended as the sporty two-door model. The 1600 TI had a 175 km/h (109 mph) performance, but the allure of low-down acceleration and inserting the 1990 cc engine in either single-carburettor 100 bhp trim (2002) or twin-carburettor 120 bhp form (2002 TI) proved irresistible, particularly outside Germany.

From its introduction in 1966 to the end of the economy-conscious 1502 in 1977 (this was made alongside the later 3-series for two years), the 02 derivatives seemed endless. Anticipating future styling, there was even a version with a hatchback third door: the Touring model of the 1970s; the 02 was also available, in limited quantities, as a convertible by Baur in Stuttgart. The success of the 02 cars and the rapid expansion of BMW's car manufacturing capabilities can be judged from the fact that the four-door series of 1962–72 (to 1974 in South Africa) had a total production figure of 364,378. By comparison 863,203 of the 02 machines were made in 11 years. By far the most popular were the 2002 types: nearly 400,000 of these were made between 1968 and 1976.

This sales success is not surprising, for the 2-litre engine provided a balance of speed, some 173 km/h (107 mph), and overall pulling power that was made even more acceptable by good road manners and a fuel consumption of 12.5 litres/100 km (22.6 mpg). Customers kept calling for more power, even though a twin-carburettor 2002 ti, with a 185 km/h (115 mph) maximum speed, was offered from 1968 onwards. Such demands were satisfied in the 1970s, but even during the first years of its life the 02 series could be obtained with power outputs of 85 bhp (1600-2); 105 bhp (1600 TI); 100 bhp (2002); and 120 bhp (2002 ti). The same basic principles found in all the 02 series—but with impressive braking and suspension improvements where appropriate—eventually coped with power outputs ranging from 75 to 170 bhp, and maximum speeds from 157 km/h (97 mph) to 211 km/h (131 mph). Simply to state that the 02 cars were versatile does not adequately convey their merits: these 02 BMWs were truly outstanding cars that satisfied widely differing public taste and demand.

BMW 2500
1968–77

ENGINE	
No. of cylinders	6
Bore/stroke mm	86 × 71
Displacement cc	2494
Valve operation	Single overhead camshaft
Compression ratio	9:1
Induction	Twin carburettor
BHP	150 at 6000 rpm
Transmission	Four-speed manual

CHASSIS	
Frame	Unitary construction
Wheelbase mm	2692
Track—front mm	1446
Track—rear mm	1464
Suspension—front	Independent, MacPherson strut
Suspension—rear	Independent, semi-trailing arms
Brakes	Hydraulic disc

PERFORMANCE	
Maximum speed	190 km/h (118 mph)

THE ROAD TO PROSPERITY

Although four-cylinder cars had powered the BMW renaissance of the 1960s, the company was not likely to forget its tradition of in-line six-cylinder units when there was finance to expand the range of cars further. The year 1968 was the most important in BMW's recovery and the link between the BMW of old and the expanding and prosperous company of the 1980s. Within those 12 months many plans at BMW were realized, including the manufacture of over 100,000 cars in a year; the continued transfer of motorcycle production to Berlin; the renovation of the Glas factory at Dingolfing which BMW had taken over, along with the firm, in 1966 (of today's major models only the 3-series is made in Munich); and the unveiling in September 1968 of the six-cylinder model.

BMW's rapidly increasing wealth was reflected in the stylish press launch at the Tegernsee lakeside of not just one six-cylinder saloon but three new models available in coupé (CS) two-door or four-door saloon bodies. Developed under the overall control of Bernhard Osswald, engineering director from 1965 to 1975, the big new BMWs amounted to an expansion of the basic principles found in the four-cylinder range. The single overhead camshaft was chain driven and operated the aluminium cylinder head's inlet and exhaust valves in the same V-arrangement with BMW's unique combustion chamber shape. The smaller 2494 cc six that was installed in the 2500 saloon, and in the much later economy model, the 2.5 CS of 1974–5, had much the same short-stroke proportions as the four-cylinder engine—71.6 mm, only fractionally more than on the original 1500 saloon and the later 1600 and 1600-2 designs. The bore of the 2.5-litre unit was some 2 mm longer than in the previous 1800 and 3 mm shorter than in the widely used 2-litre engine of the 2000, 2002, and 2000 CS.

At that 1968 launch the new BMW 2.5-litre six appeared only in saloon form, although it subsequently did stout work in

BELOW *The BMW 2500 six-cylinder model was built between 1968 and 1977. Provided by L and C Auto Services.*

The BMW 3.0 CSi of 1971–5 had a 3153 cc engine with Bosch D Jetronic fuel injection. Provided by Mrs H. Gates.

TKP 797N

LEFT *The final version of the BMW 3.0 CSL, though of 3153 cc. This lightweight version of the stylish coupé is distinguished by its 'Batmobile' aerodynamic rear wing. Provided by L and C Auto Services.*

BELOW RIGHT *The rare 2002 turbo of 1973–4, introduced the now familiar turbocharger to the European market. It boosted output of the 1990 cc engine from 100 to 170 bhp. Top speed was 211 km/h (131 mph), but only 1670 examples were made.*

many other BMW designs. In addition the 2500 proved the longest-lived of the original 1968 saloons in production terms, being offered until 1977 in much the same 150 bhp form. The larger 2.8-litre engine also shared the basic BMW principles of overhead camshaft, alloy cylinder head and an iron cylinder block 30° from vertical; with its extra 20 bhp it was installed in the sporting 2800 CS as well as the 2800 saloon. The 2788 cc capacity was achieved by the alliance of the 2.5-litre's 86 mm cylinder bore and the same 80 mm stroke as used in the 2-litre four-cylinder unit. The result was so successful it has been described by many experts as the world's best six-cylinder unit. The engine remained in continuous production for the next 14 years, and fuel injection versions appear in today's 5-, 6- and 7-series.

Underneath their shiny new bodies the 2800 CS and 2800 saloon shared engine, gearbox and rear end transmission through differential and halfshafts, but the running gear to support the 170 bhp sixes in their respective two- and four-door bodywork was very different. The 2800 CS ran on the shorter 2625 mm (103 in) wheelbase that owed most to the 2000 C/CS and therefore to the generation of four-door saloons that had founded BMW's recovery. Worthy as those had been, they were not the best base for a new six-cylinder coupé of sporting inclinations, a fact reflected in the use of drum brakes at the rear of the CS, while the saloon had a new four-wheel disc braking system.

The suspension principles that BMW has used since the 1500 (but with a significant number of modifications over the years to keep pace with improved tyres and higher customer expectations) were retained in the new sixes. MacPherson strut front suspension was used with trailing arm rear. This was an all-independent layout that featured an optional front roll bar for the saloons until 1971, when it became a production item, although it had been standard from the start on the CS. In the same way, power steering was a production item on the CS while it was an option for both saloons.

High performance

Although the new engines had to haul 1360 kg (2998 lb) in the saloons and 1355 kg (2987 lb) in the 2800 CS, none of the cars could be described as slow, even by the standards of today. The 2800 saloon could exceed 200 km/h (124 mph) and reach 100 km/h (62 mph) from rest in 10 seconds, the acceleration standard that many motorists used to divide the really sporty cars from the pretenders. Yet BMW was providing such performance in an ostensibly upright saloon with plenty of luggage space and accommodation. Even the less powerful 2500 was expected to provide 190 km/h (118 mph) and reach 100 km/h only a second after its big brother; the 2800 CS was credited with a 206 km/h (128 mph) maximum speed and was also capable of accelerating from 0 to 100 km/h in 10 seconds.

Fuel consumption was estimated at between 16 and 16.5 litres/100 km (17.7 and 17.1 mpg) under the worst conditions the factory could manage, but many owners stayed happily between 13.5 and 14.9 litres/100 km (21 and 19 mpg).

The new sixes were well received, but BMW was almost embarrassed by demand, making only 140 of the 2800 saloons in 1968, and also failing to contain the lengthening waiting lists with the manufacture of 2560 of the smaller-engined saloons that same year. By 1969 all BMW motorcycles were manufactured in Berlin.

However, 1969 saw BMW set new company records, including the output of just over 20,000 BMW 2500s and 16,611 2800 saloons. That year the company employed more than 20,000 people for the first time since the wartime peak of 42,346 in 1942, and overall car production reached nearly 150,000. Such rapid progress, aided by increasing export sales, has been the hallmark of BMW virtually ever since.

The 1968 six-cylinder range contributed a great deal to the company's turnover, total production of the various types reaching 252,559, including 44,254 coupés. However, it was not all glittering success, particularly in America where, from the 1969 introduction of the six-cylinder saloon, sales proved rather lethargic. By 1971 BMW had dealt with this problem by introducing the Bavaria, a cocktail of cheaper 2500 equipment and the 2800 engine. The 1971 Bavaria even had a European-style power output and the nameplate was carried on to its 3-litre carburated and fuel-injected successors, which stayed on the American market until 1975.

In Europe, development of the six-cylinder saloons followed logical lines but they were given the usual baffling system of numbers and suffixes. BMW and Mercedes excel at this arcane badgework, although BMW did return to more logical designations after the demise of the large six-cylinder saloons in 1977.

The 2500 had the simplest production record, running from 1968 to '77 with the few minor changes already noted. The 2800 remained officially in production until 1974, but was continued in the guise of the 2.8L of 1975–7. The L stood for *lang* and referred to the long wheelbase, which was extended by 100 mm (4 in) to give a total of 2792 mm (110 in). Like Jaguar and Mercedes, BMW had concentrated the extra length behind the centre pillar to the benefit of the rear passengers and to the detriment of kerb weight, which went up by 80 kg (176 lb). Long-wheelbase examples of the saloon subsequently included two 3.3-litre models: the 3.3 L of 1974–6 with 190 bhp from the 3295 cc engine, and the 3.3 L fuel-injected version of 1976–7, which developed 196 bhp from a marginally shorter-stroke version of the rugged 3210 cc six. Such slight changes in engine capacity do occur repeatedly in BMW history—in 1982 just such an adjustment was made to the 635 CSi, and the 1800 had two engines during the 1960s.

Although the 2800 was still being made in 1974 on the normal wheelbase, it had truly been supplanted by the 180 bhp 3.0 S; in this case the S stood for Saloon, although Sport might have been appropriate because of the extra 10 bhp. The 3-litre version of the six was ready for the German market in April 1971, and immediately revived the popularity of the bigger-engined BMW saloon. Yet it was soon outshone by the definitive 3-litre BMW six, the 3.0 Si of September of that same year! The fuel injection system on the Si was made by Bosch, as always on BMW six-cylinder power units (Kugelfischer mechanical injection systems were used in the four-cylinder power plants from 1969 to '75), yet two different Bosch systems were utilized for the 3.0 Si. Originally the engine was rated at 200 bhp and ran a 9.5:1 compression ratio with Bosch D-Jetronic injection. From September 1976 the compression was lowered slightly to 9:1, the injection system updated to Bosch L-Jetronic, but the power dropped to 195 bhp. Similarly the maximum torque figure was also slightly amended, but with over 265 Nm (196 lbf. ft) there was plenty of pulling power available in either version.

The 210 km/h (130 mph) 3.0 Si was a superb four-door saloon that had vigour, balanced by four-wheel ventilated disc brakes, and a turn of speed that continued to surprise right up to the end of its production life in 1977. In production form the 3.0 Si could sprint from rest to 100 km/h (62 mph) in only 8.5 seconds.

Coupé: towards a racing base

Development of the 2800 CS ran parallel to the saloons, although production did not begin until December 1968. The 3-litre carburettor and Bosch electronic fuel injection versions of the engines arrived in 1971, accompanied by a welcome conversion to four-wheel disc brakes, which made the CS series safer. Because of the coupé's 20 mm (¾ in) narrower body and 80 mm (3 in) lower roofline, BMW always claimed it had a better performance than the saloons, resulting in a top speed of 220 km/h (137 mph) for the 3.0 CSi.

Now that the 3-litre CS machines were the fastest BMWs in the range, it was not long before the legendary series of special coupés began to make an appearance under the generic CSL badge. This time the L stood for *leichtgewicht* (lightweight), which referred to a specially made Karmann coupé bodyshell. It utilized alloy skins instead of steel for components like doors, boot and bonnet to reduce weight from the standard 1400 kg (3086 lb) to 1200 kg (2645 lb) in the original carburated model of May 1971, or 1270 kg (2800 lb) in the more common fuel-injected CSL versions that ceased production in 1975.

For the public, the CSL road cars that had to be made to support that racing effort became valuable collector's items, although it should be noted that at least 500 of the cars exported to Britain were in a luxurious specification that made a mockery of the lightweight suffix. However, a 3.2-litre CSL of the 1973–5 period made a formidable mileage-eater, capable of close on 225 km/h (140 mph). During independent tests in Britain it dashed from 0–60 mph in a little over 7 seconds.

Turbo pioneer

The four-cylinder 02 models of the late 1960s provided a base on which to expand into the following decade: six cylinders may have had glamour and speed, but BMW's fours proved appealing in balancing sport with affordable economy. Thus the 02 derivatives continued to multiply with astonishing speed. Using engines of 1600, 1800 or 2000 cc, BMW built new bodies on that 02 basis, including the 1971–4 hatchback Touring models and a series of convertibles produced by Baur at Stuttgart from 1971 to '75. Engine power of the slant fours could be anything the customer demanded between the 75 bhp of the economy-conscious 1975–7 1502 and the 170 bhp of the ill-fated 1973–4 2002 turbo. This aggressive 211 km/h (131 mph) BMW appeared in the fuel crisis years and contributed to a public outcry against performance cars in Germany. In fact the 2002 turbo deserved a better production run than the 1670 examples recorded, for it was not only a landmark in BMW's history as the company's first turbo-charged road car, but it was also Europe's first production turbo to be offered to the public. If you remember that everyone from Renault to Porsche now offers such exhaust-driven turbines to enhance the performance and image of their wares, you can see BMW paid a very high price indeed

for pioneering. This 2002 special, with its stripy body, was immensely fast, its 2 litres of KKK turbocharged power producing 0–100 km/h (62 mph) figures of around 8 seconds or less and also gave owners the opportunity to cruise at 190 km/h (118 mph) alongside the disconcerted drivers of larger BMWs and Mercedes—at least for the rather short life of the turbocharger. The car is now rated highly by collectors, but it had no motor sport pedigree.

A far more significant year in BMW history was 1972. In the year that Munich was host city to the Olympic Games, BMW displayed its spectacular 'four-cylinder' office block and adjacent eggcup-styled museum. In September 1972 BMW also had a new four-door car to offer faithful customers of the previous 2000, together with a new numbering system that persists to this day. Under the control of current chairman Eberhard von Kuenheim (appointed from an industrial engineering background in 1970), BMW began to reveal the path it would follow to success, and the straightforward styling of the initial models, the four-cylinder 520 and its Kugelfischer-injected brother the 520i, reflected this exactly.

Built on a 2636 mm (104 in) wheelbase with an overall length of 4620 mm (182 in) the 5-series cars have proved among the most versatile and most enduring of BMW designs. Retaining the MacPherson strut and trailing arm independent

LEFT *BMW 520i, introduced in 1981 with 1990 cc engine.*

ABOVE *1981 M535i which was top of the original 5 series range.*

suspension, with adequate room for four adults, this series has catered perfectly for middle-class families all over the world in an amazing variety of power and equipment guises. Even though the 5-series was extensively revised with a far more aerodynamic body of 2625 mm (103 in) wheelbase in June 1981, its appearance has altered little in more than a decade of production, which included over 700,000 of the original series.

BMW played the power and options game with a vengeance on the 5-series, which also established the family look that BMWs carry today. The 520 lasted with four-cylinder power (and a subsequent insertion of Bosch fuel injection for the 520i) until 1977, when it inherited one of the new generation of small M60 six-cylinder engines that had been designed for the smaller 3-series. That engine, but with Bosch mechanical K-Jetronic injection, lives on in the 1980s' version of the 520i.

In September 1973 the 2.5-litre six of 2500 saloon fame became a 5-series alternative, and that too lived on in fuel injection form for the 1982 model range, badged as 525i and resplendent with the four-wheel disc brakes that used to be reserved for the 528 of 1975. In August 1977, the 528 became the 528i with Bosch L-Jetronic injection, 176 bhp and a maximum speed of 208 km/h (129 mph).

There had always been a limited number of BMW Motorsport GmbH 3- and 3.3-litre specials made to satisfy more enthusiastic customers (although the 530i was both an American and South African production reality), but BMW made perhaps the finest ever 5-series car by inserting the 3.5-litre 218 bhp six and uprating both suspension and braking for the M-for-Motorsport M535i in 1980–1.

Unfortunately the 225 km/h (140 mph) 535 was not carried over to the revised 1981 models, but the basic 518 of 1974 vintage was still represented in the 90 bhp and 1766 cc four-cylinder trim: it was the only new 5-series without fuel injection in a line-up that read 518, 520i, 525i and the now 184 bhp/209 km/h (130 mph) 528i. The later 5-series cars combined an admirable improvement in both performance and economy, plus the pioneering use of electronic Service Interval Indicator to replace fixed maintenance mileage.

The smallest BMW grows

The next débutant in BMW's current range was the 3-series, the smallest car from Munich today. Production started on 2 May 1975 and German sales began in August 1975. Right-hand-drive cars were available by October of that year. Once more the basics of a single overhead camshaft engine, with trailing arm rear-wheel drive, plus MacPherson strut front suspension, were adhered to. However, there were some important changes, such as the use of rack-and-pinion steering in place of the worm-and-roller layout BMW had used in all its four-cylinder cars since the original 1500. BMW also made no secret of the fact that the 3-series had been designed with the forthcoming small six-cylinder engine in mind. Thus initial criticism of the size and weight of the 3-series when compared to the 02 did not bother BMW unduly. Yet Anglo-German reaction to the rather soft initial suspension settings did result in a crisper response from the chassis by the time the six-cylinder 320 and 323i arrived in August 1977 (the following year for Britain).

Compared with the 02s the 3-series cars were built on a 63 mm (2½ in) longer wheelbase and were also longer overall and wider, although the height was the same. The 2002 was also 90 kg (198 lb) lighter than the similarly engined 320. Therefore it was quite a relief to BMW when the two M60-coded sixes became available, with their belt-driven overhead camshafts. The 2-litre M60 was a very over-square 80 × 66 mm design providing 122 bhp with one Solex carburettor. The 2315 cc M60 engine simply had a longer stroke (76.8 mm) and Bosch K-Jetronic injection allied to electronic ignition, sharing the 30° slant installation of all modern BMWs, except the exotic mid-engined M1 introduced in 1978, although only 450 were built.

BMW's concept of a more comfortable yet still sporty small car was a tremendous success. Always a top contender in

LEFT *A 1982 BMW 320 cabriolet by Baur of Stuttgart. They were produced in 1.6-, 2.0- and 2.3-litre forms. Provided by Romans of Farnborough.*

BELOW *The BMW four-door 3 series model followed the two-door 323i (below left) into production in 1983. All these new 3 series cars have revised rear suspension, and extensive use is made of fuel injection. Handling and noise levels are noticeably improved over the previous series, and increased use is made of electronics.*

Germany, the 3-series sold an astonishing 1,527,256 examples from the 1975 début to the end of 1981. By autumn 1982 BMW had prepared a new body with revised aerodynamics, reminiscent of the 5-series modifications of June 1981. A two-door version was offered from November 1982 with a four-door model in 1983.

Today's big BMWs

Almost too similar in looks for sales comfort, the big BMWs that top today's prestige offerings from Munich were introduced separately. The two-door 630 and 633 CSi of March 1976 rested on the 2625 mm (103 in) wheelbase used for the previous CS cars, but the 6-series actually owes much of its running gear and floorpan to the 5-series. This is particularly true today where the latest 5- and 6-series share the same wheelbase. However, in the cause of style, the 6-series is 135 mm (5 in) longer and appreciably lower than the four-door 5s.

The 6-series lacked some of the sporting panache of its predecessors, so in July 1978 the 218 bhp six of 3453 cc was installed in the BMW 635 CSi, to provide 222 km/h (138 mph) and 0–100 km/h (62 mph) sprint performance of 8 seconds. From July 1982, by which time BMW was able to report 'approximately 35,000 vehicles of this series have rolled off the assembly lines', the company offered Europeans the choice of the 2788 cc 628 CSi of 212 km/h (132 mph) capability, or a new 3430 cc version of the fabled straight-six. The latter was still known as the 635 CSi but was a very much more economical and refined car with many of the electronic features of the revised 5-series. Power output remained at the same quoted level, but weight was down by a claimed 60 kg (132 lb) and the aerodynamics slightly modified. *Autocar* carried out an independent test on the car that showed a 227 km/h (141 mph) maximum speed, 0–100 km/h (62 mph) in a startling 7.3 seconds, and a fine 12.95 litres/100 km (21.8 mpg) overall, including the rigours of performance testing. However, it was an expensive car to buy.

The biggest BMWs offered today, the 2795 mm (110 in) wheelbase 7-series, went into German production in May 1977 to supersede the 3.0 range. By December 1981 some 129,804 7-series cars had been made, including the original carburated 728 and 730, plus the 3210 cc 733 CSi model that topped the range until the arrival in July 1979 of the lighter (by up to 70 kg, 154 lb) 728i, 732i, 735i and the left-hand-drive only 745i. Now all the models in the 7-series had Bosch fuel injection for those durable in-line sixes, but the 3.2-litre 745i had a single KKK turbocharger to provide BMW's most powerful current production engine (only the limited production M1 had more power) with 252 bhp and 36 Nm (265 lbf. ft) torque. The 745 designation refers to the engine capacity multiplied by 1.4, which is the factor used in international motor racing to classify turbocharged cars. It was certainly true that the 745i

RIGHT *1982 BMW 635 CSi. The tradition of the BMW sports coupé, which began with the 2000 CS of 1965, was maintained when the 6 series was introduced in the spring of 1976. A 2985 cc six-cylinder engine was employed for the 630, and the series was also available in 633 CSi form. For 1979, engine capacity was increased to 3453 cc and the car redesignated 635. This used the big-bored block of the M1 sports racer, but with two rather than four valves per cylinder. A five-speed gearbox featured, along with spoilers front and rear, stiffer suspension, and wider wheels. In mid-1982 the 635 CSi benefited from 5 series-derived suspension modifications. At the same time engine capacity was reduced slightly to 3430 cc which resulted in a somewhat smoother power unit. Top speed is 225 km/h (140 mph).*

BELOW *The new M535i, the latest 5 series offering, has a 3.5-litre six-cylinder single overhead camshaft engine. Aerodynamic refinements include front and rear spoilers and fairing over the boot, bringing the drag coefficient down to 0.38. Maximum speed is 233 km/h (145 mph) with an impressive 0–60 mph performance of 7 seconds.*

PJM 6X

ABOVE *Another new offering: the 518i with 175 km/h (109 mph) maximum speed and 1766 cc four-cylinder 105 bhp fuel-injected engine.*

BELOW *Introduced in 1977, the 7 series model evolved into the 745i in 1979, the turbocharged 3.2-litre six developing 250 bhp.*

with its automatic transmission performed like many 4.5-litre cars, rushing to 'over 220 km/h' (137 mph) and reaching 100 km/h (62 mph) in 'less than 8.0 seconds' in the justifiably proud words of its manufacturer. The 745i was never exported to Britain and the 218 bhp 735i was left to head the UK range in lavish extra equipment trim.

The future

BMW has largely met the most challenging automobile regulations in the world by ensuring that Americans can buy at least one example from each current line. For the 1982 season there was the fuel-injected 1.8-litre 320; the new high efficiency, low revving Eta 2.7-litre six for the BMW 528e; and the 733i and the 633 CSi shared emission control, 181 bhp versions of the faithful 3210 cc six. BMW's American horizons also stretched to provide Ford with examples of the M60 diesel engine the company produced with Steyr in Austria from 1983. Europeans get the stretched M60 Eta petrol engine before being able to sample all-BMW diesel motoring.

Current offerings include a 518i—fuel-injected from 1984—and there is also a new 535i with 3.5-litre single overhead camshaft 218 bhp engine. In addition, there is talk of a four-wheel-drive BMW in the near future.

The company's sports activities have always allowed its customers a foretaste of the future, so it is fitting to conclude by highlighting aspects of the BMW motor sport story.

THE SPORTING SIDE

BMW became a force in motor sport with the advent of the six-cylinder 315/1 in 1934. These cars made their début in that year's Monte Carlo Rally and went on to take the 1.5-litre class and team prize in the *Alpenpokal* of that year. The 315/1 was also successful under the British Frazer Nash badge, and in races such as 1600 km (1000-mile) events in Czechoslovakia. However, the 1936 début of the 1971 cc BMW 328, with motorcycle ace Ernst Henne at the wheel of one of two such cars made that season, was the point at which BMW started to have a real international impact on motor sport.

As a 2-litre sports racing car the 328 was a most promising contender for class honours wherever it raced: from 1936 until after the war, the 328 won events outright or came first in class all over the world. It was no fragile sprinter either, claiming 2-litre category wins in the 1938 Spa-Francorchamps and the 1939 Le Mans races, both 24-hour events. The most serious factory effort largely went unnoticed, for it was 1940, and wartime, when BMW entered five purpose-built 328 racers for the Mille Miglia. These were very advanced cars, three of them open and two exceptionally streamlined coupés. A very light tubular frame was hidden beneath their aluminium bodies and power was increased from the production 80 bhp to 135. All but one of the BMW 328s completed the 1484 km (922-mile) Mille Miglia, Huschke von Hanstein and Walter Bäumer winning in the Italian-bodied (Touring) 328 at an *average* of over 160 km/h (100 mph) on a closed circuit made up of public roads. The same coupé, which weighed under 650 kg (1433 lb), had also finished fifth at Le Mans the previous year—BMW's best result in the French classic to date.

After the war, as we have seen, simply getting a BMW car into production was difficult, let alone finding the money for a factory competition programme. Privateers, often former personnel who returned to the fold in the 1950s (such as Ernst Loof and Alex von Falkenhausen), used pre-war BMW parts from the 328 series in a variety of racing specials that competed in the immediate post-war period.

However, subsequently BMW fielded its 700 model with some hill climb and track successes. There followed a decade of works participation in touring and Formula 2 racing, but in 1971 BMW decided to withdraw from motor sport. The move was shortlived and the firm was soon successfully back in the competitive fray.

The motor sport professionals

In spring 1972 Jochen Neerpasch, former Porsche factory sports car racer and competition director for Ford in Cologne, took up his appointment at BMW: directing a new, separate company within the Munich factory complex (he was to hold the post until 1979). Called BMW Motorsport GmbH, the enterprise would have the substantial backing of the parent company in endeavouring to wrest the European Touring Car Championship from Ford's team of Capris. It was also given the task of securing the European Formula 2 Championship, using a 2-litre version of the successful 16-valve engine

LEFT *BMW won the 1940 Mille Miglia, with other lightweight 328s in third, fifth and sixth places. This is the Brudes-Roese car which was third.*

BELOW *In 1929 BMW won the* Alpenpokal *team prize with 3/15s driven by (left to right) Max Buchner, Albert Kandt and W. Wagner.*

ABOVE *The BMW 700 with its all-independent suspension and rear-mounted engine proved an agile performer in its class on the motor racing circuits of Europe. With no less than 63 per cent of the car's weight over the rear wheels, it proved to have surprisingly good handling.*

RIGHT *Hubert Hahne at the wheel of a 1966 BMW 2000 TI at Coram curve at the British Snetterton circuit. On this occasion he took second place, but by the end of the year he had taken the European Championship title in the 2-litre class. In addition, a 170 bhp racing 2000 won the prestigious Spa 24-hour race with Hahne and Jacky Ickx driving.*

developed before BMW's official withdrawal from the sport in 1971. All this was to be achieved in the following season, so BMW was back in an official racing capacity after a break of less than two years.

That historic 1973 Ford vs BMW saloon car season began with the two sides fairly evenly matched. In March Niki Lauda and Brian Muir won the opening event at Monza, North Italy, in the orange Alpina BMW. The faster factory Fords and BMWs wilted under the strain of matching the reliable 202.87 km/h (126.06 mph) pace established by the Alpina CSL over 4 hours and 816.5 km (507.35 miles). The fastest lap was shared between the two camps, Jackie Stewart's 3.0 Capri RS 2600 and Vittorio Brambilla's Schnitzer BMW roaring around the parkland circuit at an average speed of 208 km/h (130.69 mph).

Because of bad weather the next European Championship round of 1973 was delayed until the Austrian Salzburgring could be cleared of snow. Ford won that round in May and the June event at Mantorp Park in Sweden, but BMW had been beating Ford in their battles within the German and world long-distance championship races held in between these European saloon car races. At Le Mans the 350 bhp, 3331 cc works CSL of Hezemans and Quester handsomely held off the

Fords and surprised many with its 257 km/h (160 mph) pace along the Mulsanne straight. Besides winning the saloon car section of the classic *vingt-quatre heures*, the BMW was 11th overall.

The watershed for Ford and the beginning of total BMW domination in the European Championship came on 8 July 1973. Working at astonishing speed to prevent any Ford counter-move, BMW's Martin Braungart devised and had produced a complicated set of wings, spoilers and air dams that provided the big saloon with such tremendous stability that lap times around the hilly Nürburgring track dropped by nearly 15 seconds. This enormous margin was established with the 3.3-litre racing engine, but by the Nürburgring 6-hour race on 8 July, Paul Rosche's engine team had added a 94 × 84 mm bore and stroke derivative of the racing Kugelfischer-injected straight-six. From 3498 cc and an 11:1 compression ratio they extracted 'a lot more torque than before' and 370 bhp as the big six revved heartily to 8000 rpm.

The new 3.5-litre racing sixes were used to demoralize Ford in practice, with Lauda and Stuck seconds clear of Jochen Mass in the fastest Capri. Reverting to 3.3 litres for the actual race, Stuck and Amon won for Munich at an average of 158.4 km/h (98.4 mph), which was a higher speed than the lap record a Capri had established a year earlier! BMW also found that the wings gave the cars astonishing cornering consistency so that they could run tyres with softer compounds and more grip than before. This led to an amazing Nürburgring run from Lauda who repeated his lap times to a tenth of a second for

ABOVE *This CSL coupé had been prepared for American IMSA events. It had 450 bhp available and had a successful 1975–6 season.*

ABOVE LEFT *1969 Brands Hatch 6-hours race with the BMW 2002 TIK (left) which fractionally beat the opposition in which works Ford Escorts predominated.*

LEFT *This European hill-climb car was developed by BMW for 1967–8. It has a Lola sports car chassis and 2-litre Ludwig Apfelbeck-designed engine.*

RIGHT *The 1973 European Championship CSL.*

ABOVE *BMW and Ford battle it out in June 1975 at the German national championship race at Norisring. In the front row are Hans Stuck in a BMW and Jochen Mass in a Ford. Unfortunately, Stuck retired after a hectic battle, lacking the water-cooled brakes of his opponent!*

LEFT *The Jägermeister BMW 320i in action on the Belgium Zolder circuit was a typical example of the 320i racer produced for the 1977 season.*

RIGHT *The Ford and BMW teams continued their duel in 1974. This was their first confrontation of the year at the spring Salzburgring Austrian event of the European Touring Car Championship. The winning BMW was driven by Hans Stuck and Jacky Ickx.*

three tours of the crowded race track: the Austrian also established a record at nearly 164 km/h (102 mph) average.

Ford did not win any of the remaining four European Touring Car Championship events of 1973, BMW taking the manufacturers' title by a crushing 6–2 score. And Hezemans won the drivers' title as well. The crowds, from Silverstone in Britain to the super-fast Spa-Francorchamps public road circuit in Belgium—where the winning BMW *averaged* 192.62 km/h (119.6 mph) for 24 hours!—could feast on their memories of the sliding, wheels-airborne, motoring they had witnessed as Ford fought to get back on terms. For 1974 both Ford and BMW planned a return bout, Ford this time equipped with the tail spoiler for the Capri RS3100 and over 400 bhp from a Cosworth 3.4-litre variant of Ford's V6. Paul Rosche and his men were not idle in Munich either; they had a four-valve-per-cylinder version of the BMW 3.5-litre six producing 405 to 420 bhp by September 1973, ready for winter testing—and 1974. But BMW partipication that year was low key in the wake of the oil crisis. However, subsequent BMW Motorsport activities included wins in the 1975, '76 and '77 European Touring Car Championship, although latterly the competitive emphasis has shifted towards Formula 1.

Castrol

BOSCH
BOSCH
2

Formula 2

BMW had developed a 1.6-litre Formula 2 engine during the winter of 1966–7, though the cars performed badly and were withdrawn. In 1968 things improved with the T102 Lola chassis powered by a BMW engine and Diametral re-designed cylinder head. But when later united with a Len Terry-created Dornier single-seater chassis, the engines showed their worth with five international Formula 2 victories in 1969.

Meanwhile, how did a BMW-March alliance shape up in Formula 2? Tremendously, in a word. In fact the results were so good in 1973, and for every season since, that March-BMWs were still racing and winning the European Championship more than ten years after the alliance was formed. During that period the iron block fours, progressively developed from that M12/6 into the 1974 M12/7 specification still used to this day, battled against purpose-built V6s from Honda, Renault and Ferrari, plus the Brian Hart 420R racing unit that went on to become the basis of the first Toleman F1 turbo engine.

BMW engines did not win every time against these opponents, but they always gave a good account of themselves, despite an apparent power deficiency by the 1980s. That inaugural 1973 season saw Jarier win eight times and finish second twice to take the European Formula 2 title easily from the Ford Cosworth-powered Surtees cars of Jochen Mass and Patrick Depailler.

Since then, over 300 BMW Formula 2 engines have been built and the company has won the European title seven times: 1973, '74, '75 (a Schnitzer-developed engine with BMW block), and 1978, '79, '82 and '83. The winning drivers for BMW were Jarier, fellow Frenchmen Patrick Depailler and Jacques Laffite, Italian Bruno Giacomelli, Swiss Marc Surer, Italian Corrado Fabi and Austrian Dieter Quester, who won in 1983. In most of these championship wins the chassis were provided by March as part of that loyal alliance, with an exception coming from Martini in France for 1975. The BMW engine has won about half the championship races it contested since the 1973 début, which is a competition record to be proud of. By 1982, the engine was developing 315 bhp or more and was capable of withstanding 10,000 rpm. With Michelin tyres on the March chassis, Fabi and former motorcycle champion Johnny Cecotto scored eight wins against the best Honda opposition. Nineteen eighty-four saw engine output rise to 330 bhp.

Politics, heartbreak and victory

It was the Austrian former editor of the Swiss weekly *Powerslide*, Dieter Stappert, a BMW competitions administrator from 1977, who got Neerpasch's job after Jochen's departure for Talbot. Stappert knew that his first priority was to retain a recently developed Formula 1 engine for BMW's own use, for it would be the jewel in any sporting crown.

LEFT *This is the third version of the 1.6-litre racing engine with which BMW achieved more power – 252 bhp at 10,700 rpm – and reliability. The crossflow M12/1 competition engine of this BMW 270 racing car helped Austrian Dieter Quester to fourth place in the 1970 championship for ungraded European Formula 2 drivers.*

ABOVE RIGHT *Jean-Pierre Jarier showing his form on the Pau street circuit when he scored most March-BMW wins in 1973. The March BMW combination, plus Michelin tyres, continued into the 1980s when it beat the Honda-powered Ralt and Team Spirit V6s for the 1982 European Formula 2 Championship title.*

RIGHT *In 1969 the fast Hockenheim circuit provided BMW with hope for its Formula 2 programme. Hubert Hahne, seen here ahead of the opposition, secured two second places in his traditional slip-streaming manner that season.*

LEFT AND RIGHT *The mid-engined BMW M1, introduced in 1978. This glass fibre-bodied sports racer was engineered by Lamborghini, while the body styling was by Ital Design. The mid-located engine was a BMW six of 3453 cc, but with four valves per cylinder and twin overhead camshafts. The M1 was built in the Baur bodyworks at Stuttgart until the beginning of 1981: only 450 were made. Developing 227 bhp, the top speed was about 261 km/h (162 mph).*

BELOW *One-marque M1 racing became popular as supporting events for the European Grands Prix of 1979–80. The former year saw Niki Lauda win the ProCar series for M1 racers, and in 1980 it was Nelson Piquet's turn to take victory laurels.*

BMW M1 ROAD CAR
1979–81

ENGINE	
No. of cylinders	6
Bore/stroke mm	93 × 84
Displacement cc	3453
Valve operation	Twin overhead camshaft
Compression ratio	9:1
Induction	Mechanical fuel injection
BHP	277 at 6500 rpm
Transmission	Five-speed manual
CHASSIS	
Frame	Tubular stressed
Wheelbase mm	2560
Track—front mm	1550
Track—rear mm	1576
Suspension—front	Independent, wishbone and coil spring
Suspension—rear	Independent, wishbone and coil spring
Brakes	Hydraulic disc
PERFORMANCE	
Maximum speed	261 km/h (162 mph)

LEFT *1973 March 732-BMW which brought the firm the European Formula 2 title. It was powered by BMW's 275 bhp M12/7 racing engine.*

RIGHT *This 1969 Formula 2 racing BMW 269 with its Diametral 1.6-litre competition engine brought BMW a considerable change in its racing fortunes. Provided by the Auto & Technik Museum, Sinsheim.*

BELOW *1982 Canadian Grand Prix at Montreal. Nelson Piquet, in a year of rapidly changing fortunes, achieves victory at the wheel of the BMW-powered Brabham GP car.*

Stappert succeeded in convincing both his immediate superior, Hans Erdmann Schönbeck (BMW sales director since 1974) and Karlheinz Radermacher, the engineering chief appointed in 1975, that the 1.5-litre Turbo F1 engine should be for BMW's use in a chassis of the company's choice.

In 1980 there came a liaison with Brabham and the result was the Brabham-BMW BT 50. On 12 June 1982, the 1499 cc KKK-turbocharged Bayerische Motoren Werke's Grand Prix engine won the Canadian GP in Montreal. Fittingly, the driver was Nelson Piquet and he was supported in second place by Riccardo Patrese, his Brabham BT49D Ford Cosworth V8 team mate.

It had not been easy for either Brabham or BMW, especially while they tried to achieve race-winning reliability in the middle of the season—always a desperately difficult task. But by mid-season the combination had emerged as one of the most formidable in the GP world and it seemed clear that BMW was on the threshold of a long involvement in Formula 1. This proved triumphantly successful in 1983, when Nelson Piquet in his Brabham-BMW won the world championship title, although, in contrast, the 1984 season was not a particularly successful one. Better things are anticipated for 1985. If BMW's history is anything to go by, it will be well worth watching...

Dieter Quester
BOSCH
Castrol
BILSTEIN
DUNLOP

Santal
parmalat
BMW

MERCEDES-BENZ

Gottlieb Daimler created the high-speed internal combustion engine in 1885 and his firm later went on to produce the Mercedes car in 1901. Carl Benz simultaneously built a powered tricycle and, like Daimler, went on to found a manufacturing dynasty. Both firms participated in racing in pre-First World War days and later, in 1926, their divergent paths combined to create Daimler-Benz. During the 1920s somewhat unadventurous models were offered, although the fabled SSK sports car was a glorious exception. In the 1930s the cars became technically more interesting and Mercedes-Benz, rekindling an established tradition, produced some of the most powerful racing cars that the world has ever seen. Following the Second World War the silver cars were again supreme on the motor racing circuits of the world, while the saloon car range was progressively expanded and refined. Today the cars from Untertürkheim are world famous for their superlative engineering, outstanding quality and unique, indefinable, but very special character.

MERCEDES
BENZ

S HP 5107

The three-pointed star of Mercedes-Benz is far more than a symbol of prestige and success, more even than an epitaph to Gottlieb Daimler's dream of conquering travel on land, sea and air. Since this world-famous trademark was first embossed on the radiators of Mercedes cars in the early 1900s (it was not encircled by a ring and raised proudly above the bonnet until 1923), it has stood for the very finest in engineering and craftsmanship. Yet the origin of the name Mercedes which, as we shall see later, has nothing to do with the marque's founding fathers, does less than justice to the pioneers, Daimler and Carl Benz, the two geniuses whose early endeavours not only laid the foundation of the great Daimler-Benz empire that now bears their name, but also the modern automobile as we know it today.

Neither Benz nor Daimler exactly invented the car. What sets them apart from their contemporaries is that they succeeded where others had failed. What is more, they did so quite independently, neither man being remotely involved in the other's work. Indeed, they never even met, though their epoch-making experiments were conducted barely 100 km (60 miles) apart in the Neckar valley. Daimler, 12 years older than Benz, died in 1900, over a quarter of a century before the concern he founded merged with that of his early rival. Carl Benz lived on not only to see the amalgamation of 1926, but also to become an active part of it as a director. He died three years later in his eighties.

It was in 1886 that Daimler and Benz coincidentally produced a petrol-powered vehicle that actually worked, though they reached this common goal by very different routes.

Carl Benz

Benz, the son of a railway mechanic who died of pneumonia when Carl was only two, had a tough childhood and a determined mother who gave her bright son a sound education despite great financial hardship. Benz's interest in the newfangled gas engine, running on piped town gas and used for industrial power, was kindled by his tutor at the Karlsruhe Polytechnic, Ferdinand Redenbacher, and fanned by work on an early Lenoir 'gasmotor' in 1861. He graduated in 1864, worked briefly for a locksmith and then as a fitter in a locomotive works. The valuable experience he gained here served to underline his faith in the internal combustion engine: he saw little future in steam. After several more engineering jobs, the dedicated, hard-working Benz set up workshops to develop his own gas engine. The business foundered, but not before progress had been made on a two-stroke design with which he persevered despite the success of Dr Nikolaus Otto's patented four-stroke (hence the Otto cycle), the forerunner of modern car engines.

Following a dispute with business partners, he started afresh with funds from friends and established Benz & Co.: gas-

ABOVE *Carl Benz (1844–1929), who was intent on producing a self-propelled vehicle and did so in 1886. The son of an engine driver, who died when he was a child, Benz went on to attend the Karlsruhe Polytechnic and to found his own gas-engine business.*

RIGHT *The famous Benz three-wheeler of 1886, a combination of bicycle and gas-engine technology. The single-cylinder engine developed 0.9 hp at 250–300 rpm, while drive was through a differential gear, belts and chains. When driven for the first time on the public highway it achieved a speed of 14 km/h (9 mph).*

LEFT *Benz remained faithful to a three-wheeler layout until 1893 when he followed Daimler's four-wheeled system. The engine was also more powerful, being of 5 hp and 2.9 litres capacity. The unequal wheel sizes still follow carriage practice.*

BELOW *Gottlieb Daimler's first car of 1886. It is a converted horse-drawn carriage powered by Daimler's water-cooled engine of 1.1 hp. Not a very practical vehicle...*

engine manufacturers, though it was the application of the engine in a vehicle, rather than the motor itself, that obsessed Benz. By 1884 his high-speed two-stroke was running with advanced battery and trembler-coil ignition (the 'problem of all problems' he wrote later) rather than primitive hot-tube ignition used by Daimler and others. Benz turned to the four-stroke after the validity of the famous patent concerning Dr Nikolaus Otto's design had been questioned. And it was a four-stroke 'single' that powered the first Benz car, a three-wheeler tailor-made for the job rather than an adapted horse carriage.

To call Benz's first car a horseless carriage does less than justice to what was a primitive but remarkably well-conceived design. Remember, Benz had to start from scratch and work out for himself where to put the engine and how to transmit its puny 0.9 horsepower. The cumbersome single-cylinder engine, mounted behind a two-seater bench perched atop a flimsy chassis, had a huge horizontal flywheel to avoid any undesirable gyroscopic effects (good thinking but misguided as it happens), and drove the big-diameter wire-spoked rear wheels through a belt clutch to a remarkably advanced differential gear and then by chain from a countershaft. The water-cooled engine with its electric ignition and mechanically operated inlet valves, not to mention the clever differential, are all still with us on modern cars.

Benz's first tricycle (he failed at first to resolve the steering problem presented by a four-wheeler) achieved 12 km/h

(7½ mph) in 1886 and was in regular use in Mannheim the following year, much to the consternation of the police. Bureaucracy bedevilled development and also deterred customers, which caused Benz's business partners to grow impatient and withdraw. Once more he had to start afresh—and again he was rescued from oblivion, financial support coming this time from two men of greater vision, one of whom, Julius Ganss, was a persuasive salesman who soon opened up new markets for the Benz three-wheelers. Meanwhile, the stationary petrol-engine business flourished, especially where there was no town gas laid on, allowing Benz—now in his forties—to concentrate on the development of his cars. He overcame the steering problem and built his first four-wheeler in 1892. His technical assistant August Horch was responsible for improving the performance of Benz's cars by increasing output by one horsepower, though Benz himself was not really interested in speed. In 1897 the first twin-cylinder engine was made, soon to power the famous 5 and 8 hp Benz models, and the cumbersome horizontal flywheel was abandoned. The wire wheels of his first tricycle were replaced by more conventional wood-spoke ones; Benz was, however, opposed to Michelin's early pneumatic tyres, introduced in 1896.

Despite important technical innovations, like the use of ball-bearing races in the back axle, not to mention quite a good range of cars, the conservative Benz, wedded to his own ideals, was slow to respond to advances elsewhere and was openly hostile to the quest for more power and speed. He stubbornly persevered with designs that were outmoded, resolutely sticking to his rear-mounted horizontally opposed twin-cylinder engine when in-line fours were all the rage.

Gottlieb Daimler

Daimler was born in 1834, the second of four sons of a prosperous baker. As a boy, he shone at mathematics and geometry and was apprenticed to a gunsmith who developed young Gottlieb's innate creative gift. The pair of double-barrelled pistols he made, with carved walnut butts and chased barrels, are testimony to the skill and precision of his work. Nothing less than perfection was good enough for the diligent Daimler, who thrived on hard work and had no time for slackers. He left gunmaking to further his studies, won a scholarship, and in 1856 joined a locomotive works for a brief period.

Like Benz a little later, Daimler was not interested in steam and left to seek experience elsewhere. He spent two years in England (with Armstrong Whitworth and Roberts and Co.) and held other engineering positions in Germany before being appointed technical director of the Deutz works of Otto & Langen, makers of four-stroke gas engines. The relationship between Otto and Daimler was at best uneasy, but Daimler had a strong ally and lifelong friend in Wilhelm Maybach who was to play a leading role in the Daimler firm's fortunes later on. It was at Otto & Langen that Daimler instituted a quality-inspection system still used today.

The gas-engine business prospered but Daimler's relationship with Otto & Langen did not: he wanted to do more research and development, his employers were more concerned with production. Daimler was eased out. After a period in Russia in the oil business, he set up his own workshop in 1882 at Bad Cannstatt, first in a converted summerhouse, later in a small factory, and persuaded Maybach to join him. By 1883 they had perfected their hot-tube ignition, as far as the intrinsic

LEFT *In 1897 Benz went to a two-cylinder horizontally opposed 'Kontra' engine which was originally of 1.7 litres, later increased to 2.7 litres. This is a Dos-à-Dos four-seater.*

RIGHT *Diversity: Daimler displayed this two-cylinder five-tonne truck in 1898. Gottlieb Daimler is in the foreground with Wilhelm Maybach on his right.*

BELOW *This mid-1890s Daimler has a centrally pivoting steering for the luckless, unprotected driver. The engine is rear mounted.*

shortcomings of so crude an arrangement would allow. Nevertheless, by using its own tanked fuel (benzine or petrol, obtained from chemists in those days) Daimler's single-cylinder engine was the first to run without piped mains gas. Moreover, it ran at unheard-of speeds of up to 900 rpm.

Unlike Benz, Daimler was not obsessed solely with the automobile. His vision was to provide powered transport for everyone and everything, on land, sea and air. His first self-propelled vehicle, built in 1885, was a motorcycle, or 'single track' as it was then known. This ungainly wood-and-iron contraption, powered by an air-cooled ½ bhp engine, was successfully ridden by Daimler's eldest son Paul, but the patented design was not developed. His first powered boat, which so impressed Prince Bismarck that he later bought one, led to a flourishing marine division. In 1886, while Benz was completing his three-wheeler, Daimler installed one of his more powerful engines in a converted horse-drawn carriage to produce the world's first successful four-wheel car. Its 1½ bhp water-cooled engine drove through a system of belts, pulleys and a simple slip-disc differential to pinions that engaged with large toothed rims attached to the rear wheels. It was crude but it worked. So, too, did the tram he built for the local Cannstatt authorities, and the taxi that went into service at Stuttgart station in 1888. Daimler engines were soon powering fire engines, timber saws and the world's first dirigible, built with balloonist Dr Karl Wolfert.

Daimler's third car was a specially made four-wheeler, the tubular frame of which acted as the radiator for the rear-mounted V-twin engine's cooling water. A cone clutch transmitted the 1½ bhp through a four-speed gearbox and the wire-spoked front wheels were carried by cycle-type forks with proper steering geometry, although it was tiller operated.

Soon four-cylinder 10 bhp Daimler engines were successfully powering railcars, and in 1892 came the first vertical twin, later to oust the V-twin, with improved valve gear and speed control. The engine business flourished, but, after a dispute with his co-directors, Daimler and Maybach cut themselves adrift from the company in 1892 and returned to more research and development, which resulted in Maybach's jet carburettor and patented belt-drive car. Three years later, the two engineers returned to a reconstituted Daimler Motoren-Gesellschaft with a strong new programme for car production.

BELOW *Gottlieb Daimler's engine used in his so-called 'single track' to create the world's first motorcycle in 1885 and thus predating his own automobile by a year. It had an air-cooled 264 cc power unit.*

BOTTOM *The engine of an 1893 Daimler with exposed crankshaft and big end bearing and still horizontally located. The engine's radiators on either side of the compartment and chain drive can be clearly seen.*

The Mercedes name

Daimler was by now a sick man but before his death in 1900 he saw several important developments: the adoption of low-tension magneto ignition instead of hot-tube after Robert Bosch had solved the problem of accurate spark control; the use of pneumatic tyres on the front-engined Phœnix, Victoria, Phaeton and Vis-à-Vis (face to face) models; a return to dirigible propulsion, which ended tragically with a fatal accident to Dr Wolfert, though not before attracting the attention of Count Zeppelin; and, in 1896, a four-cylinder 6 hp speedster in response to an enquiry from the rich and influential Austrian banker, businessman and diplomat, Emil Jellinek (pronounced Yellinek). This adapted 6 hp Phaeton, which did not meet with Daimler's wholehearted approval, handled well and did 42 km/h (26 mph)—but it was not fast enough to beat the speed-crazy French. The upright, short-wheelbase Daimler Phœnix 23 hp racer of 1899 was not the final answer either, and, when works driver Wilhelm Bauer was killed while competing in one of these hard-to-handle cars on the La Turbie hill climb, the Cannstatt works withdrew from the competition: but not for long. Consul-General Jellinek, who was a Daimler enthusiast as well as a distributor (a director and backer too later on), was not deterred. He advocated something even more powerful with a longer wheelbase and a lower centre of gravity. What is more, he pledged to buy 36 such cars in return for the selling rights in Austria, Belgium, Hungary, America and France, provided he could name the cars after his daughter, Mercédès—the name under which he had previously raced Daimler cars.

It was not uncommon for the gentry of the period to use such pseudonyms, often to avoid conflict with a disapproving family for social or safety reasons. Jellinek may well have originally chosen the name lightheartedly on the spur of the moment out of nothing more than sentiment. If so, it was a momentous whim. Whether Gottlieb Daimler, by now a very sick man, approved of Jellinek's proposals is uncertain, but Maybach and his co-directors did and the deal went through.

A 1902 Mercedes 20/28 though with later bodywork. The model was inspired by the revolutionary 35 hp Mercedes of the previous year. It is powered by a four-cylinder engine. Provided by J. Lightfoot.

It is thought that Maybach based his design for Jellinek's racer on that of Paul Daimler's small twin-cylinder car of 1899 which, among several advanced features, had a honeycomb radiator, an integral crankcase/gearbox, column-mounted gear lever and a foot-operated throttle. The new 35 hp four-cylinder car was a sensation, and immediately outdated everything else on the roads. The 5.9-litre engine was relatively small compared with that of some rival monsters, but very powerful for its size and weight. Its mechanically operated inlet valves ensured good filling of the T-shaped combustion chambers through two carburettors, one for each pair of cast cylinders with integral heads. The Bosch low-tension magneto ignition could be advanced and retarded as required, and the large honeycomb radiator cooled the small volume of water that was pumped around the engine. A coil-spring clutch transmitted the 35 bhp, developed at 1000 rpm, through a four-speed gearbox operated by a gate change, to a countershaft that drove the rear wheels by sprockets and chains. Deep-section chassis pressings gave greater strength and rigidity than on previous cars, resulting in better roadholding and handling. This new car was so impressive that the name was actually adopted by the Daimler company for all its cars.

MERCEDES V. BENZ

Gottlieb Daimler's death, said to have been caused by overwork, at the age of 66, left the Daimler Motoren-Gesellschaft under the control of financier Max Duttenhofer; Daimler's sons Paul and Adolf, later to become directors, at this stage played no more than supporting roles to Wilhelm Maybach, generally recognized as the most talented automobile designer of his day.

Not that Daimler's activities were confined to cars: the company was by 1907 firmly established in the truck, bus, marine and stationary engine fields, with manufacturing plants in Berlin and Austria (run for a time by Paul Daimler) as well as Bad Cannstatt.

In the early 1900s Daimler's great Mercedes racers overshadowed the activities of Carl Benz, whose modest cars of outmoded design were better known for their reliability and comfort than for speed. Not that they had been commercially unsuccessful: the Velo and Comfortable were among the best-selling models of their time and, as a volume producer, Benz was in the big league in 1899 with agencies throughout the world. But Benz was not a racing man and sales of his outdated cars began to fall sharply in the early 1900s. Even then it was co-director Julius Ganss rather than the conservative Benz who forced a change of direction with a front-engined, shaft-driven car based on a Renault design. For a time this completely new Benz, called the Parsifal, was built alongside the old-fashioned cars by French fitters under the direction of Marius Barbarou. However, the Parsifal, in its original two-cylinder form, was underpowered and a commercial failure. The company's fortunes went from bad to worse and Carl Benz and his son Eugen resigned after a boardroom dispute. Ganss had been on the right track but, with the company now well in the red, he too was compelled to resign.

Carl Benz's period of exile was brief. He returned to the board, reworked the Parsifal's chassis and replaced its two-cylinder engine with a new in-line four-cylinder of advanced design with mechanically operated inlet and exhaust valves: something of a novelty as many cars still employed automatic inlet valves opened by suction.

By 1904 Benz had a range of touring cars to match that of Mercedes. Both manufacturers included in their range quality cars of modest size and power but they concentrated on the

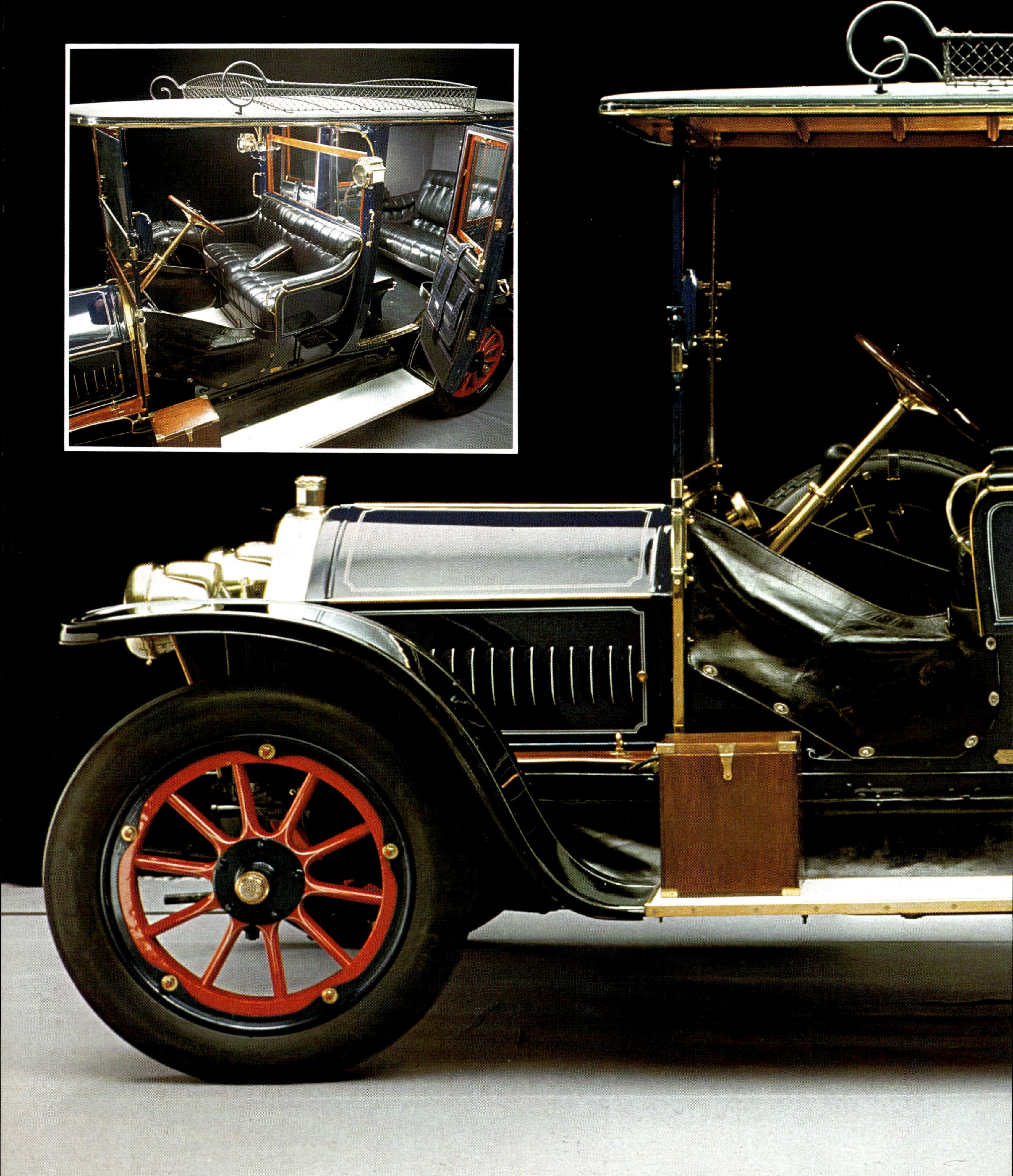

As one of the leading makes of its day, Benz soon attracted a wealthy clientele who required closed rather than open cars. This is a 1909 20/35 limousine (note the magnificent interior). The figures in the model's title reflect the horsepower taxable in Germany and the actual output of the engine.

large, exclusive market. From 1908 Hans Nibel became to Benz what Maybach had been to Daimler and as chief engineer he headed the company's design team for the next 20 years. Under a new racing formula that limited the bore of four-cylinder engines to 155 mm, Benz produced a long (200 mm) stroke engine of 15,095 cc that developed 150 bhp. Its cylinders were cast in pairs and the overhead valves were operated by an enclosed camshaft and pushrods and rockers.

It was in one of these cars that Hémery finished second to Christian Lautenschlager's Mercedes in the 1908 French Grand Prix, with another Benz third, making it a resounding clean sweep for the Germans. This was the last great Mercedes victory for some years, however, because Daimler thereafter withdrew from racing because of the enormous costs. Several other manufacturers pulled out at the same time as a result of an international pact to abstain from the big events. Not so Benz who, far from cutting back, committed even bigger sums of money to the company racing programme.

The legendary Blitzen Benz

The 150 hp car captured several records in America, the great Barney Oldfield taking the standing-start mile at Indianapolis in 43.1 seconds. But it was Nibel's incredible 200 hp Blitzen ('Lightning') Benz with its thin, torpedo-like body that stole

the limelight from 1909 on, taking several new world speed records. It achieved a remarkable 205 km/h (127.4 mph) at Brooklands in 1909, 210.9 km/h (131.1 mph) at Daytona in 1910, and a resounding 228 km/h (141.7 mph) there the following year. In fact this legendary Benz held the world speed record for 15 years from 1909 to 1924.

Although Daimler had withdrawn from racing in 1908, the company was very active in other spheres. Paul Daimler took over as chief engineer when Maybach retired (later on, in 1913, he also assumed the responsibility of technical director when his brother Adolf died at the age of 42). From 1908 to 1913 Daimler built up an extensive range of shaft-drive cars—the 18/18, 10/20, 14/35, 21/35, 22/40 and 28/60—though chains were still used to drive the more powerful models. Daimler also introduced a new range of engines with overhead inlet valves and side exhausts to improve breathing, piston-type carburettors with preheating, high-tension ignition and a plunger oil pump, driven by the water-pump shaft to force-feed all the engine bearings.

It was in 1909 that the three-pointed star was adopted as Daimler's trademark. The story goes that Gottlieb Daimler had once told his young sons of a star that would rise from the family home to bring happiness and fortune. It was a tale that caught the imagination of the Daimler board who adopted the star as a tribute to the company's founder, though not without some difficulty as many other firms had already registered a trademark of similar design.

In the quest for quietness and refinement, Daimler introduced a series of sleeve-valve engines in 1909, built under licence from the American Charles Knight. Instead of using noisy poppet valve gear, induction and exhaust was by means of ported cylindrical 'sleeves' that slithered between pistons and cylinders, giving not only quieter running but, claimed Daimler, more power in the 500–1500 rpm range.

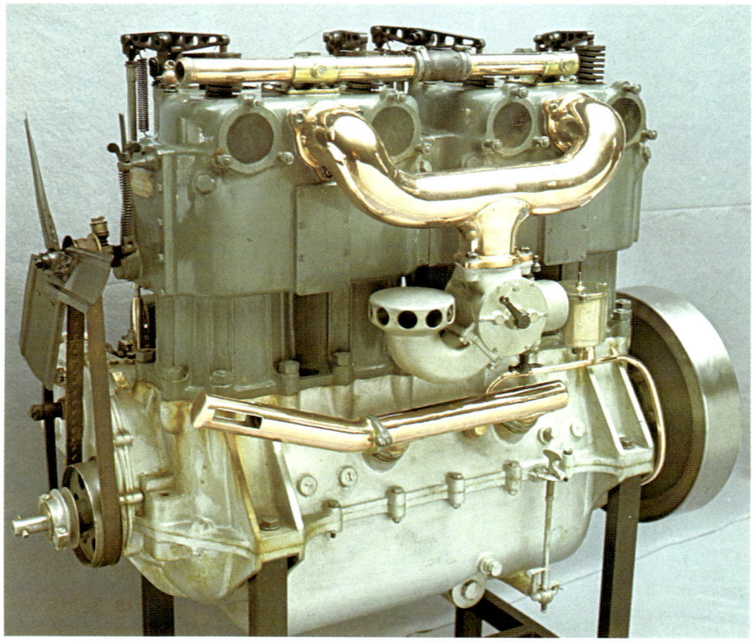

ABOVE *The famous 'Blitzen Benz' which held the world land speed record at 211.25 km/h (131.27 mph) in 1909. Also shown is the massive 187 × 200 mm four-cylinder engine with a capacity of 21.5 litres and developing 200 hp.*

ABOVE RIGHT *The famous 1914 French Grand Prix when Mercedes took the first three places. The mechanics of Wagner's car, which finished second, managed a complete wheel-change in under a minute.*

A memorable victory, 1914

With the stormclouds of war gathering over Europe, the 1914 French Grand Prix became more than just another motor race. It was a battle for national pride and prestige. Six countries and many more manufacturers were represented by 47 cars.

The Mercedes cars entered for the race had four-cylinder long-stroke Daimler engines, with four valves per cylinder operated from a single overhead camshaft, developing some 115 bhp at 3200 rpm—a very high speed for those days. What is more, the engines, with their steel cylinders surrounded by welded-sheet water jackets, could sustain high revolutions for long periods.

The cars started two at a time at half-minute intervals, with 20 laps, over 750 km (466 miles), ahead of them. By the end of the first lap it was evident that the new Mercedes, even without front-wheel brakes, said to be worth a minute a lap, were the fastest cars. Max Sailer's white machine led Boillot's blue Peugeot by an ever-increasing margin until the engine of the leading Mercedes 'hare', intended to stretch the opposition, failed. Strictly to order, Lautenschlager, Louis Wagner (who was French) and Otto Salzer then moved up, Lautenschlager, winner of the 1908 French GP, taking the lead from Boillot on the 18th lap and pulling away comfortably. The Peugeot, now harassed by Wagner for second place, failed on the 19th lap, giving the German cars a sweeping one-two-three finish in front of a stunned and stonily silent French crowd. It was a splendid victory for the Mercedes team. Soon after, France and Germany were at war.

ABOVE *In 1909 Daimler obtained a licence to manufacture the Knight sleeve-valve engine, and Mercedes models appeared from 1910 so equipped. It was used on the 10/30, 16/40 and 16/45 cars and gave quiet (as the usual poppet valves were dispensed with), smooth performance at the expense of high oil consumption. The Knight was to remain a feature of the Mercedes range until 1923. A tourer of the immediate pre-First World War era is illustrated.*

RIGHT *The supercharged 1923/4 Mercedes 24/100/140 Sportwagen. The supercharger was not permanently engaged but came into operation when the throttle was fully depressed and did so via a multi-plate clutch. This meant that the blower was operating at three to four times crankshaft speed. It was to feature on selected Mercedes-Benz passenger cars until 1939 and was incorporated in all the racing cars.*

AFTER THE WAR

Although her factories were not destroyed by air attacks as they were to be later in the Second World War, the Kaiser's defeated Germany was in financial ruins after the 1914–18 conflagration. The far-reaching political, economic and social changes caused by the war, succeeded by the total collapse of Germany's monetary system, meant a new approach for the old car manufacturers, if not new models. To begin with, both Daimler and Benz resumed small-scale manufacture of tried and trusted pre-war cars, though evolutionary new models were introduced in the early 1920s. Cars like the Mercedes 28/95 and the Benz 10/30 soon appeared on the market.

The war had curtailed all motor racing in Europe, but in America, which was not drawn into the conflict until later, Mercedes cars continued to win important races, notably in the hands of Ralph DePalma, who had acquired one of the successful 1914 GP cars. His most famous victory was in the Indianapolis 500 of 1915. After the war, Mercedes cars soon made their mark again in Europe. Max Sailer, hero of the 1914 French GP, drove a short-chassis 28/95 from Stuttgart to Sicily in 1921 and there won the Coppa Florio, the Targa Florio's companion event for touring cars. The following year Count Giulio Masetti, driving a 1914 GP Mercedes, won the Targa itself against a strong field, including the first of Mercedes' 1.5-litre supercharged racing cars.

The Benz company, too, was quick to re-establish its name in racing. A special 10/30 won the first post-war race at the AVUS in 1921, and an advanced 'teardrop' twin-cam, six-cylinder, 2-litre, rear-engined racer with independent swinging rear axles and inboard drum brakes foreshadowed the shape of things to come, although it attracted more attention for its design on its one works appearance at Monza.

In 1906 Paul Daimler had been succeeded as technical director of the Austro-Daimler works by a brilliant engineer called Ferdinand Porsche. In 1923, when the war-weary Daimler retired as chief engineer at Untertürkheim, it was again the great Ferdinand Porsche who took over from him to head the company's design team. One of his first tasks was to complete the 2-litre straight-eight supercharged racing car, started by Paul Daimler, to replace the 1.5- and 2-litre four-cylinder blown cars that scored a number of successes in the early 1920s.

At the Berlin motor show of 1921, two supercharged models were exhibited: a 10/40/65 with poppet valves, and a sleeve-valve 6/25/40. (The third figure indicates the maximum developed horsepower with the supercharger engaged.) The Roots air pump—two closely meshing figure-of-eight vanes—was mounted vertically at the front of the engine and driven at about three times engine speed from the crankshaft through bevel gears and a small multi-disc clutch which, by means of a mechanical linkage, engaged only when the accelerator was fully depressed. So the supercharger did not operate all the time, but only when extra power was required. In 1922, the now outdated 1914 28/95 was also supercharged for racing, followed by the small 1.5- and 2-litre overhead-camshaft four-cylinder supercharged racers complying with international formulae of the time. Although they were very fast, the 2-litre cars proved difficult to drive and were soundly beaten in the 1923 Indianapolis 500 where Daimler, engaged in an American sales campaign, had hoped to excel. The following year Christian Werner, driving an improved 2-litre four, scored a notable double in Sicily, winning both the Targa and Coppa Florio races outright. The company's official records show a total of 93 wins for these 1.5- and 2-litre supercharged cars in 1924, though most of them were in minor events in the hands

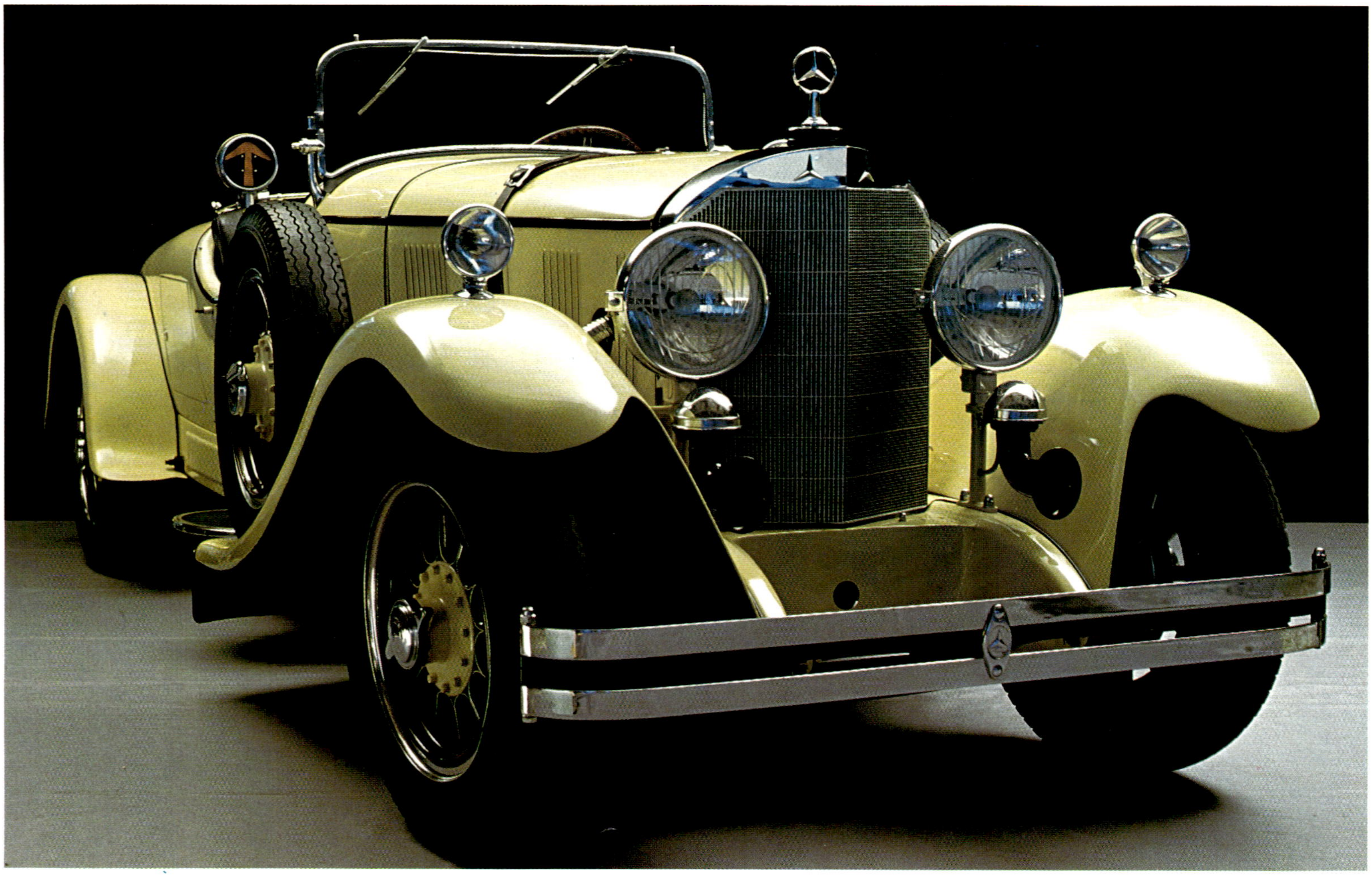

of privateers, among them a young apprentice called Rudolf Caracciola who was destined for much greater things.

Porsche's eight-cylinder 2-litre cars made an inauspicious début, the whole Mercedes team being withdrawn from lowly positions in the 1924 Italian GP after the popular Zborowski was killed in a crash. Their failure here serves to underline that the Germans were not always invincible first time out. Despite their many victories, neither Mercedes nor Benz really ruled the tracks in the early 1920s.

The straight-eight was a potent piece of engineering. Its very stiff built-up crankshaft, running in nine roller bearings, was lubricated by a dry-sump system and stressed to 6000 rpm. With twin overhead camshafts operating four valves per cylinder, it developed over 160 bhp: rather too much, according to contemporary reports, for the leaf-sprung, live-axled chassis and cable-operated drum brakes. By all accounts, it was a demanding car to drive on the limit, though Caracciola mastered it. Another young German with a flair for organization and attention to detail, who had put in some competent rather than brilliant drives for Mercedes earlier, was at this time appointed to head the racing department. For the next 30 years under the legendary *Rennleiter*, Alfred Neubauer, the Germans really did become all but invincible.

MERCEDES-BENZ SSK
1928–32

ENGINE	
No. of cylinders	6
Bore/stroke mm	100 × 150
Displacement cc	7069
Valve operation	Single overhead camshaft
Induction	Twin carburettors, via Roots-type supercharger
BHP	225
Transmission	Four-speed
CHASSIS	
Frame	Channel section
Wheelbase mm	2946
Track—front mm	1397
Track—rear mm	1397
Suspension—front	Half-elliptic
Suspension—rear	Half-elliptic
Brakes	Mechanical drums
PERFORMANCE	
Maximum speed	202 km/h (126 mph)

RIGHT *Now a Mercedes-Benz, this 1926 K model has a 6.25-litre six-cylinder supercharged engine. The wooden wheels are a very American feature and typical of German cars of their day. Provided by Coys of Kensington.*

FAR RIGHT *Al Jolson was the original owner of this 1928 SS (for Super Sports) model with 7.1-litre supercharged engine which developed 200 bhp. The bodywork was far removed from the more functional coachwork usually on offer. Provided by Brian Classic Ltd.*

BELOW *1928 SSK with familiar chromed exhaust pipes. Again a 7.1-litre supercharged engine is employed.*

The merger

The big news of 1926 did not come from the race tracks, though, but from the boardrooms of Daimler and Benz. Amalgamation of the two great rivals had been mooted as early as 1919. By 1923, when both firms were fighting for the same precarious market against crippling economic factors, hostility to the scheme originally proposed by Dr Jahr of Benz had softened. An 'agreement of mutual interest' was signed in 1924 between Daimler Motoren-Gesellschaft and Benz & Cie, and a director of co-ordination appointed. In June 1926, the two companies merged as Daimler-Benz AG. The encircled three-pointed star of Daimler was combined with the circular laurel wreath (symbolizing victory) of Benz to form a trademark that was soon to stamp its authority throughout the world.

For five years after the merger, until 1931, the mainstay of the Daimler-Benz range was the Stuttgart and Mannheim series of medium-sized saloons and tourers. They were dull but dependable cars of conventional design and rather bland styling, recognized by their flat radiators carrying the new emblem, and pressed-steel 10-spoke wheels. They were the last of what the company calls its 'classical' cars, with U-section frames, live axles front and rear supported on leaf springs, and mechanically operated brakes that contemporary road tests criticized as inadequate.

These rather dated, live-axled saloons and tourers were Daimler-Benz's bread and butter until the revolutionary 170 series was introduced in 1931. It was the great supercharged sports cars at the other end of the price scale that provided the German jam. A short-chassis version of the big, blown tourer was brought out in 1926. Known as the K (*kurz*: 'short') model, its 6.25-litre overhead-valve six-cylinder engine developed 160 bhp at a lazy 2600 rpm with the supercharger engaged. Its top speed was about 160 km/h (100 mph) but it was the relaxed, long-legged cruising and surging acceleration in top from walking pace that marked it out as something extraordinary. Like other Mercedes cars of the period, though, it had poor brakes—so poor that it became known as the 'death trap'. Even so, it was in a Type K that Caracciola and others started to make an impact in racing and hill-climbing that the heavier, less powerful 24/100/140 had failed to do: a works team of these cars had been humbled by lesser machinery in the touring-car race accompanying the 1926 Spanish GP.

In 1927, the K was succeeded by the redoubtable 36/120/180, more simply known as the S (for Sport). The enlarged 6.8-litre engine developed 180 bhp and was carried in a chassis that was acutely arched over the rear axle to give a very low centre of gravity and much better handling and roadholding, according to contemporary tests. The car could accelerate swiftly and cleanly from 8 to 170 km/h (5 to 105 mph) in top gear. Still the brakes were the Achilles heel, but that did not prevent Caracciola from winning the opening event on the Nürburgring—beating Christian Werner in one of the eight-cylinder 2-litre grand prix cars in the process. In 1928 came the larger capacity 7.1-litre SS, for Super Sports, also supercharged, and the more powerful SSK, while the SSKL of 1931 was a short-wheelbase potent racing version of the latter.

Although the big blowers were to win many more sports-car and Formule Libre events, they were no match for some of the new thoroughbred single-seaters of the early 1930s like the P3 Alfa Romeo and Type 51 Bugatti. Their last great international victory was in the 1932 AVUS race before an estimated 250,000 spectators, when Manfred von Brauchitsch in an SSKL carrying streamlined bodywork designed by an aircraft engineer beat Caracciola—not in his usual Mercedes but at the wheel of an Alfa Romeo—by a mere four seconds.

The 170 series

In racing, Mercedes was temporarily on the wane, but the company's road-car programme went from strength to strength, and advanced dramatically in 1931 with the introduction of a revolutionary new range of cars designed by Hans Nibel. Both Daimler and Benz had hitherto excelled in engine design but Nibel was first and foremost a chassis man, and it was the all-independently sprung lightweight chassis, first seen at the Paris Salon, that made the new 170, backbone of

Mercedes' range for years to come, rather special in its ride and handling.

The Depression had knocked the bottom out of the luxury-car market and the 170 was conceived and built as an advanced contender in the medium-sized, medium-priced sector, a market strongly contested by Mercedes ever since. Its pressed-steel box-section chassis frame was deeply arched over the back wheels to allow ample movement for the independent rear suspension. Twin coil springs, one each side of the swinging drive shafts, were anchored under the frame arch. A pair of upper and lower transverse multi-leaf springs located and sprung the independently suspended front wheels. The wishbone arms of the shock absorbers also acted as emergency wheel locators in the event of a spring breakage. The chassis was centrally lubricated and fitted with hydraulic brakes, and an all-synchromesh gearbox, built under Maybach patents, transmitted the modest power of the six-cylinder 1692 cc, 32 bhp side-valve engine to a differential and final drive assembly rubber-mounted to the rigid chassis. Reasonably priced, the 170 put Mercedes cars within reach of a much wider market. In the next five years, 14,000 170s were made and, from 1932, an even greater number of 40 bhp 200s of

LEFT *The rather sombre 170 of 1931 was the first Mercedes-Benz to employ a rear swing axle, and its 1.7 litres capacity is a reflection of the bleak economic climate. A box-section chassis was also used.*

RIGHT *Kaiser Wilhelm II owned this 1932 Super (or Grosser) Mercedes powered by a 7.7-litre supercharged straight-eight engine.*

BELOW *1934 500K Special Roadster. This magnificent creation has an eight-cylinder 5-litre supercharged engine and all-independent suspension.*

I. 15237

ABOVE *The 500K was introduced in 1934 and replaced the 380 sports model. It was in turn succeeded by the 540 car. The 5-litre straight-eight engine developed 100 bhp and 160 when the supercharger was engaged. This right-hand-drive 500K model is still in regular use in Britain. Note the twin spare wheels; ideal for continental touring. Provided by Richard Grey.*

similar design. In 1933 came the introduction of the 2.9-litre 290—the policy now was to base model nomenclature on the engine size—in normal and short-chassis form with new independent front suspension combining inboard coils compressed by upper pivot arms, and a lower transverse leaf spring. Much further up market came the all-independent straight-eight 380 sports tourer with coil-and-wishbone suspension like that pioneered by Cadillac in America. This advanced system, still in use today, separated as three independent elements the wheel location, springing and damping, with consequent benefits to the car's ride and roadholding.

In the late 1920s, Daimler-Benz had constructed some small prototype cars with integral body-chassis units, but financial constraints curtailed development. In 1932, the company also manufactured a small, horizontally opposed four-cylinder engine for a utility runabout. Following these lines of development, which clearly foreshadowed the Volkswagen, the rear-engined 1.3-litre 26 bhp 130 saloon, based on a single-backbone chassis tube, was seen for the first time at the 1934 Berlin show, and was later supplemented by a 1.5-litre, 55 bhp 150 sports car with a mid-mounted engine ahead of the rear wheels. The independent swing-axle rear suspension of these cars was similar to that of the front-engined 170/200 series, and the four-speed gearbox, which was an integral part of the engine, had a semi-automatic overdrive which could be engaged without the clutch.

Although very advanced, indeed ahead of their time, the small 130/150 cars, supplemented by a 170 version in 1935, did not sell well and were soon dropped from the range. The great success of the 170V, a 1936 development of the original front-engined 170 with a new all-independent X-frame chassis of tubular steel powered by a three-bearing, four-cylinder engine, accelerated the demise of the rear-engined cars. Over 90,000 170V models, the cheapest Mercedes ever built, were sold from 1936 to 1947 with open tourer and saloon bodywork. At the other end of the scale came the mighty Super Mercedes, first produced in 1930 and completely modernized in 1938 with an all-independent chassis, five-speed gearbox and supercharged engine of 230 bhp. The 7.7-litre 770, or Grosser Mercedes, of the late 1930s still ranks as one of the world's great luxury cars. At the other extreme was the 230, which was a 2.3-litre six-cylinder and introduced in 1936. By the outbreak of the Second World War, 20,000 had been produced.

Capitalizing on its diesel expertise in the light and heavy commercial fields, Daimler-Benz showed a diesel-engined car at the Berlin show in 1936. Three years earlier, a 3.8-litre, 82 bhp six-cylinder diesel had been fitted to a Mannheim saloon chassis, but the vibration proved too much for it. Further development resulted in the successful 260D, forerunner of Mercedes' highly successful range of diesel cars that were to come later.

With the rise of Hitler's Nazi party, Daimler-Benz received the means, through government subsidies, of demonstrating Germany's might and technical prowess on the racing tracks of Europe. It was an invincible onslaught, the like of which the world had never seen—and probably never will again.

THE GREAT RACERS

With government encouragement, Hans Nibel and his team designed and built the W25 racing car in ten months. By January 1934 the prototype, which was shown to an approving Hitler, was ready for testing. It is just as well that Nibel was a chassis expert because the key to success was not simply power, for German technology was so advanced and her engine expertise so great that there would be no shortage of that, but how best to use it while keeping the car on the road. Calling on experience gained from the company's all-independent road cars, the W25 had an extensively drilled, lightweight box-section chassis frame with enclosed swinging rear axles pivoted on universal joints each side of the combined four-speed gearbox/final drive assembly. Transverse quarter-elliptic leaf springs also helped to locate the wheels. Independent wishbone suspension was used at the front, where bell-crank arms acting on horizontal coil springs enclosed in a chassis cross-member helped to minimize frontal area. Friction dampers controlled spring movement at both ends. Unlike most other racing cars of the day, which used mechanically operated brakes, the W25 had a Lockheed hydraulic system to work the big, outboard drums carried by the large wire-spoked wheels. At first, the straight-eight engine had bore and stroke dimensions of 78× 88 mm to give a capacity of 3360 cc. With a Roots blower running at over twice engine speed, four valves per cylinder operated by twin overhead camshafts, and Bosch ignition, the engine developed 314 bhp in its original form, and 354 bhp when bored to 3.71 litres. In 1935, when the capacity was increased again to 3990 cc, the power went up to a remarkable 430 bhp. The W25 was built to the formula, introduced in 1934, which limited the car's weight, less fuel, oil and tyres, to 750 kg (1653 lb).

The W25 was a big car, but despite its size it just complied with the 750 kg ruling, thanks to the extensive use of expensive light alloy castings and a no-expense-spared design philosophy. The engine, for instance, was built up from two steel forged blocks welded to cylinder barrels and water jackets to give an immensely strong, rigid but light structure. Even so, it was right on the limit. Mercedes-Benz's great rival was the

MERCEDES-BENZ W125
1937

ENGINE	
No. of cylinders	8
Bore/stroke mm	94 × 102
Displacement cc	5664
Valve operation	Twin overhead camshaft
Induction	Carburettor, via Roots-type supercharger
BHP	646 at 5000 rpm
Transmission	Four-speed

CHASSIS	
Frame	Oval tube side members
Wheelbase mm	2794
Track—front mm	1473
Track—rear mm	1397
Suspension—front	Independent, coil springs and wishbones
Suspension—rear	De Dion axle with torsion springs
Brakes	Hydraulic drums

PERFORMANCE	
Maximum speed	322 km/h (200 mph) on highest gearing and largest tyres

ABOVE *The Mercedes-Benz Grand Prix car reached its pre-war peak when the W125 arrived in 1937 with a possible 646 bhp on offer. Here Rudolph Caracciola is at the wheel of an example in the 1937 Monaco GP. The event was won by Manfred von Brauchitsch, who can be seen behind second-placed Caracciola, while another W125 was in third. It was Mercedes-Benz's third win on the twisting Monaco circuit.*

LEFT *Monaco again, this time 1935. The car is the W25 model and the driver is Luigi Fagioli who went on to win the event ahead of an Alfa Romeo. Here he is lapping Soffietti in a Maserati at the gasworks hairpin, after leading all the way, although he dropped his speed slightly after setting a lap record of 96.68 km/h (60.07 mph).*

mid-engined Auto Union, designed by Ferdinand Porsche, their former technical director!

The Germans, still ironing out teething troubles, failed miserably in the 1934 French Grand Prix, which was a walkover for Alfa Romeo, but they were ready again for their own premier event on the Nürburgring in July. Caracciola led until his car broke down, giving Hans Stuck's Auto Union an easy victory ahead of Fagioli. Caracciola took the Kausen hill climb from Hans Stuck, but the Auto Union driver got his revenge on the Freiburg dash soon after. Stuck was a master on the long Continental hill climbs, which in those days counted towards the European drivers' championship. At Pescara, where Caracciola (who crashed) was timed at 290 km/h (180 mph) it was Fagioli's Mercedes that won; but the Mercedes were outclassed—in fact one of them finished last—in the Swiss Grand Prix at Berne where Auto Union took the first three places.

And so it went on with the now all-conquering German teams sharing the honours, Mercedes taking the Spanish and Italian Grands Prix, Auto Union winning at Brno in Czechoslovakia. In all, the W25 won four of the big internationals in 1934, and rounded off the season with several speed records using a streamlined 3992 cc GP car driven by Caracciola.

Sadly, Hans Nibel died in November 1934 at the age of 54, so he did not live to see the remarkable 1935 record of the cars he had created. Now with well over 400 bhp and any problems having been sorted out, W25s won nine of the ten big internationals in which they ran.

The tables were dramatically turned in 1936. By now the Daimler-Benz racing department, with almost unlimited funds (like Auto Union's), employed several hundred people. The W25, with shorter wheelbase, revised suspension, more streamlined body and 450 bhp, was faster than ever and, with two early wins at Monaco and Tunis, appeared set for another invincible season. It was not to be. Thereafter the racing was dominated by the much-improved 16-cylinder Auto Unions, led by the brilliant Rosemeyer.

The W125 and W154

Grand prix racing was to have run under a new 3-litre formula for 1937, and it was for this that the W125 Mercedes was originally designed. But in a late and muddled change, the AIACR extended the 750 kg formula for another year and, instead of a 3-litre motor, for the 1937 season the W125 appeared with a 600 bhp 5.6-litre straight-eight developed from the W25's. With some 200 bhp more than its predecessor, drastic chassis and suspension changes were called for to utilize all the power, not least to minimize wheelspin, said to be possible at 240 km/h (150 mph) in top in the W25. This required a new chassis with coil-and-wishbone independent front suspension and torsion bar sprung de Dion rear axle. It was a long and exciting season, with many memorable races, the honours just going to Mercedes with 7 wins and 9 seconds in 13 races, the fastest of them won by Lang in a special W125 streamliner at the AVUS where he averaged 262 km/h (162.6 mph). Auto Union, led by the inspired Rosemeyer, won

everything else, including the British Grand Prix at Donington in a year that was totally dominated by the big German cars. He died, alas, on a flying kilometre record attempt in October 1937.

For 1938, the grand prix formula was for 3-litre supercharged cars or 4.5-litre unblown ones, with a *minimum* weight limit of 850 kg (1874 lb) with tyres, the idea being to slow the cars down by making them less powerful as well as heavier. Partially to offset the lost capacity, Mercedes increased the engine piston area with a 60-degree V12 supercharged 3-litre, with two overhead camshafts per bank operating four valves per cylinder. The crankshaft and con rods ran on roller bearings and no fewer than nine oil pumps lubricated this masterpiece of engineering. With twin superchargers to increase the boost pressure to 12.25 kg (27 lb), more than double that of the W125, the engine developed 450 bhp at 8000 rpm.

Although not as powerful as the W125, the W154 was almost as quick, thanks to better handling, brakes and streamlining. It made a bad start though. In the 1938 Pau Grand Prix, the first race held under the new formula, the 4.5-litre unblown V12 Delahaye of René Dreyfus, though a slower car, completed the distance non-stop, and neither Lang nor Caracciola could close the gap on the French car after stopping for fuel. The prodigious fuel consumption of the Mercedes necessitated a huge tankage, which none of the drivers liked.

Thereafter, Caracciola, Lang, von Brauchitsch and British driver Seaman—who won the German Grand Prix, which was said to have displeased Hitler—had things much their own way on the circuits, if not the hill climbs where Hans Stuck was virtually unbeatable. Without Rosemeyer, though, the Auto Unions were not the force they once were until the little Italian maestro Nuvolari got the hang of the rear-engined monsters and beat the Mercedes in the season's last two grands prix, at Monza and Donington. Even so, out of ten major events, Mercedes won six and Caracciola, for the third year running, took the European drivers' championship.

The W154 was replaced in 1939 by the W163 with many detail improvements, a wonderfully sleek new body and some 480 bhp with the help of a new two-stage supercharger that sucked rather than blew through the carburettors. It was a year of triumph and tragedy for the Mercedes team, who won most of the big races. Lang was the undoubted star in this final act but Dick Seaman, who had joined the team in 1937, crashed at Spa while leading the Belgian Grand Prix and died the following day.

Mercedes was not fooled by the Italians' ruse of restricting the prestigious Tripoli Grand Prix to 1.5-litre supercharged cars to give their Alfa Romeos (now led by Enzo Ferrari) and Maseratis what they thought would be an unrivalled run. The

A magnificent study of Rudolf Caracciola at the wheel of a W125 during the Coppa Acerbo race at Pescara, Italy in 1937. The car gave piston trouble and Caracciola handed over to Seaman, who finished fifth. Von Brauchitsch, in another W125 racing car, was placed second.

Germans wheeled out their superb 1.5-litre V8 W165, designed and built in eight months, and Lang and Caracciola utterly defeated the Italians with their mini-Mercs, beautiful scaled-down versions of the 3-litre 163.

For five years, from 1934 to 1939, German GP cars had ruled supreme. It was another 15 years before the Mercedes were to do so again in grand prix racing.

HOSTILITIES INTERVENE

As in the 1914–18 conflict, development of the car came to a standstill during the Second World War while aero-engine technology advanced dramatically. However, Germany's great expertise in this field was of little immediate help to Daimler-Benz when the crippled company came to pick up the pieces in the spring of 1945. This time, Germany was not only in financial ruin but flattened as well. Factories at Untertürkheim, Sindelfingen and Gaggenau were largely destroyed by Allied air raids, though that at Mannheim escaped the worst of the bombing. For a brief period, Daimler-Benz officially ceased to exist in the immediate post-war period of chaos and disruption, but as the staff filtered back and the lines of communica-

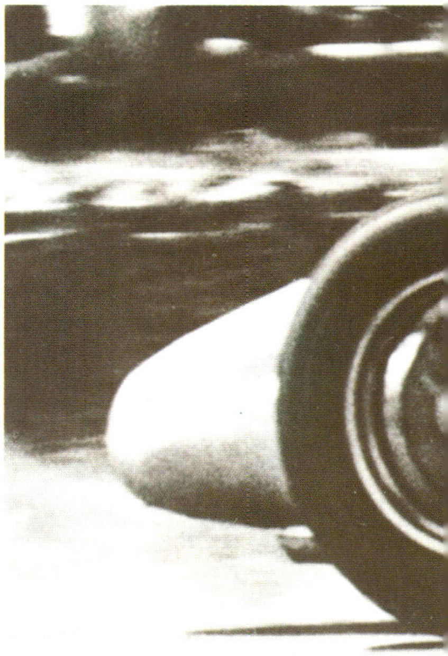

RIGHT *Caracciola putting a W154 through its paces during the 1938 French Grand Prix when he was placed second behind von Brauchitsch in another W154, while Lang in a further example was third. The 3-litre V12 engine developed 450 bhp and the model proved more than a match for the D type Auto Union*

BELOW *The W154's successor was the W163, introduced for the 1939 season. With two-stage supercharging it developed 483 bhp, as opposed to its predecessor's 450, while the nose was re-designed and the driveline offset to permit the driver to sit lower than previously.*

TOP *This Mercedes-Benz brochure depicts the Type 170S in convertible form and built between 1949 and 1951.*

ABOVE *The 170V model was built between 1946 and 1953, and this Cabriolet A dates from 1947.*

tion were re-established, so the round-the-clock job of clearing the debris and rebuilding got under way. It was a monumental task, tackled with typical Teutonic thoroughness and vigour, and it was not long before at least some of the works were operating again, doing general repair work.

Car manufacture restarted in 1948 with the pre-war tubular X-frame 170V which, along with the 230 six, had accounted for most of D-B's production in the late 1930s.

In 1949 came the extensively revised 170S that had in fact been running in prototype form, with the works type number of W136, before the war. The modified chassis retained the cruciform layout of oval-section tubes with outriggers to carry the saloon or cabriolet body, but the rear track was increased by nearly 127 mm (5 in) to reduce the tricky effect of swing-axle camber changes, and the old transverse leaf-spring front suspension, which could induce shimmy caused by undesirable gyroscopic effects, was replaced by a coil-and-wishbone layout similar to that first used on the 540K and GP cars. Improved breathing and a small capacity increase helped to raise power of the 1777 cc side-valve engine by 37 per cent to 52 bhp at 4000 rpm. Even then, the 170S was not a fast car but, thanks to thermostatic control of inlet manifold temperature, a ribbed sump to cool the oil, new lead-bronze bearings for the main and big-end bearings, and fairly high gearing, it could sustain 120 km/h (75 mph) indefinitely on the growing network of *Autobahnen*, one of Hitler's few beneficial legacies.

It was the 170S, and the 1700 cc diesel derivative of it, that not only put Mercedes back in big business, but reaffirmed the company's standing as a manufacturer of high-quality cars.

From the 170S (by 1950 Mercedes was producing 800 cars a week from a workforce of 3200) the company progressed steadily up market as the period of hardship and austerity gave way to more affluent times in West Germany's remarkable recovery to prosperity. The 220, introduced in 1951 at the Frankfurt show along with the 300 and 300S, was based on a strengthened 170S cruciform chassis with wider track, powered by a new 2.2-litre six-cylinder engine developing 80 bhp at 4600 rpm. By early 1952, over 1000 a month were being made.

Although it had faired-in headlights and more room, the first 220 retained the dignified but dated pre-war body styling of the 170. But in its performance and behaviour, it established the character of other Mercedes to follow: its smooth, short-stroke, high-revving engine with a chain-driven overhead camshaft operating staggered valves feeding high-turbulence combustion chambers gave a good specific output at the expense of relatively modest torque at low engine revs. The ability to sustain high cruising speeds without risk of mechanical failure or premature wear stemmed not only from high-quality engineering and manufacture but also from very careful attention to cooling and lubrication. The 220's suspension was similar to that of the 170's, the coil-and-wishbone front end invariably being described in contemporary reports as a direct development of that on the pre-war grand prix cars, adding support to the old adage about racing improving the breed. It would be more accurate, however, to describe the front suspension as an updating of that on the big 540K sports tourer, which was copied on the GP cars.

The bigger 300, again based on the now familiar cruciform chassis and all-independent suspension of coil and wishbones at the front, and swinging half-shafts at the back, represented Mercedes' post-war comeback to the luxury-saloon market, and its more powerful short-chassis derivative, the 300S, carried on the tradition of the great pre-war sports cars.

The 300SL and the return to racing

It was the six-cylinder engine of the 300S that provided the basis for Mercedes' long-rumoured comeback to European racing in 1952 with the 300SL, or 3-litre Sport Leicht to interpret the nomenclature. And light it was, with a small, closed coupé body with gullwing doors clothing a space-frame chassis of thin steel tubes powered by an inclined (for a low bonnet line) development of the 300S engine with raised compression and three downdraught Solex carburettors, developing a relatively modest 175 bhp at 5200 rpm. The suspension was similar to that of the production cars; even the flexible kingpost mounting, which allowed slight fore and aft cushioning of the front wishbones, was retained, though the car had bigger drum brakes and a close-ratio four-speed gearbox.

Modest or not, the 300SL was strong, well engineered and very successful. If not the fastest sports car of its day, it could certainly claim to be the most dependable and best supported, paving the way for greater things to come. Of the five events in which it was entered in 1952 before being withdrawn, the 300SL won four. Its only 'failure' was on its difficult début in the Mille Miglia when Karl Kling and Hans Klenk, newcomers to the team, finished an honourable second to Giovanni Bracco's Ferrari, with Caracciola (a past winner) and Kurle fourth. In the Grand Prix de Berne, Kling, Lang and Fritz Riess took the first three places after the only serious opposition—a works-supported 4.1-litre Ferrari—had failed on the line with a broken transmission. Caracciola was injured in a crash just before the end in what proved to be his last appearance in the Mercedes racing team, so he did not compete in the 1952 Le Mans soon after. While Jaguar, Cunningham, Ferrari, Talbot and Gordini fought for the lead in the 24-hour race, the three Mercedes coupés gave a demonstration run in regularity and reliability, gradually climbing the leader board as faster cars failed until only the 4.5-litre Talbot, driven solo by Frenchman Pierre Levegh, was ahead. Within sight of victory after an epic drive, his Talbot ran a big end, handing the race to the 300SL of Kling and Klenk.

The Germans were not represented in their own 1952 Grand Prix, a walkover for Ferrari, but in the accompanying sports-car race 300SLs, some with open bodies, filled the first four places. The fifth and final appearance of the little gullwings was in the gruelling Mexican Panamericana, success in which would mean a boost in prestige and sales in the United States. Again Ferrari fielded the fastest car, Mille Miglia winner Bracco building up a useful lead. But in the end it was the 300SL's reliability, Neubauer's slick organization and the dependable Kling and Klenk that won the day again for Mercedes.

There was certainly an element of luck in the 300SL's 1952 successes. It could so easily have been reduced to a respectable placing at Le Mans had faster cars not failed, and there was little to oppose it at Berne where, as in the Panamericana, less fragile Ferraris might well have beaten it—as one did in the Mille Miglia. But the Mercedes company had made its point: without the fastest car, it had still fielded a winner in what was really little more than a trial run for a bigger onslaught to come.

In 1953 the factory withdrew from racing, but that was not the end of the 300SL: far from it. Capitalizing on its victories, particularly in America, Mercedes introduced a limited production 300SL that retained several of the competition version's unusual features, including the gullwing doors and removable steering wheel that facilitated entry and exit. Its big advantage over the racers, though, was in the first-time use of

RIGHT *The 300S (for super) model was introduced at the 1951 Paris Motor Show for 1952 and remained in production until 1955. Aimed at the sports enthusiast, it was powered by a 3-litre six-cylinder overhead camshaft engine, while the chassis was cruciform with the proven Mercedes-Benz formula of front wishbones and a swing axle rear. Available in drophead coupé, coupé and convertible forms, it was replaced in 1955 by the 300Sc with Bosch fuel injection rather than triple Solexes and with bhp increased from 150 to 175. Production ceased in 1958 after a total of only 760 examples of both types had been built.*

MERCEDES-BENZ 300SL
1954–7

ENGINE	
No. of cylinders	6
Bore/stroke mm	85 × 88
Displacement cc	2996
Valve operation	Single overhead camshaft
Compression ratio	8.55:1
Induction	Bosch fuel injection
BHP	215 at 6200 rpm
Transmission	Four-speed

CHASSIS	
Frame	Triangulated tubular spaceframe
Wheelbase mm	2400
Track—front mm	1385
Track—rear mm	1435
Suspension—front	Independent, coil springs and wishbones
Suspension—rear	Independent, coil springs and swing axles
Brakes	Hydraulic finned drum, servo-assisted

PERFORMANCE	
Maximum speed	265 km/h (165 mph)

Bosch fuel injection, developed from that of the aero engines. With improved induction and optimum fuel-air mixture throughout all operating conditions, allowing the use of a higher 8.55:1 compression ratio, the power of the seven-bearing, dry-sump overhead-cam 3-litre six was increased to 215 bhp at 6200 rpm, 40 bhp more than the racing cars developed with Solex carburation. With the highest of three possible axle ratios, intermediate maxima were 82, 138 and 203 km/h (51, 86 and 126 mph), with a top speed of over 258 km/h (160 mph): astonishing figures for 1954, although clean aerodynamics and an inclined engine that gave a very low frontal area were in part responsible for the car's great speed. The Bosch injection also made it very docile, with the ability to accelerate cleanly from 24 km/h (15 mph) in top gear on low-grade petrol.

It was with the relatively humdrum companion 190SL (1.9-litre Sports Leicht) that Mercedes attacked the volume specialist market. Although the hood, windscreen and bumpers could be removed, and the doors replaced with lightweight cutaway ones for competition use, the 190SL was much more of a civilized open tourer than an out-and-out sports car, even though its dry-sump engine—basically an overhead camshaft 300 six with two cylinders removed to make a four—developed a respectable 110 bhp at 5500 rpm with two

The fabled 300SL with distinctive gullwing doors required by the use of a spaceframe chassis. The engine is a 3-litre fuel-injected six and the suspension is all independent.

horizontal Solex carburettors, to give a maximum speed of 190 km/h (118 mph). Although the wheelbase was the same as the 300SL's, the track even wider, and the body styling strongly reminiscent of the open 300SL racers of 1952, the 190SL was in fact based on the chassis of the new 1953 180 saloon.

The advantages of an integral body-chassis unit, among them great strength from a lightweight structure, were being widely exploited by other manufacturers in the early 1950s, but all post-war production Mercedes cars had hitherto been based on the separate cruciform oval-tube chassis first seen in 1936. The 180 represented a radical departure from that design, with a pressed-steel floorpan stiffened by a central backbone and boxed side members, integrated with a full-width five-seater body of modern design.

The 180 was soon followed by the 220a using an improved 85 bhp 220 six-cylinder overhead camshaft engine with better low and mid-range torque in a roomier integral body-chassis unit based on the 180's. Effectively increasing the length of the drive shafts, by doing away with the pivot each side of the final drive assembly and introducing instead a single central joint, reduced camber changes of the rear wheels still further. This design, which gave better roadholding and safer handling (even in the mid-1950s swing-axle suspension had its critics), was soon adopted on the 180.

So, by 1955 Daimler-Benz was firmly re-established as the manufacturer of a wide range of quality cars, including the 170/180 four-cylinder petrol and diesel saloons, the faster up-market 220a six based on the 180 shell, the luxury 300 saloon and 300S tourer—both dignified and desirable though by now rather dated—and the ultra-modern 190SL and 300SL sports cars.

Back to the track

The Daimler-Benz concern committed itself to an ambitious and astronomically expensive grand prix racing programme in 1952 when the new 2.5-litre formula, effective from 1954, was announced. Rather than produce a carbon copy of the dominant Italian Ferraris and Maseratis, which would no doubt have worked but offered insufficient scope for development, the Mercedes designers characteristically shunned current GP design practice and started from scratch, basing their ideas on a great deal of original research and calculation.

Despite a worldwide trend towards V-type engines, Mercedes rejected this layout because the duplication of auxiliary drives for the valve gear meant unnecessary weight, and opted instead for a straight-eight which, if laid on its side, had the added advantage of being very shallow, allowing a very low bonnet line. The engine was in effect two back-to-back 'fours' with a central gear train to drive the two overhead camshafts, as well as a central power take-off to eliminate torsional vibrations in the long built-up crankshaft running in ten roller bearings and carrying forged con rods in ball races. A geared-down subshaft from this central delivery transferred the drive to the clutch and rear-mounted five-speed gearbox.

In its construction the engine followed traditional Mercedes practice, with one-piece forged cylinder bores and combustion chambers, welded together in groups of four, with the ports welded on top of the hemispheres and then surrounded by welded-on steel-sheet water jackets. The invincible 1914 GP engine had been built along similar lines. In detail design, though, the new straight-eight broke fresh ground. Instead of the expected four small valves per cylinder disposed at 60 degrees, there were only two large ones at an included angle of 90 degrees, positively opened *and* closed by a unique and ingenious desmodromic arrangement of cams and rockers, removing the need for space-consuming return springs and the limitations they impose on valve lift and peak accelerations. By eliminating the risk of a destructive encounter between valves and pistons during, say, a missed gear change, safe engine speeds of up to 9000 rpm were possible, though this was a useful bonus rather than a design objective. The primary purpose of the desmodromic valve gear was optimum filling of the combustion chambers.

One predictable carry-over from the 300SL was the use of Bosch direct fuel injection, with the nozzles placed some way down the cylinder bores so that they were protectively shrouded from intense thermal loads by the pistons at the moment of ignition.

By laying the engine almost on its side the W196, as it was called, had a very low build and centre of gravity. Like the 300SL, the lightweight spaceframe was constructed from small-diameter tubes, suspended at the front by upper and lower wishbones fabricated from the solid in Mercedes' traditional way. The rear suspension raised a few eyebrows, though. Instead of the de Dion layout, pioneered on pre-war Mercedes GP cars and by the 1950s almost standard practice for racing machinery, Daimler-Benz reverted to a sophisticated and unusual swing-axle design, which could at least be related to that of the latest road cars. The wheels were laterally located by curved arms swinging from a common, low central pivot beneath the rear gearbox casing only a few inches above the ground, thus effectively increasing the radius of the swinging arms to reduce wheel-camber changes as well as lowering the car's roll centre. Fore and aft location was by upper and lower longitudinal arms forming a Watts linkage. As at the front, springing was by torsion bars, not because of any innate advantage conferred by this medium but because there was really no room for anything else. The brakes, too, were a surprise. The factory had always mistrusted anything it had not developed itself, so rather than risk disc brakes, still in their infancy but showing great promise elsewhere, the racing

MERCEDES-BENZ W196
1954

ENGINE	
No. of cylinders	8
Bore/stroke mm	76 × 68
Displacement cc	2498
Valve operation	Twin overhead camshaft, desmodromic actuation
Compression ratio	9:1
Induction	Bosch fuel injection
BHP	290 at 8000 rpm
Transmission	Five-speed

CHASSIS	
Frame	Spaceframe
Wheelbase mm	2286
Track—front mm	1320
Track—rear mm	1346
Suspension—front	Independent, wishbone and torsion bar
Suspension—rear	Independent, low pivot swinging arms
Brakes	Hydraulic drums

PERFORMANCE	
Maximum speed	Approx 290 km/h (180 mph)

RIGHT *The 196's 2.5-litre engine, distinguished by its desmodromic valve gear and fuel injection.*

BELOW *The W196 Grand Prix car in its later bodied form built for the 1954 2.5-litre formula.*

department opted instead for tried and trusted drums, albeit very sophisticated ones developed from those of the 300SL, with an inner cast-iron ring bonded to a light-alloy drum, heavily finned to dissipate heat. To minimize unsprung weight, these huge drum brakes were mounted inboard, driven at the front by shafts from the wheels.

Few of these technical details were known when pictures of the car were first released early in 1954: what attracted most attention then was the sleek, incredibly low, all-enveloping streamlined bodywork. Mercedes had recognized early in the development programme that efficient aerodynamics, evolved from wind-tunnel tests, would help them win races on fast circuits: and the first on which they were to compete, at Rheims for the 1954 French Grand Prix in July, was very fast indeed. Even so, Mercedes left nothing to chance for Neubauer had recruited as his number one driver the great Argentinian maestro, Juan Manuel Fangio.

The W196s on the circuits

Although Alberto Ascari's open-wheel Maserati was only a fraction of a second slower than the Mercedes streamliners in practice, Fangio and Kling ran away from the Italians in the race. This memorable début victory pointed towards the sort of invincible comeback that the pundits had forecast. Yet three weeks later the Mercedes were soundly trounced in the British Grand Prix at Silverstone. Although Fangio started from pole position, it was the Ferrari of Froilan Gonzalez that set the pace. In the heat of battle Fangio found the W196 a bit of a handful, and on more than one occasion hit the circuit marker barrels that were hard to see from the central cockpit of the low-slung streamliner. Fangio dropped even further back after a mid-race downpour, eventually to finish fourth, with team mate Kling a lowly seventh. The opposition took heart. The new Mercs were not, after all, unbeatable, though the Silverstone debacle was arguably the result of a tactical error in using enclosed cars on a circuit for which they were unsuited, rather than the squat open wheelers which the drivers preferred. These were raced for the first time in the German GP on the Nürburgring. Fangio, Kling and Lang were entrusted with the new cars, aesthetically less pleasing than the enclosed streamliner that Herrmann drove, but demonstrably more effective on this sort of track. Even so, only Fangio made the front row of the grid, shared with Hawthorn's Ferrari and Moss's Maserati. It was not the dogfight between the Italian and German cars that made this a memorable race, however, so much as the meteoric drive of local hero Kling who, starting from the back row after missing official practice, swept through the field to overtake Fangio for the lead. After breaking the lap record several times, he unfortunately also broke his car and eventually finished fourth, much to the displeasure of Neubauer who had planned on a clean sweep in front of the home crowd.

Fangio won again in the Swiss Grand Prix, though Moss had beaten him in a wet practice session and was already attracting the attention of Neubauer, just as Dick Seaman had done in the late 1930s. Nor were the works Ferraris by any means outpaced. The Mercedes team was certainly having to work for its wins, never more so than in the Italian Grand Prix at Monza where Ascari's Ferrari led Fangio until Stirling Moss overtook them both to hold the lead for 45 laps before his Maserati failed within sight of victory. Ascari also retired, so once again Fangio took the chequered flag for his fourth win of the season. This was Mercedes' last GP victory that year. In the Spanish event at Barcelona, it was the new and very fast F1 Lancias that set the pace until they retired, leaving Fangio to contend not only with other Italian cars ahead but also with a tiresome wind that whisked leaves and waste paper into the radiator air scoop, causing the engine to overheat and spew oil. He eventually finished fourth behind Hawthorn's winning Ferrari.

In its first season, the W196 had proved itself to be fast and reliable—but not unbeatable. Had it not been for the driving talents of Fangio, the record books might well have shown a very different story. Nevertheless, a Mercedes had helped to carry Fangio to his second world title, and Daimler-Benz, largely through the Argentinian's efforts, clinched the manufacturers' championship. After such a long lay-off from grand prix racing, it was a pretty devastating comeback.

With a season's valuable experience behind the team, lighter and more powerful cars, and Stirling Moss now enlisted to support Fangio, it was hard to see who or what could beat Mercedes in 1955. In addition, Daimler-Benz now had a second Silver Arrow to a powerful bow in the shape of the 300SLR (designated the W196-S), a derivative of the grand prix machine rather than a development of the gullwing 300SL racer of 1952, to contest the great sports-car classics. Like the W196, the 300SLR had a straight-eight inclined engine with desmodromic valve gear and fuel injection. But instead of

ABOVE *Monaco 1955; the W196s of Stirling Moss (6) and Fangio (2). Fangio retired but Moss was placed ninth.*

LEFT *Hans Herrmann in a W196 in its original streamlined form.*

forged fabricated cylinder barrels, the cylinder block was cast in light alloy with chrome-plated bores. Bore and stroke dimensions were greater than those of the 2496 cc GP engine, giving a capacity of 2976 cc. Valve timing, too, was altered to provide greater mid-range torque—295 Nm (220 lb ft) at 5950 rpm—at the expense of absolute power (296 bhp at 7450 rpm). In chassis, suspension and brake design, the 300SLR was very similar to the grand prix car, though the spaceframe chassis (weighing a mere 59.8 kg—132 lb!) was a little wider to accommodate two people, and the inboard front brakes, driven by angled double-jointed shafts, were moved slightly forward so that the engine could be mounted further forward too. Outboard front brakes were also available. So, too, was a novel hydraulically operated air brake that flipped up behind the driver's head for especially demanding braking from high speeds, like that needed at the end of the Mulsanne straight at Le Mans where the the 300SLR could reach 290 km/h (180 mph).

Mercedes started the year in fine style in South America,

Fangio winning the Argentine Grand Prix in January, and the Buenos Aires GP (a non-championship race) two weeks later from Moss. The European campaign began in May with the famous victory of Stirling Moss in the Mille Miglia, navigated by journalist Denis Jenkinson from a roller map of pace notes. Moss's average speed of 157.2 km/h (98 mph) in the début appearance of the 300SLR was 16 km/h (10 mph) faster than the race had ever been won before, and not even Fangio—driving solo even though he did not much care for sports-car racing—could match the pace of the young British ace. He finished 30 minutes adrift in second place after the fast but fragile Ferraris of Piero Taruffi and Eugenio Castellotti had given up. It was an epic win for Moss.

For a time it looked like yet another Mercedes one-two walkover in the Monaco GP three weeks later for Fangio and Moss, both driving W196 open wheelers with outboard front brakes in order to shorten the chassis for the twisty Monte Carlo circuit. The two German cars were well ahead of the Lancias and Ferraris but, to the astonishment of everyone, not least Neubauer and his pit crew, both cars suddenly failed: Fangio's with transmission trouble, Moss's with a blown engine. Not even Mercedes cars were infallible. A week later the team's spirits were back to their normal level when Fangio and Moss almost dead-heated their 300SLRs in the Eifelrennen on the Nürburgring, and early in June they scored another one-two in the Belgian Grand Prix.

The Le Mans tragedy and its aftermath

Things were now running pretty well according to plan again for Mercedes until that fateful moment on 11 June 1955 when poor Pierre Levegh, invited to join the 300SLR team at Le Mans as a tribute to his epic drive two years before when he so nearly beat the 300SL, cannoned off a slower car in front of the pits and scythed into the packed terraces. Over 80 people, including Levegh, died in the worst accident in motor-racing history. At 2 am, orders were received from Stuttgart to withdraw the remaining cars as a mark of respect when Moss and Fangio had a two-lap lead over the disc-braked D-type Jaguar of Hawthorn and Ivor Bueb.

The Le Mans tragedy, through no fault of Mercedes, cast a shadow over motor racing for a long time afterwards. Switzerland was never to hold another motor race and the 1955 French and German Grands Prix were cancelled, though such was the form of the W196 and its two ace drivers that it is hard to imagine anything but a Mercedes winning either. To underline the point, the German cars finished first and second in the next three Grands Prix to be held—Fangio, Moss at Zandvoort in the Dutch GP; Moss, Fangio in a photo finish at Aintree in the British GP; and Fangio, Taruffi in Italy's premier event at Monza where Fangio and Moss (who retired) once again drove enclosed streamliners.

Nothing could stop the 300SLR either. In the Swedish GP at Karlskoga, Fangio and Moss took the first two places in another photo finish driving air-braked cars; and Mercedes were first, second and third in the Dundrod Tourist Trophy after the Jaguar and Aston Martin challengers had wilted. In a bid to wrest the sports-car championship from Ferrari—the F1 drivers' and constructors' title were already in the bag—Neubauer dispatched two 300SLRs to Sicily for the Targa Florio. When Moss went off the road and lost nine minutes, it looked as though the race and title were beyond reach. But with co-driver Peter Collins, Moss not only recovered that lost time but went on to win by nearly five minutes from the sister car of Fangio and Kling, and so clinch the title.

So Mercedes' two-year racing programme was completed just as it had started with a one-two victory. No name in the motor industry commanded greater respect, no emblem was more highly revered than the three-pointed star—the only decal carried by the great eights throughout their racing life. Mission was accomplished: the factory withdrew from racing.

TECHNICAL EXCELLENCE

While Mercedes was whipping all comers on the track with the world's most advanced grand prix machinery in the mid-1950s, the company was producing a range of road cars that were superbly engineered and commercially very successful but hardly technical trendsetters. The base 180 saloon, for instance, still used an antiquated side-valve engine of basically pre-war design. D-B was not slow to capitalize on its racing reputation, however. The company's abrupt withdrawal from competition, which had absorbed a great deal of engineering time and talent, not to say a vast sum of money, was followed by the release of several new and revised production cars. Late in 1955 came the convertible version of the 220a with a shorter wheelbase than the saloon. Early in 1956 Mercedes announced the 220S with twin carburettors and 112 bhp, which demoted the old single-carb model to a 219.

The 180a of 1957 was not an improved 1.8-litre saloon as its name suggests but an economy low-compression version of the 190, introduced the year before with a detuned version of the original full-width 180. Updating existing bodyshells with new engines and running gear—and similarly equipping new body styles with existing mechanical components—is the key to Mercedes' evolutionary policy.

With the adoption of the 190 engine, the old side-valve unit, which had been in service for 20 years or so in one form or another, was at last dropped from the range. At the other end of the market spectrum a more powerful 250 bhp 300SL roadster lost its gullwing doors and gained a new version of the low-pivot rear suspension that was later to be adopted on lesser models.

It was for the introduction of fuel injection, however, that Mercedes' mid-1950s passenger-car programme is perhaps best remembered. Developed in conjunction with Bosch, and perfected for use on the 300SL, 300SLR and W196 GP car, fuel injection soon filtered down the range. The 300 saloon and coupé were so equipped in 1955, increasing mid-range torque and top-end power by 1957 to 180 bhp, when a completely new injection system, squirting into the ports rather than the combustion chambers and sensitive to ambient temperature and atmospheric pressure, was standardized in a lengthened 300. The 130 bhp injected 220SE (E for *Einspritz*, injection) came the following year.

The 300SLR derived from the W196. Its first victory was in the 1955 Mille Miglia when Stirling Moss with Denis Jenkinson as navigator won the event at 157.6 km/h (97.9 mph); a record that stands for all time, since the race ceased in 1957. This is the number of the winning car which is on display in the Daimler-Benz museum.

New body styles for the 1960s

By the late 1950s, with an overhead camshaft diesel 'four' in the base model—now well established for taxi use, but also popular with private and business buyers for its economy and longevity—and high-performance injected sixes at the other end of the scale, Daimler-Benz had a fine line-up of modern powertrains but a somewhat dated range of body styles. That shortcoming was to a large extent answered by the introduction of a new 220 series at the 1959 Frankfurt show. Although the existing rounded bodies remained in production for the base cars until 1961, the 220 had completely new and elegant bodywork, longer, wider and lower than before. Flanking the traditional Mercedes grille were distinctive vertically stacked headlights contoured into wings that swept back to an angular tail treatment embracing vestigial fins. The 220 (105 bhp), 220S (124 bhp) and 220SE (130 bhp) all had this new, more roomy unitary body structure, as well as revised suspension.

It was not until the introduction that same year of the advanced 300SE—based on the 220's new bodyshell but with a self-levelling air suspension, a limited-slip differential, all-disc (Dunlop) brakes operated by a hydraulic servo, D-B's own

FAR RIGHT *The 230SL, introduced in 1963 and built until 1967 with a total of 19,831 manufactured. The engine was a 2.3-litre overhead camshaft six, while the Pagoda roof was a distinctive feature. The model won the Spa-Sophia-Liège rally on its 1963 introduction. Provided by David Prior.*

BELOW *Introduced for 1960, the 220SE was mechanically the same as the previous 220SE model but with horsepower rated at 120 instead of 115. It had a 2.2-litre six-cylinder overhead camshaft fuel-injected unit. Provided by R.D. Lloyd.*

MERCEDES-BENZ 220SE 1959–65	
ENGINE	
No. of cylinders	6
Bore/stroke mm	80 × 72
Displacement cc	2197
Valve operation	Single overhead camshaft
Compression ratio	8.7:1
Induction	Bosch fuel injection
BHP	120 at 4800 rpm
Transmission	Four-speed or automatic
CHASSIS	
Frame	Unitary construction
Wheelbase mm	2750
Track—front mm	1470
Track—rear mm	1485
Suspension—front	Independent, coil springs and wishbones
Suspension—rear	Independent, coil springs and low pivot swing axle
Brakes	Hydraulic front disc, drum rear
PERFORMANCE	
Maximum speed	177 km/h (110 mph)

new four-speed automatic transmission and power steering—that the last of the tubular chassis-framed cars of pre-war ancestry was finally ousted from the range. The first post-war full-width body, introduced nearly a decade before for the 180, was also dropped around the same time, and the 190 petrol and diesel base models acquired the new square-cut look of the up-range cars, albeit with a simplified front-end treatment. D-B's policy of continuous improvement and updating was now in full swing, and reaping dividends in the market place.

Still the new shapes and models kept coming. The 230SL, faster and more luxurious than the 190SL it replaced, but less of an all-out sports car than the 300SL, was introduced at the 1963 Geneva show. In performance, price and character it was a brilliant compromise, though mechanically it owed far more to the 220SE saloon than to either of the superseded sportsters. If D-B had followed its labelling code to the letter, this Sport Light model should have been called the 230SEL, for its 2306 cc engine, identical in stroke to the 220's but larger in

bore, also had Bosch fuel injection of an improved six-plunger type. Power on a raised compression ratio of 9.3:1 was 170 bhp against the 220SE's 134, good enough to give a top speed of over 193 km/h (120 mph). This elegant, wide-tracked roadster, squatting on big 185 × 14 tyres made specially for it by Continental and Firestone, had disc/drum brakes, low-pivot swing-axle rear suspension with the new transverse compensating spring and, in closed form, a delectable slim-pillared hardtop with a distinctive concave roofline that later 250 and 280SL derivatives were to inherit.

Compared with D-B's range of the 1930s, only one model was now missing from the line-up: a super prestige saloon to equate with the great 7.7-litre Grosser Mercedes. That niche was filled in 1963 by the remarkable 600 twins—the 5/6-seater saloon and 7/8-seater Pullman limousine of almost railway-carriage proportions, a massive car outranking even the Rolls-Royce Phantom V in size and possibly in prestige too. Both models were also endowed with a vigorous performance.

The model changes, 1965–70, and the 'new generation'
Mercedes' prestige and reputation following its string of rally successes, including the 1960 Monte, '61 Safari and '63 Spa-Sofia-Liège events, were never higher than when a bewilderingly comprehensive new range of graded models was introduced in 1965. The improved base cars, now 2-litre 200s in petrol and diesel form, retained the old fintail body style but the new middle and upper range 250/280/300 series, still with vertically encapsulated headlights, had improved running gear and new, low-waistline bodies with curved side windows and a

LEFT *The 3.5-litre V8-engined 350SL of 1970 and the 1971 SLC coupé replaced the 230/250 and 280SL.*

BELOW *The 6.3-litre V8 eight-seater 600 intended for tycoons. Provided by Bruton's of London.*

RIGHT *The 3-litre six-cylinder 300SE appeared in 1965 and was, from 1968, fitted with a 6.3-litre V8 and re-designated the 300SEL 6.3. It remained in production until 1972. Provided by John de Grave Cars.*

LEFT *The diesel-engined 240D 3.0 was introduced in 1974 and, while it was no great performer, running costs were low. It had a five-cylinder 3-litre overhead camshaft engine which was, in effect, a 240D unit with an extra cylinder. Suspension was all independent with wishbones at the front and a swing axle rear. Cars in this cheaper W123 series were distinguishable by their round rather than rectangular headlights. This is a 1978 example in long-wheelbase form.*

FAR RIGHT *In 1961 Daimler-Benz acquired a licence to manufacture the Wankel rotary piston engine. It was used in triple-rotor form in the C111 mid-engined coupé, first unveiled in 1969. Further examples followed and later a diesel-powered record-breaker version appeared.*

crispness of line that was echoed, perhaps a little too closely, two years later in the much-vaunted cars for 1968.

On the last-in, last-out principle, it was predictably the old fintailed body that was now ousted in a range change that affected every model in the line-up except the big 600s and sports cars. Everything else was subdivided into two groups. The more powerful cars—250S, 280S, 280SE (saloon, coupé and convertible) and 280SL (successor, through the 250SL, to the original 230SL)—were basically the same in appearance and design as the previous 250/300 series introduced three years earlier in 1965, though the 280 had a new, more powerful six-cylinder engine developing 140–170 bhp according to specification. It was the down-range cars—the 200/220 petrol and diesel fours and the 230/250 petrol sixes—that were most changed with their new bodies and suspension. The swinging rear axles, which had been progressively developed over a period of 30 years from a pre-war design, were replaced on the new generation of small models by a viceless semi-trailing independent layout.

The model line-up was soon expanded still further in 1968 with the exciting 300SEL 6.3. This astonishing luxury slingshot was the brainchild of development engineer and competition driver Erich Waxenberger. The story goes that Waxenberger, working on his own initiative, shoehorned the big V8 into an existing 300 bodyshell and then invited chief engineer Uhlenhaut to try the car without telling him what it was. Uhlenhaut set off in his usual press-on style and was amazed and mystified by the car's incredible performance. He lifted the bonnet at the first set of traffic lights to see what was beneath. That the car went into production is a tribute to Waxenberger's foresight and initiative and to Uhlenhaut's forbearance with a staffman experimenting on the side. So formidable was the car's performance that a team of works 6.3s was entered for the Spa 24 hours saloon race. When it became obvious that breaking up of the tyres would mean failure—unthinkable to Mercedes—the cars were withdrawn after practice and little more was heard of them in competition, though Waxenberger himself won the Macau GP in one.

RIGHT *Specialists converted Mercedes saloons to estate cars before Daimler-Benz did the job itself. This is the 240TD and is diesel powered, while the T series also came with petrol engines. It was mechanically similar to the saloon, although there was a self-levelling device on the rear suspension, and other refinements included different rear seat options, rear wash/wipe system and built-in roof rails.*

The following year, in 1969, a high-revving short-stroke single overhead camshaft 3.5-litre V8 was introduced as an alternative for the same saloon shell and new coupé and convertible versions of it.

Some 50,000 230/250/280SL roadsters had been made when the series was replaced in 1971 by the V8-engined open 350SL and 350SLC coupé, both with striking new wedge-shaped bodies and new-generation running gear, including semi-trailing rear suspension, leaving very little of the market spectrum uncovered from the 200/220 diesels (accounting for the bulk of base-car production) upwards. There were carburettor fours, normally aspirated and fuel-injected sixes from 2.3 to 2.8 litres, and injected V8s of 3.5 and 6.3 litres powering a range of saloon, coupé and convertible body styles. It was a line-up that no other manufacturer of quality cars in the world could match. Nor did it end there.

Two low-emission twin-cam 2.8-litre sixes—super-efficient engines capable of meeting America's stringent exhaust emission regulations—were introduced in 1972, one giving 160 bhp on carburettors, the other 185 bhp with Bosch fuel injection. First they powered new versions of the existing saloons and coupés. Later in 1972 they were to be used in the first models of a new up-market series of super saloons called the S-class, which Mercedes heralded as the closest reasonable approach to attainable perfection at an affordable price. Seven years' intensive research and development, in which an exciting experimental C111 Coupé played a major part, went into the design of these big, luxurious cars, which replaced the previous generation of seven-year-old 280/300 models after some 350,000 had been made.

In shape, the solidly elegant S-class cars, still showing some family resemblance to the 'new generation' of small models—perhaps a little too much according to some critics—incorporated many detail design improvements affecting strength, safety, aerodynamics, comfort and refinement. The 'safety-cell'

body, welded to a floorpan frame along now familiar lines, was immensely strong and carried new running gear, with double-wishbone suspension at the front incorporating zero offset steering, developed on the C111, to give run-straight stability even with, say, the inside wheel locked in the gutter under braking. At the back the old low-pivot swing axles, already replaced on the smaller cars, gave way to a fashionable semi-trailing layout. An improved version of Daimler-Benz's own power steering, which set the standard others were judged by according to contemporary road-test reports, was fitted, and there was a choice of transmissions: four-speed manual or automatic for the six-cylinder cars, and a new three-speed automatic for the 200 bhp V8-engined 350SE.

A 450 series of 4.5-litre V8s—acclaimed Car of the Year by an international jury of motoring journalists—supplemented the twin-cam 280 and 350 models in 1973, the long wheelbase version later spawning the redoubtable 225 km/h (140 mph) 6.9-litre 450SEL 6.9, a luxury slingshot that provided a combination of performance, comfort and refinement to a degree that no other car in the world could match, with the possible exception of Jaguar's XJ12. Even-keel suspension that prevented nose dive under braking, and tail squat when accelerating hard, was a 450 refinement, although in most other respects the V8s were much like the smaller S-class cars.

Continuing development and research

Daimler-Benz by now led the world in diesel-car manufacture. The company had built more than a million since the first 260D of 1936, and 1974 saw the production of nearly 150,000 diesel cars, which accounted for almost half D-B's output of passenger vehicles. Mercedes consolidated that position in 1974 by taking the diesel up market with the introduction of a 3-litre 80 bhp five-cylinder saloon, confusingly called the 240D 3.0 to indicate that the unusual new engine powered one of the small-bodied cars. The demand for more economical luxury models in the wake of the first fuel crisis of the 1970s also prompted the introduction of 2.8-litre twin-cam versions of the sporting SL and SLC, hitherto powered only by 3.5- or 4.5-litre V8s. Such permutations have enabled Mercedes effectively to fill almost any emergent niche in the market with little delay, helped by computer-controlled production lines that have allowed considerable flexibility.

RIGHT *450SLC of 1980 in fixed-head coupé form. A 5-litre V8 engine was employed.*

BELOW *The Mercedes-Benz Experimental Safety Vehicle, coded ESF 13, of 1972.*

By 1976 the 'new generation' of middleweight cars, now not so new after a production run of eight years and 1.8 million units, was replaced after a short period of overlap by the W123. Predictably, the new perceptibly wedge-shaped series, spanning the 200–280E range, resembled scaled-down S-cars and represented another evolutionary step forward rather than a revolutionary one. The top 280E model had rectangular head- and foglight nascelles to establish its position immediately below the similarly styled S-cars. Horizontally arranged circular headlights helped to identify the lesser models.

Coupés and the T-car estate—the first Mercedes had made, though specialist converters had produced them before from saloons—followed later; the estate was offered with a choice of five engines and self-levelling rear-suspension to keep an even keel under load.

Daimler-Benz also joined the growing ranks of turbo manufacturers in 1979, not with a high-performance petrol engine but with a blown 300SD diesel unit in a W123 body, manufactured with the economy- and emission-conscious North American market in mind. Technical director Hans Scherenberg confirmed that the new turbo, which in 200 bhp form had powered the special C111 Coupé to several international speed records the year before, was part of a vigorous programme of diesel-car development.

A new all-alloy 5-litre petrol V8 announced at the same time, although lighter and more efficient than the elderly iron-block 4.5- and 6.9-litre engines it was designed to replace, may have a less certain future. It was first used, almost as a trial run, in the 450SLC. The car it was primarily intended for, though, was the new S-class, announced in the autumn of 1979. The shape was unmistakably Mercedes, but it was sufficiently different and striking to answer previous criticisms that the most expensive cars had not been distinctive enough, not sufficiently different from the cheaper models.

Such a complaint could not be levelled at the latest, superbly proportioned flagship, designed for a production run that could well span the 1980s. The narrower body, strongly tapered front to rear, was distinctly shovel-nosed and wedge-

LEFT *The 1981 coupé was available in 380 and 500SEC forms with 3.8- and 5-litre V8 engines respectively.*

RIGHT *The 190 saloon of 1983 is offered with a choice of 2-litre four-cylinder carburettored or fuel-injected engines.*

BELOW *The 280SE with 2.8-litre six-cylinder engine produces 185 bhp and has a top speed of 211 km/h (131 mph).*

shaped in profile, resulting in a 14 per cent reduction in drag compared with the previous cars. Slightly less weight also helped to reduce the fuel-guzzling tendencies of a car that, in a worsening fuel crisis, could yet finish up as a diesel. The new S models were announced, however, with a rationalized range of petrol engines in normal and long-wheelbase forms (and no anomalies in the nomenclature either): 280S, 280SE/SEL, 380SE/SEL and 500SE/SEL, the 380 being a smaller version of the new 5-litre alloy V8 rather than an enlarged 350.

In autumn 1981, new V8-powered 380 and 500SEC models, based on the floorpan and running gear of the S-class saloons, supplanted the old coupés after 60,000 had been made over a production run spanning a decade. The elegance and efficiency of the new coupés, which echoed the lines of the S-class saloons, were best reflected by the aerodynamic body, designed to slice through the air with the minimum of resistance.

The new coupés were not the only cars to benefit from Mercedes' 'energy concept' measures. By increasing gear ratios, introducing a new five-speed gearbox and improving engine efficiency (by, among other things, lowering the idle speed and cutting the fuel supply on the overrun), other models were also made more economical.

It was intelligent foresight that prompted initial design studies for a new small fuel-efficient Mercedes, code-named W201, in 1973—before the big energy scare. Nearly a decade later, Daimler-Benz launched the 190, the smallest car the company had made since the 1950s. The design objective was to retain D-B's traditional standards of build quality, durability and charisma with a compact four-door saloon that was relatively inexpensive to buy and run, and also fun to drive.

In style and character, the 190 was every inch a Mercedes, with a strong family resemblance to the S-class. But it was 270 kg (600 lb) lighter than the 200 and much more streamlined, its rising waistline body giving a drag factor of only 0.33. Strength was not sacrificed for weight or safety, though. Computer-aided design and new structural materials helped to give the 190 the crash-worthiness of an S-class car.

With new all-independent suspension and a two-programme economy/performance automatic transmission, there was nothing small about the 190's road-ability. Initially, the car came only with a 2-litre, four-cylinder engine giving 90 bhp on carburettors, or 122 bhp with fuel injection. Later on came a 230 km/h (143 mph) high-performance version called the 190E 2.3-16, powered by a 185 bhp 16-valve Cosworth-developed twin cam engine.

For 1985 the 200, 230, 250 and 280 range was replaced by the new W124 with engine options starting at 109 and rising to an eventual 197 bhp.

Thus Daimler-Benz remains in the very forefront of motor vehicle technology, a century after Daimler and Benz ignited the spark that triggered the birth of the automobile.

MERCEDES-BENZ 280SE
1980 to date

ENGINE	
No. of cylinders	6
Bore/stroke mm	86 × 78
Displacement cc	2746
Valve operation	Twin overhead camshaft
Compression ratio	9:1
Induction	Bosch mechanical fuel injection
BHP	185 at 5800 rpm
Transmission	Four-speed or automatic

CHASSIS	
Frame	Unitary construction
Wheelbase mm	2930
Track—front mm	1540
Track—rear mm	1520
Suspension—front	Independent, coil springs and wishbones
Suspension—rear	Independent, semi-trailing arms and coil springs
Brakes	Hydraulic disc

PERFORMANCE	
Maximum speed	211 km/h (131 mph)

OPEL

Adam Opel established a sewing machine business in Rüsselsheim in 1862 and then progressed to bicycle manufacture. Although an initial diversification into motor cars proved disappointing, the department was soon established on a sound footing so that by the 1920s Opel was far and away Germany's largest car maker. In 1929 the American General Motors Corporation bought the firm, and the 1930s witnessed a dramatic expansion of production which, coupled with technical refinement, saw Opel emerge as Europe's largest vehicle maker. Although badly mauled during the Second World War, Opel rose again and in the 1950s, with the firm once more in GM control, expansion again gathered pace. Further growth, along with new factories, came in the following decade with a wide range of models employing straightforward, no-nonsense mechanics. Now Opel, an important firm in General Motors global strategy, is spearheading the Corporation's assault on the European market with an impressive and increasingly popular range of models.

GG·D 46

NCH · BJÖRBO BIL · NCH
Mobil
Rally Formula
ENEM
ENEM
24
BOSCH
BOSCH
BOSCH
BOSCH
BOSCH
NCH
ZHK 321
Mobil
Mobil

2
2

MANTA GT/E
A489 LTM

Opel has been in the forefront of the German motor industry since the 1920s. By then a productive momentum had been established which, fortified and enriched by subsequent General Motors ownership, continues to this day.

Yet, ironically, Opel's initial involvement with the automobile was so unsuccessful that the firm, which had come to the horseless carriage via sewing machines and bicycles, closed down its motor car department. Fortunately the company persevered with the idea, and the Rüsselsheim factory was soon producing an extensive range of models.

The Opel story begins in 1835, when Wilhelm Opel set up in business as a locksmith in the town of Rüsselsheim on the Main river, about 25 km (15½ miles) west of Frankfurt. Soon afterwards he married Anna Katharina Diehl and she bore him three sons, Adam, Georg and Philipp. It was thought that Adam, the eldest, would follow in his father's footsteps, as indeed he did for a time, but he had the good fortune to be granted a travel permit by the Grand Duchy of Hesse. So Adam went first to Belgium and then in 1858 found himself, as a 21-year-old, in Paris. The French capital was buzzing with the news of the sewing machine that had been seen in a recent Paris exhibition and, although for a time Adam pursued his lock-making craft, by 1859 he had joined a sewing-machine manufacturer. This gave him an invaluable insight into the workings of the device and, by the time he returned to Rüsselsheim in 1862, he was fully conversant with the machine's intricacies.

Adam had hoped to begin manufacturing sewing machines from his father's locksmithing shop, but Opel senior had other ideas, so the young man had to start his own business in a nearby disused cowstall belonging to his mother's brother. His brother Georg had moved to Paris in 1862, and there he obtained the special steels that Adam required to begin production. This started in 1863, and Wilhelm Opel was to see the results of his eldest son's enterprise before he died in 1867. By this time Adam was planning to expand his production facilities and a two-storey factory was subsequently built not far from Rüsselsheim's railway station.

It was in 1867 that Adam married and three years later, in 1870, he introduced a new line of sewing machines, named 'Sophie' after his wife. Output increased, as did the size of the Opel works, and production soared at such a rate that, by 1899, half a million sewing machines had been made there. Sophie presented Adam with five children, all of whom were boys. They were Carl, Wilhelm, Heinrich, Friedrich and Ludwig, who were all destined to enter the family firm. Ludwig, however, was killed in 1916 while serving in the First World War.

Meanwhile, Adam was always looking for new product lines for his fast-growing company. He had diversified into machinery for corking wine bottles and, on one of his visits to Paris, he became interested in the bicycle and ordered a set of parts for an Ordinary, or Penny Farthing bicycle from England. Even though Adam found the machine, with its different sized wheels, almost impossible to ride, his interest was re-kindled when he found that he had little difficulty in selling the new product, and at a good profit, while his sons plagued him for two-wheelers of their own. This was in 1884, and by 1886 Opel was producing his own bicycles. Soon the five Opel brothers were enthusiastic cyclists and did much to publicize the family name by competing in races all over the country.

The firm was becoming world famous, and in 1893 Wilhelm went to America to uphold Opel laurels at the Chicago World's Columbian Exposition. His brother Friedrich, by then universally known as Fritz, and the most engineering orientated of the family, also found much to interest him there. Adam Opel died in 1895 at the age of 58, having seen the firm that he had established back in 1862 become one of Germany's foremost manufacturing companies.

However, the Opel story is not one of uninterrupted growth. A dip in bicycle production came at the end of the 19th century, but the brothers stuck to their guns, and two-wheeler output was subsequently increased to such an extent that, by the 1920s, the firm was the largest bicycle manufac-

A bicycle made for five. The Opel brothers aboard one of the firm's two-wheelers. Left to right: Carl, Wilhelm, Heinrich, Fritz and Ludwig.

ABOVE *Opel's 19th-century success was built on sewing machine production which began in 1863. Seven years later Adam Opel launched a new model named Sophie after his wife.*

ABOVE *Opel's first car, brought out in 1899, was based on the designs of Friedrich Lutzmann.*

turer in the world. However, in 1936, Opel sold its bicycle business to the Neckarsulm-based NSU company. By then Opel was Europe's leading motor car manufacturer, and space at the Rüsselsheim factory was desperately needed for automobile production.

Enter the motor car

The motor car, as is well known, was born in Germany. It was in 1885 and '86 that Carl Benz and Gottlieb Daimler produced motor vehicles, quite independently of each other, at Mannheim and Stuttgart respectively. But, although Germany was the cradle of the automobile, it was the French who enthusiastically took up the new industry. Germany, ironically, was rather slower to develop the new invention and was represented by only one firm, in addition to the pioneering Benz and Daimler, at Germany's first motor show, held in Berlin in 1897. This was Friedrich Lutzmann's which had begun vehicle production at Dessau three years previously in 1894. Like Adam Opel's father, not only was he a locksmith but he also held Carl Benz in high regard, so his four-wheeler with horizontally mounted 5 hp engine and chain drive closely resembled the Mannheim-produced Victoria of 1891.

In addition to this 1897 display, there was also a road run held between Berlin and Potsdam at which the official observers were none other than the Opel brothers. They were particularly impressed with the Lutzmann's performance and, as a result, a visit was arranged to Friedrich's Dessau works. An outcome of this meeting was that Lutzmann and his manufacturing operation were transferred to Rüsselsheim, where a motor car department was set up.

It was in 1898 that the first cars to bear the Opel name and based on the Lutzmann design were made, and 11 were sold in the following year. The 1.5-litre engines were of slightly smaller capacity than the Dessau-built cars and produced 4 hp. There was also a two-cylinder version, and in 1900 Opel took a stand at a show held at Nuremberg where the best German and French designs were on display. The brothers did recognize, however, that their own horizontal-engined cars were archaic when compared with a new generation of front-engined automobiles, as pioneered by the French Panhard company. This perhaps accounted for Opel's newly formed car department failing to pay its way and, at the request of Sophie, Adam Opel's widow, it was shut down in 1900 after production that year had reached 24 cars. This meant that there was little for Lutzmann to do so he left Opel, dying, a forgotten pioneer, in 1930.

BELOW *The firm began motorcycle production in 1902; this is a 1903 3/4 PS model.*

ABOVE *By Darracq out of Opel. Rüsselsheim's second attempt at car production was based on the French Darracq car, and this is a 1903 9 PS model. These front-engined cars represented a considerable improvement over the old-fashioned Lutzmann-based Opels with their power units mounted amidships.*

LEFT *This 1912 13/30 PS model with special bodywork was known as 'The Egg'. It was a year that saw annual Opel production reach 3202 cars. By then the firm was Germany's second largest car maker with only Benz producing more vehicles.*

One outcome of the shutdown was the firm's decision to enter the motorcycle market: a logical extension of its bicycle business. Zedel- and Fafnir-engined machines were produced in 1902, and Opel continued to build motorcycles until 1932. Despite the short life of their car division, the Opels did not give up their interest in the horseless carriage. It was to Paris, by then the motoring capital of the world, that the brothers looked for inspiration, just as their father had so often done. At the Paris Salon they signed up the agency for the new Renault company and also took up the Darracq concession for Austro–Hungary and Germany. It was just as well that they had two strings to their marketing bow, for Renault was not sufficiently large at that stage to service their needs. They therefore concentrated their resources on the Darracq, importing the make in chassis form and then building their own bodies. Sold as Opel-Darrracqs in Germany, the 8 hp single-cylinder cars of 1100 cc were joined in 1903 by a 9 hp 1360 cc model.

Using a two-cylinder Darracq as its starting point, Opel began to develop its own designs and, in the autumn of 1902, the Type 10/12 PS made its appearance. There was also an additional 12/14 PS model with the earlier car's 1884 cc displacement increased to 2365 cc. In 1903 came the firm's first four-cylinder model, again of Darracq inspiration, which was effectively a pair of 12/14 blocks mounted on a common crankcase. These cars soon began selling in encouraging numbers with output standing at 252 in 1904, an increase of 74 over 1903. This was sufficiently encouraging for the firm to proceed, in 1905, with the construction of a purpose-built car factory, named the Ludwigsbau after the Hessian Grand Duke Ernst Ludwig.

American influence

The subsequent Opel model range grew in complexity and variety. The Darracq-inspired single- and twin-cylinder models were strong sellers, although at the other extreme the company produced a 6.8-litre four which was an altogether more exclusive and expensive offering. In 1909 the singles and twins were dropped and three small fours then introduced. The respective capacities were achieved by juggling standardized bores and strokes, the outcome of another transatlantic visit by Wilhelm Opel during which he found the American practice of standardization and parts interchangeability very much the order of the day. The same principle was subsequently extended to the medium and large Opel car range.

Then, in 1911, fire ravaged the section of the Rüsselsheim plant used for sewing-machine production and this seemed an ideal opportunity to rebuild that part of the factory for the increasingly important bicycle and motor car production. This was duly undertaken but, when it was found that total sewing-machine output fell short of the million mark by just 12 units, the appropriate number was built up from spare parts. The completion of the factory rebuilding in 1912 coincided with the firm's Golden Jubilee celebrations, which were attended by Grand Duke Ludwig, accompanied for the occasion by Sophie Opel, the founder's widow; she died the following year, thus breaking a link with the firm which reached back to its unpromising origins in a Rüsselsheim cowstall.

Opel in competition

It was during the pre-First World War era that Opel began to forge a reputation for competition. From the very outset of its excursion into car manufacture, Opel competed in the many colourful road events held in those heady, carefree days. Fritz Opel finished fourth behind a trio of Mercedes in the 1905 Herkomer Trials, with a similar placing in that same event the following year, and a second in 1907. Also in 1907, Opels driven by Jörns and Michel came third and fourth in the prestigious Kaiserpreis event. Then came a triumph for the marque in the 1909 Prince Henry Trials, which Wilhelm Opel won, and there were other Rüsselsheim cars in third, fifth, sixth and tenth places.

Nineteen thirteen also saw Opel entering a car for the French Grand Prix at Amiens. It was powered by a 3.9-litre four-cylinder engine but dropped out when the unit gave trouble. The following year's event at Lyons saw a team of three impressive and sophisticated Opels entered. Their single overhead camshaft engines of 4.4 litres had four valves per cylinder, echoing the practice of the famous 1912 Grand Prix Peugeots. Two of the Opel team retired, but a third car, driven by Carl Jörns, succeeded in coming home tenth out of a field of 11 finishers which was notable for its one-two-three Mercedes triumph. Two of the Grand Prix Opels were sent to Britain in August 1914, a month after the French race, but they were overtaken by international events with the outbreak of the First World War. After hostilities, one of them was successfully campaigned by Henry Segrave, who was later to attain international fame as holder of the world land speed record.

The war intervenes

During the First World War, Opelwerke undertook the manufacture of trucks, having first produced commercial vehicles in 1910, and also built BMW aero engines under licence. Opel's own excursion into the production of these units, begun in 1911, was not proceeded with. In 1916 a prototype six-cylinder model, the company's first and designated the 18/50, was built and there were two further sixes,

TOP *Fritz Opel in a 12-litre Opel entered in the 1908 French Grand Prix; he finished 21st.*

ABOVE *Racing Opel of 1913–14 with 260 PS engine.*

BELOW *Carl Jörns in one of the three 4.4-litre Opels entered in the 1914 French Grand Prix. He was placed 10th, the other two entries retiring.*

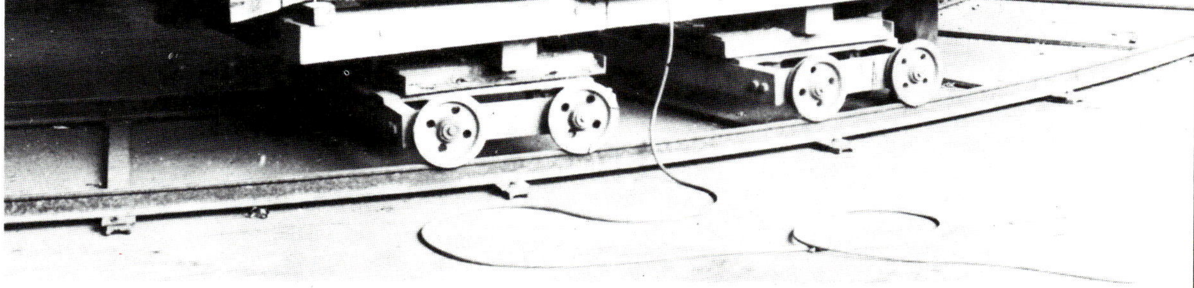

ABOVE AND RIGHT *Opel had Germany's most modern car factory as this 1927 photo shows.*

the 21/60 and 30/75 produced in the post-war era. Unfortunately, Germany in the early 1920s was gripped by political turmoil and financial instability, and these more expensive cars had a limited appeal.

The post-war era began badly, with French troops occupying the Opel works at the end of 1918, but the firm managed to introduce a model well suited to the unsettled climate. This was the 8/25 with side-valve four-cylinder engine which evolved into the 10/35 model, with larger capacity unit. Next there came an additional model, the 14/38, also a four, and a sports design of 3.4 litres based on the 8/25 chassis. Total output was small, however: only 1154 vehicles were produced in 1920, and 476 more in 1921.

Nineteen twenty-three was a year of terrible inflation in Germany, echoed in Opel's production figures as only 910 vehicles left the Rüsselsheim works. With the coming of financial stability in 1924, Opel's prospects began to look up with 4571 cars and trucks produced. It was during these troubled times that the Opel name was kept in the public eye by the indefatigable Carl Jörns, who actively campaigned an aged 12-litre Opel two-seater, powered by a potent four-cylinder overhead camshaft engine which boasted four valves per pot. It accordingly bore some resemblance to the 1914 Grand Prix car, although the valve springs, being placed above the rocker arms, projected through the bonnet. This 225 km/h (140 mph) car participated in hundreds of hill climbs and speed trials, but by the mid-1920s Opel was again forging ahead and the driver and his faithful car took a well-earned retirement.

The change in Opel's fortunes was, in part, due to Germany's more settled financial climate and the fact that the firm had decided to update its Rüsselsheim factory by introducing a moving track assembly line of the type that Henry Ford had employed to make his Model T, the world's best-selling car. Opel decided, like Ford, to concentrate on just one model, which meant ruthlessly scrapping the dated four-cylinder cars along with the low-production sixes. What Opel wanted was a simple, cheap model that was easy to build and likely to appeal to a mass market. Not for the first time, the Rüsselsheim company looked to Paris for its inspiration.

A Citroën copy

It was in the French capital in 1919 that André Citroën, who during the First World War had brought mass-production methods to shell manufacture, transferred the process to car production. The first Citroën, the Type A, was a straightforward economy-conscious design with a 1.3-litre four-cylinder engine, detachable cylinder head, unit-construction gearbox and quarter-elliptic springs front and rear. It was succeeded in 1922 by the improved Model B, and there was an 856 cc 5CV model on similar lines. The 5CV helped Citroën to sell 150,000 cars in 1924 and made him France's largest manufacturer, much to the distaste of Louis Renault who had been in the business since 1898.

Opel decided to take the concept of the 5CV Citroën and, quite blatantly, copy it, although there were some very minor differences in specification. The French car had a 55 × 90 mm engine of 855 cc, while the new Opel's was 58 × 90 mm giving 951 cc. However, the Citroën's 6-volt coil ignition system was replaced by 12-volt electrics and magneto on the cars from Rüsselsheim. There were also minuscule differences in track and wheelbase, the Opel's being 1176 mm (46¼ in) and 2255 mm (88¾ in) respectively, while the 5CV had 1181 mm (46½ in) and 2250 mm (88½ in). The French car was mostly offered in yellow livery, when it was known by the punning nickname of *Citron*, French for 'lemon'. As the new Opel was usually resplendent in green it quickly became known as a *Laubfrosch*, or 'tree frog'. The car made its début in the spring of 1924 and soon after its appearance, in 1925, the engine's capacity was increased from 951 to 1016 cc. This brought about a re-designation from 4/12 to 4/14. The wheelbase was lengthened to permit the fitment of four-seater bodywork. It was at about this time that Citroën, understandably annoyed that its design had been so blatantly copied, brought a court

LEFT *A simple but highly effective Opel advertisement of 1911.*

BELOW *A Citroën in everything but name: the 1924 4/12 PS Opel, an almost nut-for-nut copy of the Type C Citroën 5CV. It therefore had a small four-cylinder engine of 951 cc, compared with the French car's 855 cc, unit construction gearbox and all-round quarter-elliptic springs. As examples were usually painted green, the German car acquired the nickname* Laubfrosch *which is German for tree frog. Not surprisingly Citroën protested at this blatant piece of plagiarism, sued Opel for infringement of patents and, incredibly, lost the action.*

case against Opel on the grounds of infringement of patent and, amazingly, lost the action.

With the model selling strongly – production figures of 16,466 in 1925 were the best ever for Opel – the firm introduced an additional model, the 10/40, a variation on the Laubfrosch theme. There was another new model for 1927, and Germany's more stable economy resulted in the arrival of a six-cylinder car, the 4170 cc 15/60. Opel, never a firm to ignore a good design, borrowed its 89 × 112 mm dimensions from the Packard Six (89 × 127 mm) which it also resembled externally. For 1928 there came a fashionable small six of 1735 cc and, like its predecessor, this had a side-valve layout. Packard also served as the inspiration for the firm's first straight-eight model, the 5.9-litre Regent, but a mere 25 were built between 1928 and 1930.

Nineteen twenty-eight proved to be a boom year for Opel when 42,771 vehicles were built: a ninefold increase over 1924. This made Opel Germany's largest car maker by far and was a triumphant vindication of the 1924 change of course.

Quicker by rocket

Opel was destined for even greater expansion in the following decade, but, before considering this extraordinary growth, we must pause to look at a bizarre corporate diversion which gained Opel much publicity in 1928 and 1929. In 1927 the firm had been approached by Max Valier, an arch enthusiast for rocketry and inter-planetary travel. The Austrian Valier wrote to Fritz Opel for financial support and subsequently presented himself at Rüsselsheim. Fritz was himself an aviation enthusiast, and he too warmed to the idea of an Opel rocket-powered car which Valier said he would cooperate in building.

The programme could not support the construction of purpose-built rockets, so Friedrich Sander, based in Wesermünde, who manufactured distress rockets used by ships, was approached and agreed to supply them for the project. The tripartite team of Opel, Valier and Sander met at Rüsselsheim in March 1928, the rockets having arrived by truck because the railway authorities would not allow them on board a train. Although the intention was to use an old racing car chassis as a test bed, it was not ready in time so a conventional chassis was pressed into service. The first test took place on the following day, 12 March, and two small rockets were used. An Opel engineer, Kurt Volkhart, had the doubtful distinction of being the first to drive the rocket car, and he accordingly sat at the controls, while a mechanic lit the rockets and then dived for cover. The rear of the car disappeared in a cloud of smoke and the vehicle inched forward and took a little over half a minute to cover 150 m (500 ft).

Not surprisingly, the apostles of rocketry came in for a certain amount of criticism as the first trial had turned out to be something of a damp squib, so to speak. Therefore, an hour later, the car, duly primed with new rockets, was again tested, although on this occasion the charges were fired when the car was moving at a speed of 32 km/h (20 mph). This time the

During 1928 Opel experimented with rocket-powered motorcycles, aircraft and cars, with some of the latter projects shown left. The top and middle photos show Fritz Opel at the AVUS circuit in Rak 2 on 23 May 1928. He reached 225 km/h (140 mph) on this highly publicized occasion. Shown below left is the unmanned Rak 3 which ran on a railway track and eventually crashed.

ABOVE RIGHT *1931 1.8-litre with side-valve six-cylinder engine.*

intrepid Volkhart felt the car buck as a racing car might have done, and it managed to attain a speed of 75 km/h (47 mph) before the rockets fizzled out.

This second test run was sufficiently encouraging for Opel to press ahead with the construction of a purpose-built rocket-powered car which was named Rak, an abbreviation of *Rakete*, German for 'rocket'. It was a single-seater, fitted with stubby aerofoils, and there was room for 12 of Sander's rockets in the all-important tail section. The rockets were electrically ignited when the car's 'accelerator' pedal was depressed and, after some preliminary trials, the car was demonstrated to the press on 11 April. Although only seven of the 12 rockets were ignited, the display was visually impressive with plenty of smoke and noise, and Rak 1 managed more than 96 km/h (60 mph). There was yet another demonstration at the AVUS

circuit in Berlin, when no less than 2000 reporters were present to see a new rocket car, Rak 2, put through its paces. This was even more sophisticated than the original and with double the space, so that it was possible to have a total of 24 rockets stacked in the tail.

Fortunately the car behaved perfectly, and on this occasion Fritz Opel took the wheel of what effectively was a bomb on four wheels. For once, all the rockets fired correctly and the car shot forward to attain a speed of 225 km/h (140 mph), at one stage showing every sign of wanting to take to the air. Even faster was a railway-bound Rak 3 with no less than 30 rockets aboard but thankfully, perhaps, no driver. This crashed after reaching 289 km/h (180 mph) when its nose-mounted braking rockets failed to fire. A rocket-powered aeroplane suffered a similar fate with Fritz Opel at the controls and, although he emerged unscathed from the experience, this marked the end of the firm's involvement with the world of rocketry!

GENERAL MOTORS TAKES OVER

After such flights of fancy we must return to the more sober conduct of the Opel company's affairs in the late 1920s. It was at about this time that the two principal American motor manufacturers, Ford and General Motors, began looking to Europe to expand their overseas manufacturing facilities. Both firms already had presences in Germany: Ford had been assembling Model Ts in Berlin since 1925, and GM had established a factory in the capital in 1927. General Motors, in particular, recognized that there was an enormous market potential in Germany and was faced with a number of alternatives for exploiting this. It could either produce a small Chevrolet and export it to Europe, or expand its Berlin operations. There was a third alternative which was to buy an existing manufacturer, as the company had done in Britain in 1925. Originally it had wanted to buy the Austin company and, although Sir Herbert Austin was all for the transaction, his board of directors vetoed the proposal so, instead, GM bought the small Vauxhall company for a mere $2.5 million.

It may have been news of this purchase that caused the Opel management, in 1926, to write to General Motors, bringing their own organization to the attention of the American corporation. The German company had been headed by Carl von Opel in the early 1920s and on his death Wilhelm took over the day-to-day running of the firm and was the last Opel to head the family business. (Both these elder brothers had been granted the use of the aristocratic *von* by the Grand Duke of Hesse after the end of the First World War.)

General Motors took a little time to respond to this overture but, as a policy evolved, GM's president, Alfred Sloan Jr, swung towards the idea of buying an existing manufacturer and in October 1928 visited Europe with this end in view. Sloan and two colleagues sought out Opel at Rüsselsheim and were sufficiently impressed by what they saw to want to buy the company. Most of the plant was less than four years old; the firm had the largest dealer chain in Germany with 736 outlets; and, of course, Opel was the country's largest car maker. Later, in March of 1929, a further party of General Motors experts, who had paid another visit to Rüsselsheim, recommended purchase.

In view of this impending sale, Opelwerke, still a family-owned concern, changed its corporate status to become a publicly owned corporation and was renamed Adam Opel AG. General Motors then paid $25,967,000 for an 80 per cent interest in the firm in 1929, while the American company retained an option to buy the remaining 20 per cent for $7,395,000 from the Opel family; the option was finally taken up in October 1931. This brought the Corporation's total outlay to over $33 million.

Although Wilhelm von Opel remained as company president, GM brought in I.J. Reuter, who had previously been general manager of its Oldsmobile division, as managing director. Not only did Reuter have a good engineering and sales background, but he was also of German extraction and spoke the language. He made no immediate changes to the Opel model line and the first effects of the take-over were not seen until 1931, by which time the world had plunged into the pit of the economic depression. Despite this, in November Opel issued an invitation to its dealers to attend a meeting in Frankfurt to see the first results of the take-over.

In truth, the changes were fairly modest. The concept of the small four was perpetuated, although the engine was revamped, reduced in capacity to 995 mm (65 × 75 mm) and its compression ratio increased to 6:1. American production thinking was reflected in a new 1.8-litre car powered by a six-cylinder engine which shared the small model's bore, thus giving them a common piston size.

It was at the presentation that Alfred Sloan caused some jocularity among the guests by suggesting that one day Opel's output would attain the annual figure of 150,000 units. As by 1931 it had slumped from a 1928 high of around 48,000 to 26,000, the prediction seemed extravagant to say the least, but seven years later, in 1938, Opel was to become not only Germany's but also Europe's largest producer of motor vehicles.

A further model, a 1.2-litre version of the 995 cc car with a longer 90 mm stroke, appeared in 1932, a year that marked the

LEFT *1936 Opel P4 with 1074 cc side-valve four-cylinder engine.*

BELOW *1938 Admiral with cabriolet body by Hebmüller.*

nadir of the Depression as far as Germany was concerned, when Opel built only 20,982 cars and commercials, the lowest production figure since 1926. There was also a rather inappropriate sporting version of the 1.8-litre six, the Moonlight roadster, in the spirit of the American Speedster. For 1933 came a revival of the Regent name, although this related to a new body range rather than a specific model. These were roomier and more up to date than their rather boxy predecessors, and the Opel engines were now fitted with aluminium rather than archaic cast-iron pistons. A new four-speed gearbox was fitted with synchromesh on the top two cogs, to obviate the need for double de-clutching, a first for Opel and Europe. This General Motors' invention to simplify gear changing had first appeared on the 1928 Cadillac and was being offered throughout the GM range. Vauxhall, the Corporation's other European satellite, received it at about the same time.

Booming Opel

Fortunately, 1933 saw an upturn in Germany's financial fortunes and Opel production soared, so that it was nudging the 40,000 mark. There was a drastic overhaul of the cars' mechanical specifications with the exception of the 1.2-litre which remained the same. The other models received longer, more robust chassis frames fitted with Dubonnet 'knee action' independent front suspension, hydraulic brakes and again styling updates with the new bodies featuring built-in boots. Both four- and six-cylinder engines were increased in capacity

TOP *The unitary construction Olympia of 1935, named after the Olympic Games held in Berlin in 1936.*

ABOVE *An Opel advertisement for the production Admiral extolling its strength and beauty.*

by enlarging the bore size from 65 mm to 67 mm to produce 1279 and 1932 cc units.

The recently upgraded 1.3-litre engine was to find its way under the bonnet of a new and technically significant car that appeared at the 1935 Berlin Motor Show. This was the Olympia, so named in honour of the Olympic Games that were due to be held in Berlin the following year. But the model represented an impressive technological breakthrough for General Motors as it embodied an integral body and chassis, another first for Germany and Europe, which was not extended to Vauxhall until 1938. The Olympia was offered in two-door saloon and open cabriolet coach forms and featured distinctive faired-in headlights, another progressive sign of the times. Also launched in 1935 was a bottom-liner P4 model which perpetuated the 1920s theme of side valves and all-round half-elliptic spring suspension. Its engine was a robust 1074 cc four and the model remained in production until 1938. The power unit was used in yet another new Opel, the Kadett, introduced in 1936 and slotted in between the P4 and Olympia in size and price. Like the larger car there were

LEFT *The Opel Kadett, introduced in 1936. It shared the P4's 1074 cc engine and there was a family resemblance to the Olympia. After the war the Kadett's tooling was handed over to the Russians and it then reappeared as the Moskvich 400. The Kadett name is still an Opel model following this original car's success with around 107,000 examples sold pre-war.*

BELOW *The very American-looking Kapitän, introduced for 1939, had a 2.5-litre overhead-valve six-cylinder engine, unitary body construction and independent front suspension. Production resumed after the war.*

saloon and cabriolet coach versions with the latter first.

It was during the 1930s that government-supported cross-country trials became increasingly popular in Germany, and Opel fielded a team of 15 cars for these events. The six-cylinder model proved an ideal vehicle for these activities and in 1934 Opel's efforts were rewarded by a team prize in that year's Alpine Rally.

With the Opel bodies and chassis having been extensively revised, the firm's design team turned its attention to the Rüsselsheim engines, most of which were rooted in the previous decade. The power units that resulted were thoroughly up to date with overhead valves appearing on Opels for the first time along with 'oversquare' dimensions. These were designed around an 80 mm bore size and the six-cylinder 2473 cc version, with 82 mm stroke and four-bearing crankshaft, was fitted in a new Super Six model in 1937. It was available in two- and four-door saloon and cabriolet forms. The four, with a 74 mm stroke, giving 1488 cc, was introduced in the Olympia for 1938 and was notable for its robust four-bearing crankshaft. There was an additional engine, however, which did not fit in with this standardized bore size, and that was a 90 × 95 mm six which had much in common with a contemporary in-house Chevrolet unit. This was used in the top-of-the-range Admiral model of 1937, its arrival coinciding with Opel's 75th anniversary year.

Yet another new car was introduced for the 1939 season. This was the Kapitän, powered by the six 80 mm bore engine which perpetuated the Olympia's integral body concept, while the independent front suspension was fitted with an anti-roll bar, a progressive feature for the day.

War again

Nineteen thirty-eight had been Opel's top-selling year, with an impressive 140,580 vehicles produced but, two years later, in October 1940, car production ceased at Rüsselsheim. The Second World War had begun in September of the previous year and Opel declined the government's request to undertake arms production. Rüsselsheim was not used for priority war work as it was a foreign-owned firm, but aircraft parts were manufactured. A truck factory at Brandenburg had been opened in 1936 and it was soon to become Europe's largest under the direction of Heinz Nordhoff, who was to work wonders for Volkswagen in the post-war years. Just prior to the outbreak of war, in 1938, Opel had introduced its latest Blitz truck, powered by the Chevrolet-derived 3.6-litre six-cylinder engine which was also used in the Admiral. This vehicle was produced in large numbers during hostilities and was also built under licence by Daimler-Benz. Rather more unusual was the NSU Kettenkrad, a type of combined motorcycle and tracked vehicle which used the Opel Olympia engine.

The war work undertaken by Opel produced the inevitable response from the Allies, and in August 1944 both the Rüsselsheim and Brandenburg factories were devastated by bombing. When the war ended in 1945 there was not much of Adam Opel AG left, as Rüsselsheim was in ruins while Brandenburg had fallen to the Russians. The Soviet Union also obtained from the Allied Military Government, then in charge of the western sector of Germany's affairs, the jigs, tools and drawings for the Opel Kadett, and these were handed over in June 1946. The Russians had intimated that they would put the resulting vehicle into production in Leipzig, within their sphere of influence, but the next that Opel saw of the Kadett was when it appeared as the Moskvich 400. It had been used to create a new Russian marque and this 'Son of Moscow' was produced in a factory located in the Russian capital.

LEFT *The 3-tonne Blitz truck, produced at Opel's Brandenburg factory from 1938.*

BELOW *Rüsselsheim in 1945, after the Allied bombing of the factory. Production re-started in 1946.*

PRODUCTION RESUMES

If the Soviet Union had had its way it would have also scooped up the Rüsselsheim manufacturing facility, but the plant fell within the American military zone and was soon at work producing the trucks that Germany so desperately needed. This was a 1.5-tonne model powered by the Kapitän's 2.5-litre engine and the first example was built in July 1946. Car production was resumed the next year and, although it would have been easier to re-introduce the Kapitän as its engine was already being manufactured, the military government was restricting civilian vehicles to 1.5 litres capacity: this meant the Olympia. It was almost indentical to its pre-war counterpart with the exception of the Dubonnet independent front suspension which was replaced by a more conventional coil and wishbone unit. In addition, the Kapitän was also back in production for 1949 with only minor changes.

Following a report by a General Motors delegation who visited Opel in February and March 1948, the corporation, after some initial qualms, resumed control of its German sudsidiary in November of that year. Edward W. Zdunek took over as managing director, a position he held with great competence until 1961.

The effects of GM's return were seen at the beginning of 1950 when the Olympia was face-lifted with the introduction of a new horizontal radiator grille and extended bumpers. Beneath the surface the original four-speed gearbox was replaced, American fashion, by a three-speed one with column rather than floor gearchange. Wheel sizes were reduced in 1951 but the Olympia, which dated back to 1935, was discontinued in 1953. The Kapitän also received some cosmetic changes when the rather dated fastback look was replaced by a new rear end with pronounced boot. Like the Olympia, it came to the end of the road in 1953.

LEFT *Essentially the pre-war Kapitän, the model received a new radiator grille in 1951 and the original fastback was replaced by notchback styling. It continued until 1953.*

TOP RIGHT *The six-cylinder Kapitän received its first facelift for 1954 giving it more than a passing resemblance to GM's Chevrolets. There were improvements in 1955 and the model was built until 1958.*

LOWER RIGHT *The Olympia Rekord of 1953 to 1957 sold 556,500 examples and was replaced in the latter year by this radically re-styled version.*

BELOW *The Olympia's replacement was the Olympia Rekord, introduced in 1953. Mechanics were essentially carried over from the previous model and the car remained in production until 1957.*

Output soars

Nineteen fifty-three also saw Opel production exceed 100,000 for the first time in its post-war history, and output improved every successive year until 1960. For as the West German economy boomed, so did Opel. The Olympia's replacement, the Rekord, introduced at the 1953 Frankfurt Motor Show, was destined to be the best-selling Opel of the decade. The model's styling showed some similarity to that year's new Chevrolets, but underneath it was still the same old Olympia engine and transmission, although the front suspension acquired ball joints and the rear axle a hypoid drive. The two-door model was offered in saloon, cabriolet and caravan (estate car) forms, but the open car was discontinued in 1956. There came a styling face-lift for 1957 with the lines sharpened up somewhat, and there was a new radiator grille and roof line. Such was the success of the model that, by the end of the 1957 model year, in July, 556,500 Rekords had been built.

There was a new Rekord for 1958. Although the engine and transmission were carried over from the previous model, the body was longer, lower and wider than its predecessor, and for 1960 the two-door saloon was joined by a four-door example and there was a new optional 1680 cc engine. There was yet another styling update for 1961 with a fashionable coupé joining the saloon, and these were to remain in production until the spring of 1963. The Rekord's success underlined the fact that, with the enforced absence of the Kadett, Opel found itself right in the middle ground in marketing terms, with only Volkswagen's ubiquitous Beetle overhauling Rüsselsheim in production.

But what of the six-cylinder Kapitän? The car had been re-skinned for 1954 with very American styling. There came a face-lift for 1956 and modest changes to the front and rear two years later. Mechanical alterations included the arrival of an all-synchromesh gearbox in 1956, and May of the following year saw overdrive offered as an option. The Kapitän again received a new body along very transatlantic lines, with the regular face-lift arriving for 1960. There were, however, more significant changes beneath the bonnet. The Kapitän's engine, which dated back to 1937, was given its first major re-design. The bore size was increased to 85 mm while the stroke came down to 76 mm, producing 2605 cc instead of 2473 cc. Automatic transmission arrived as an option for 1961 with power steering offered from 1963. This Kapitän was to remain in production until 1964.

TOP *The Kadett model was revived in 1962.*

ABOVE *Sporting appeal: the Rallye Kadett of 1967.*

OPEL RALLYE KADETT 1966–7	
ENGINE	
No. of cylinders	4
Bore/stroke mm	75 × 61
Displacement cc	1078
Valve operation	Pushrod
Compression ratio	9.2:1
Induction	Single carburettor
BHP	60 at 5600 rpm
Transmission	Four-speed
CHASSIS	
Frame	Unitary construction
Wheelbase mm	2416
Track—front mm	1250
Track—rear mm	1280
Suspension—front	Independent, transverse leaf spring and lower wishbone
Suspension—rear	Live axle, half-elliptic springs
Brakes	Disc front, drum rear
PERFORMANCE	
Maximum speed	148 km/h (92 mph)

A Kadett again

Opel had lacked a small car since the Kadett had been purloined by the Russians, and a new Kadett finally arrived in 1962. It was a completely new car with nothing carried over from the previous models, and was built at a new factory at Bochum, located over an abandoned coal mine. The all-important new model was intended to compete head on with the Volkswagen Beetle 1200 and was a German/American design with Chevrolet input to the 993 cc 72 × 61 mm engine. It was an overhead-valve unit with a high-mounted camshaft and short pushrods, and there was a new all-synchromesh gearbox. The drive line was notable for being enclosed, with a tubular extension from the gearbox running to a universal joint. From thereon it proceeded, via a short torque tube, to the rear axle. Front suspension was also unusual, with a transverse leaf spring and lower wishbone, while the rear end was conventionally cart sprung. Rack and pinion steering was also a notable first for Opel. Initially only the two-door saloon body was available, although there was an estate car in 1963, with a coupé version arriving the following year.

In 1963, the year after the Kadett's arrival, came a new Rekord for Opel's all-important middle ground. This was wider and lower than the previous version, a two-door saloon joined by an estate in 1963 and coupé for 1964. The two-engine theme of 1488 cc and 1698 cc units was perpetuated, while power-assisted front disc brakes were a desirable option. The Rekord range was extended in June 1964 with the appearance of two new models powered by the Kapitän's 2.6-litre six-cylinder engine and available in four-door and coupé forms.

An improved version of the Kapitän, with more luxurious interior trim and called the Admiral, made its début in 1964. In addition there was a new model, the Diplomat, that retained

OPEL COMMODORE GS/E 1970–2	
ENGINE	
No. of cylinders	6
Bore/stroke mm	87 × 69
Displacement cc	2490
Valve operation	Camshaft in head, rockers
Compression ratio	9.5:1
Induction	Fuel injection
BHP	150 at 5800 rpm
Transmission	Four-speed
CHASSIS	
Frame	Unitary construction
Wheelbase mm	2668
Track—front mm	1410
Track—rear mm	1410
Suspension—front	Independent, coil springs and wishbones
Suspension—rear	Live axle, coil springs, twin trailing arms
Brakes	Hydraulic front disc, drum rear
PERFORMANCE	
Maximum speed	193 km/h (120 mph)

the Kapitän's body shell but was powered by a 4638 cc Chevrolet V8 engine. There was also the inevitable Diplomat coupé, built by Karmann, which received a larger 5.3-litre V8 engine, and in 1965 this was extended to the Admiral and Kapitän, although the smaller capacity unit was still available as an option.

By this time Opel's own four- and six-cylinder engine, which dated back to 1938 and 1937 respectively, were getting somewhat long in the tooth. New units appeared for 1966 and had overhead camshaft layouts even though Opel called them 'cam in the head' units because the shaft was located alongside the valves, actuated via conventional tappets and rocker arms. A common building block of the two engines was a 69 mm stroke, with bore size varied accordingly. Both were of larger capacity than their predecessors. The four was available in three sizes: 1492 cc with an 82 mm bore; 1698 cc and 88 mm pots; while the 1897 cc unit had 93 mm ones. The six, by contrast, was available in only one engine size with a 92 mm bore and 2785 cc.

The arrival of the new engines in 1966 coincided with the appearance of a rebodied Kadett—its first—and, although the two-door saloon option was perpetuated, a new four-door version was introduced and both models were powered by a larger capacity 1079 cc engine. The continual refinement of the Rekord resulted in yet another re-design which was wider and lower than its predecessor. This 1967 model-year offering also came in handsome coupé form and was available with a 2239 cc version of the 'cam in head' six with reduced 82 mm bore. The traditional cart-sprung rear gave way to coil springs with attendant twin trailing arms and Panhard rod.

ABOVE *The GS/E fuel-injected Commodore of 1970.*

BELOW *1967 Rekord coupé.*

OPEL REKORD 1966–72	
ENGINE	
No. of cylinders	4
Bore/stroke mm	88 × 69
Displacement cc	1698
Valve operation	Pushrod
Compression ratio	8.2:1
Induction	Single carburettor
BHP	66 at 5300 rpm
Transmission	Four-speed
CHASSIS	
Frame	Unitary construction
Wheelbase mm	2668
Track—front mm	1412
Track—rear mm	1410
Suspension—front	Independent, coil springs and wishbones
Suspension—rear	Live axle, coil springs and radius arms
Brakes	Hydraulic front disc, drum rear
PERFORMANCE	
Maximum speed	143 km/h (89 mph)

The GT arrives

Opel's sporting awareness had been highlighted, in 1965, by the appearance of a one-off 'Opel GT' which appeared on the company's stand at the 1965 Frankfurt Motor Show. The reception for this concept car was encouraging but, as Opel's production capacity was stretched to the limit, the body was provided by the French firm of Brissonneau et Lotz. The model's floorpan was based on the Kadett, with two engine options of 1.1 and 1.9 litres. The Opel GT proper appeared for the 1969 model year. In 1971 there was a cheaper GT/J version and, by the time that production ceased in 1973, more than 100,000 examples had been built with a healthy 60 per cent of output having been exported to America.

Yet another rather uncharacteristic Opel project was the Bitter CD which, like the GT, evolved from a concept car; in this instance the Opel CD displayed at the 1969 Frankfurt show. Under the sleek bonnet was a 5.4-litre Chevrolet V8, while a shortened Diplomat floorpan was employed and a de Dion rear axle featured. The car attracted the attention of racing driver and enthusiast Erich Bitter and the outcome was the Bitter CD, conceived with the close involvement of the Opel design staff and the Baur body company of Stuttgart. This Diplomat-based model entered production in 1973 and was built in limited numbers until 1979. Its successor incorporates Senator/Monza mechanics and is in production at the time of writing.

But these developments were all in the future, as yet another Opel factory was built at Kaiserslautern in 1966 to produce chassis and transmission parts for an ever-expanding range. In 1967 came the Rekord-based Commodore, also six-cylinder powered, but this time with an 87 mm bore 2490 cc option. For 1968 there was a sporting GS version, instantly identifiable by its matt-black radiator grille and special steel wheels. Another potent offering was the Rekord coupé with twin Weber carburettors and Commodore-related front end. The 1968 model year also saw some refinement of the Kadett range when 1.5- and 1.9-litre engines were introduced. In addition, there were new two- and four-door saloons with distinctive sloping rear profiles offered as the Kadett and Olympia, the latter name being an old Opel favourite. The firm kept up its policy of regular improvements to the range by

BELOW *The Opel GT of 1968, which shared the Kadett's floorpan, was inspired by a 1965 Project Car. Over 100,000 examples were built.*

OPEL GT
1968–73

ENGINE	
No. of cylinders	4
Bore/stroke mm	93 × 69
Displacement cc	1897
Valve operation	Camshaft in head/rocker
Compression ratio	9.5:1
Induction	Single carburettor
BHP	90 at 5100 rpm
Transmission	Four-speed or automatic

CHASSIS	
Frame	Unitary construction
Wheelbase mm	2431
Track—front mm	1254
Track—rear mm	1284
Suspension—front	Independent, transverse leaf spring and lower wishbones
Suspension—rear	Live axle, coil springs and trailing arms
Brakes	Hydraulic front disc, drum rear

PERFORMANCE	
Maximum speed	185 km/h (115 mph)

reviving the Kapitän, Admiral and Diplomat in 1969, with a new 2784 cc version of the six for the last two models.

A new generation of Opels arrived in 1970: the sporty Manta coupé, which was Rüsselsheim's answer to Ford's Cologne-built Capri. This was powered by a 1584 cc version of the versatile 'cam in head' four with 85 mm bore, while a 1.9-litre version was available for the Rallye model. The same year came the Ascona saloon, a mid-range offering which shared mechanics with the Manta. At the beginning of 1972 there was another Rekord update. This was a completely new body shell, which was shared with the Commodore, the latter appearing at the Geneva Motor Show in March. Later, in 1972, a diesel-powered version was produced, the 2100D, which became increasingly popular as the decade progressed.

The Kadett, updated back in 1965, had served the Opel company well, and its successor, which arrived in August 1973 for the 1974 model year, has to be seen in somewhat broader global terms. The intention was to produce a 'world car' to be assembled by General Motors manufacturing facilities in Great Britain, Japan, Brazil, America and Germany. The body would be common to all countries, although locally produced engines and drive trains would be fitted. The car was styled at Opel and the Kadett C, as it was titled, was offered with its usual engine range, along with the 1.6-litre unit from the Ascona and Manta. The C was destined to last until mid 1979, by which time 1.7 million examples had been built.

TOP *Opel's answer to the Ford Capri was the Manta, introduced in 1970, with 1.6-litre 'cam in head' engine.*

RIGHT UPPER *The Ascona, of 1970, which shared a floorpan with the Manta, lasted until 1975.*

RIGHT LOWER *The Bitter CD appeared in 1973 powered by the Diplomat's 5.4-litre V8 engine. 463 examples were sold by the time production ceased in 1973.*

RIGHT *Opel's 1972 special diesel car which broke 20 world and international records.*

ABOVE *Opel's involvement with motor sport began in earnest in the 1970s. This is a Kadett GTE shown in the 1980 Lombard RAC Rally. This particular event was won by a Talbot.*

Rally triumphs

Nineteen seventy-four also saw the creation of the Opel Euro Dealer Team, for the firm from this point was to plunge itself with vigour and enthusiasm into motor sporting activities. This policy had, ironically, not come from within the firm, in the first instance; but back in 1966 a group of Swedish rally enthusiasts had persuaded in-house GM Nordiska to back an Opel Dealers' Team. This got off to a flying start, when the group won the European Rally Championship that year. Opel's commitment at this stage was low key, but the firm's awareness of the importance of competition as publicity was reflected in 1967 with the arrival of the aforementioned Rallye version of the Kadett. Further corporate involvement followed in 1968 with the preparation of a sombre two-door Rekord saloon but, tuned to 150 bhp and named the Black Widow, it proceeded to raise eyebrows on its first appearance at Hockenheim.

After the Opel Euro Dealer team was set up in 1974, Walter Röhrl and Jochen Berger won that year's European Rally Championship in an Opel Ascona, modified by Irmscher Tuning. Next came a purpose-built rally car, the Ascona 400, which reflected the number to be made for homologation purposes. This was powered by a 2-litre 16-valve twin-overhead-camshaft version of the Ascona engine developed by Cosworth Engineering. Fuel injection and dry-sump lubrication rounded off an impressive competition specification. Opel's third European Rally Championship win came in 1979 when a 175 bhp Ascona 400 driven by Kleint and Wagner proved triumphant. Yet another development came in 1981 with the birth of the Rothmans-Opel Rally team, set up with the aim of winning the World Rally Championship. Nineteen eighty-two began with an Opel win in the Monte Carlo Rally through an Ascona 400 boosted to 260 bhp. More successes

LEFT *The Rekord D was introduced at the beginning of 1972. It was produced in four-door saloon and also coupé form, as depicted. A 1.6-litre engine was employed and there was a 2-litre diesel option.*

followed, with an ever-present challenge coming from the four-wheel-drive Audi Quattro: the tough Ivory Coast Rally was destined to be the deciding event. Although the Audis initially forged ahead, by the third stage Walter Röhrl and Christian Geistdörfer in the Ascona 400 were in third position, but a shock absorber replacement set the Opel back by about an hour. Then the Audi of lady drivers Michèle Mouton and Fabrizia Pons was out for a time with transmission problems. The rally had narrowed to a race between the two cars and, in the last stage of the event, tension heightened when both cars failed to start after a routine stop. It was only after the Ascona was fitted with new sparking plugs and distributor that the engine finally fired and Röhrl was away. The Audi's five-cylinder engine was at last started, but then a blanket of fog descended, blotting out the African landscape, and at a difficult junction the Opel went off the road. Fortunately Röhrl was soon back on course, but Michèle Mouton experienced problems at the same spot, the Quattro turned turtle, and it was all over. Opel won the rally and Röhrl clinched the world drivers' championship. It had been a sensational first year.

In the meantime, the Ascona and its sporty Manta variant had been refined over the years, and in 1975 both models were extensively re-designed. The usual engine range of 1.2 to 1.9 litres was adopted, but the Manta could be had with a fuel-injected version of the larger capacity unit which was enlarged to 2 litres in 1977. Nineteen seventy-nine saw the replacement of the 1.2-litre engine with a 1.3-litre overhead camshaft unit destined to appear in the new Kadett later in the year. A new Manta appeared in 1980 with the options of notch and hatchback profiles.

The Rekord was simultaneously progressing unabated. There had been a new body style in 1977 along with five engine options, while front MacPherson struts took the place of the long-running coils and wishbones. The Commodore arrived the following year, similar in appearance to the Rekord, but with a 2.5-litre six-cylinder engine. However, the Commodore model was discontinued in 1982 and it was not replaced by Opel.

While Opel had enjoyed considerable sales successes with its smaller models, the large cars did not receive the same public response; so the Admiral/Diplomat line was phased out and replaced by a new car, the Senator, slightly narrower and shorter than its predecessors. This, along with the prestigious Monza coupé derivative, arrived for 1978. Out went the thirsty V8 to be replaced by a revised 3-litre six with fuel injection. Suspension was all-independent; MacPherson struts at the front and rear semi-trailing arms.

TOP *The Rekord E, introduced in 1977, was offered with no less than five engine options, while there was also a 2.1-litre diesel variant.*

CENTRE *The Manta, with its facelifted front end for 1983, and fuel-injected 2-litre engine, providing 193 km/h (120 mph) for this GTE variant.*

ABOVE *The Senator replaced the Admiral and Diplomat models in 1977. It was powered by a 3-litre 'cam in head' six-cylinder engine.*

LEFT *An Ascona 400 in the 1984 1000 Lakes Rally.*

The Monza coupé is a sporty version of the Senator. This is a 1984 GSE with fuel-injected 2.9-litre engine and electronic dashboard (inset). Provided by The Patrick Collection.

OPEL MONZA

1978 to date

ENGINE	
No. of cylinders	6
Bore/stroke mm	92 × 69, 95 × 69
Displacement cc	2784, 2968
Valve operation	Single overhead camshaft
Compression ratio	9:1, 9:2, 9:4
Induction	Single carburettor; 2968 cc Bosch L-Jetronic injection
BHP	140 at 5200 rpm, 150 at 5200 rpm
Transmission	Four-speed, from 1984 five-speed

CHASSIS	
Frame	Unitary construction
Wheelbase mm	2670
Track—front mm	1440
Track—rear mm	1470
Suspension—front	Independent, MacPherson strut
Suspension—rear	Independent, semi-trailing arms, coil springs
Brakes	Hydraulic disc

PERFORMANCE	
Maximum speed	193 km/h (120 mph), 199 km/h (124 mph)

At last, front-wheel drive

Up until 1979 all Opels had followed the traditional front-engine/rear-drive layout, so beloved of the American car makers. Europe, by contrast, had a deep-rooted commitment to front-wheel drive and, late in 1979, Opel's first car to feature this configuration appeared. Back in 1974 Opel had been given overall responsibility for the design of General Motors' European product lines, and this marked a closer integration of the corporation's British and German makes. The Chevette hatchback had been Vauxhall's version of GM's world car, while the 1976 Cavalier was, effectively, a re-badged Opel Ascona, and the Carlton and Royale were, respectively, the Opel Rekord and Senator at heart.

When the Opel Kadett D, soon to take over from the Rekord as the top-selling Opel model, made its 1980 model-year début, it was sold as the Vauxhall Astra in Britain. Although the front-wheel drive model was shorter than the Kadett C, it boasted more room inside. There was a choice of three engine options: the existing 1.2-litre unit in two stages of tune, or a new overhead-camshaft 1.3-litre engine. Suspension was all-independent with MacPherson struts at the front and crank arms with a lateral strut at the rear.

LEFT *The Kadett, front-wheel-drive since 1979, acquired fuel-injection in 1984 with the 1.8-litre GTE.*

BELOW *A Kadett GTE participating in the 1984 Swedish Rally.*

FAR RIGHT, TOP *The Opel Corsa, built in a new General Motors factory at Zaragoza, Spain, entered production in 1983. This front-wheel-drive car is available with hatchback or saloon bodies and with a choice of three engines, of 993, 1196 or 1297 cc. There are also two gearbox options.*

RIGHT *The front-wheel-drive Ascona C series, introduced in 1981, is GM's J car and offered as the Vauxhall Cavalier in Britain.*

BELOW RIGHT *The latest 1984 Kadett is listed with 1.2-, 1.3-, 1.6- and 1.8-litre engines. This is the LS version.*

The next model due for revision was the Ascona. This came in 1981 and, although it bore a family resemblance to the Kadett, it had rear-wheel drive. It appeared in Britain as the Vauxhall Cavalier. Suspension was similar to the smaller car, while engines were 1.3 and 1.6 litres. Then, in 1983, came another Opel, the Corsa, intended to slot in beneath the Kadett, but by no means a mini-car, and powered by a new 1.2-litre overhead camshaft engine. The model was not made at Rüsselsheim, however, for General Motors followed in the Ford Fiesta's wheel tracks and built the car in Spain. Rear-wheel drive Opels continued to be built, the Rekord receiving a new 1.8-litre overhead camshaft and 2-litre 'cam in head' engines in 1982.

With such an impressive and versatile line-up, Opel—backed by General Motors' formidable financial and technological resources—is well placed to face the future after five decades of sustained and spectacular growth.

OPEL ASCONA
1981 to date

ENGINE	
No. of cylinders	4
Bore/stroke mm	75×73, 80×79, 84×79
Displacement cc	1297, 1587, 1771
Valve operation	Single overhead camshaft
Compression ratio	8.2:1; 9.5:1 (1.8)
Induction	1 carb; 1.8 fuel inject.
BHP	60 at 5800, 75 at 5600, 115 at 5800
Transmission	Four-speed, five-speed
CHASSIS	
Frame	Unitary construction
Wheelbase mm	2570
Track—front mm	1400
Track—rear mm	1410
Suspension—front	MacPherson strut
Suspension—rear	Live axle, crank compound, coil springs
Brakes	Hydraulic front disc, drum rear
PERFORMANCE	
Maximum speed	151 km/h (94 mph), 156 km/h (97 mph), 187 km/h (116 mph)

PORSCHE

The Porsche marque, like Volkswagen, is a product of the post-war era, but there the resemblance ends. Although before the Second World War the Stuttgart-based design bureau, established by Ferdinand Porsche in 1930, had been responsible for the utilitarian VW's design, the Beetle-based 356 Porsche of 1949 was a highly individual rear-engined sports car, destined for a 16-year production life. It was followed, in 1965, by the 911, which perpetuated the air-cooled, rear-located *boxermotor* theme, a model that is still in production 20 years after it was introduced. Active participation in many aspects of competition followed, of which the fabled 917 Le Mans victories represent a high point. The 1970s brought a new generation of front-engined, water-cooled Porsches: the popular 924, the superlative V8-powered 928 and the potent four-cylinder 944. These stylish coupés ensure that Porsche, a company that represents all the very best in engineering excellence, remains in the forefront of inspired and highly individual automobile design.

YJH 122T

ROTHMANS
PORSCHE
11
ROTHMANS
Shell

Ferdinand Porsche was a genius. He designed all manner of machines and some wonderful cars as well, such as the Volkswagen, but, until May 1948, his cars always bore someone else's name: Austro-Daimler, Mercedes-Benz, Steyr, Wanderer, Zündapp, NSU, Auto Union, Cisitalia, and of course Volkswagen. There were racing cars, touring cars and jeeps among these designs, but it was sports cars that he loved best. His designs for Volkswagen were extremely versatile: no sooner had Professor Porsche and the designers who worked for his independent company, established in 1930, finished drawings for the 'People's Car' in 1937, than they set to work on a sports car with a mid-positioned V10 water-cooled engine. Porsche had hoped to use the Volkswagen as a basis, but the German authorities turned the idea down. The outcome was a coupé, titled Type 114 in Porsche's bureau parlance, but the design was never produced because the powers that be had a change of heart and agreed to a VW-based sports car. This Type 64, similar in appearance to the 114, used a tuned version of the saloon engine mounted in its rear position. It was conceived for the Berlin–Rome–Berlin road race, intended for September 1939 but cancelled because of the outbreak of the Second World War. Three of these Type 64s, however, were produced.

Thereafter, Porsche became deepy involved with war work, but in 1944 the design bureau moved to the safety of Gmünd in Austria and continued there until the war ended in 1945. When hostilities ceased, members of the Porsche family were lured to Baden Baden in the French military zone of Germany and were asked by the ruling political party in France to design a 'people's car'. But no sooner had the Porsches arrived than a rival political party won power and they were promptly arrested for having assisted the German war effort. It took Porsche's daughter, Louise Piech, who was looking after their interests in Germany, six months to free Porsche's son, Ferry, and until 1947 to extract her father and her husband Anton, who had been assisting in the French people's car project.

BELOW *The unmistakable profile of the 356A with a photo of Dr Ferry Porsche. Provided by David Edelstein.*

RIGHT *Ancestry: the Type 64 version of the Volkswagen, built for the aborted Berlin–Rome race of 1939.*

MATHÉ

The Type 356 Porsche

It was therefore at Gmünd, in June 1947, that Ferry Porsche, assisted by Karl Rabe, his father's 'right hand', began work on the Type 356 Porsche. The Type 356 was the first real Porsche sports car and Ferry Porsche's first great work. He was much influenced by the example of Piero Dusio, an Italian who in the early post-Second World War years produced Cisitalia sports cars using modified Fiat components. As the Porsche design team worked on a Cisitalia grand prix car for Dusio, Ferry was thinking about how he could produce something like the Italian's sports cars from Volkswagen parts. He did not have much choice really. Bits and pieces of old Volkswagens were just about all that was readily available in Austria and Germany after the war.

This is why the first Porsche had a frame made from a network of tubes, like the Cisitalia sports cars: this light and rigid structure was called a spaceframe because there was so much space, or air, within the frame. A Volkswagen engine was fitted the 'wrong way round' in the rear, with its gearbox behind the axle rather than in front of it, in the manner of the pre-war Auto Union grand prix car, which Professor Porsche had designed. The idea was to concentrate the weight within the car's wheelbase to give it a better balance. The torsion-bar rear suspension also had to be turned round with the result that this first Porsche established a characteristic that was to make the marque famous: it oversteered.

LEFT *Betty Haig regularly campaigned this 1952 356 in Britain. Provided by AFN Ltd.*

BELOW *The model evolves: the 356B of 1960–3, a nicely preserved cabriolet. Provided by John Piper.*

The front suspension, steering and brakes came straight from a Volkswagen. The 1131 cc flat-four air-cooled engine was boosted to between 35 and 40 bhp from its normal 25 bhp by modifying the cylinder heads, and the first Type 356 car ran in chassis form in March 1948. When Ferry Porsche was satisfied with its handling along the mountain roads around Gmünd, he authorized the construction of a body for it. This was the work of the gifted Erwin Komenda, who produced a roadster with a very slippery shape that owed some of its inspiration to the pre-war Type 64 and that of the latter-day Cisitalia coupés. Everything was kept as simple and light as possible to ensure good performance. One of its first drivers was Ferry Porsche who took it to the family's estate at Zell-am-See in Austria. On the way, while climbing the rough roads of the famous Grossglockner Pass, the frame buckled and the rear torsion-bar housing nearly collapsed. Ferry strengthened it with two pieces of scrap iron 'borrowed' from friendly roadmenders nearby.

At the same time as this car was being developed, the Porsche designers were working on a similar machine to offer better accommodation than the spartan roadster, which had been visualized more as a competition vehicle. This car, known to the designers as the Type 356/2, bore a close resemblance to the standard Volkswagen in mechanical layout. Its engine and rear suspension were the 'right' way round, which made the car a little more tail-happy, but meant that there was room for some luggage behind the seats. It was also planned to fit either a coupé or a cabriolet body. In this form, with a cosy fixed head or with a fully trimmed drop head, the car was expected to have more appeal for touring.

This model used a platform chassis, rather than the intricate spaceframe, to make production easier. There was a weight penalty, but the car was still quite light because of its alloy body, again designed by Komenda along the lines of the roadster.

Production continued spasmodically through 1949 with Porsche re-establishing close links with the thriving Volkswagen concern.

Back to Germany

It was becoming imperative that the company find more convenient premises than those at Gmünd, so attempts were made to move back to Stuttgart, where it had been located in the Zuffenhausen district before the war. The firm's old works were occupied by the United States Forces motor pool, which was planning to move out in the near future. In the meantime, Porsche production was restarted in premises rented from the Reutter coachworks at Zuffenhausen, which had successfully bid for a contract to supply 500 bodies. Production continued there for two years from 1950 as the American plans to move out were delayed by the Korean War.

Reutter used steel for the bodies to make production easier, but they were heavier as a result. The overall lines of these Zuffenhausen cars were smoother, however, as Komenda had been following the Porsche policy of constantly trying to improve and polish existing designs. Four of the 50 Gmünd alloy coupés were retained for competition work as they did not look all that much different from the new production cars.

Mechanically, the Zuffenhausen cars were similar to the earlier 356, except that they benefited from improvements in the Volkswagen components. Tragedy came to the firm, however, with the death, in January 1951, of Professor Ferdinand Porsche at the age of 75.

Production expanded tenfold at Zuffenhausen and by March 1951 a total of 500 German Porsches had been completed. Work stopped for an hour and, in an uncanny silence, the workers gathered around their car number 500 as a wreath and placard were placed on its nose, and Dr Albert Prinzing, who had done much to re-establish production in Germany, said a few words.

One of the reasons Porsche was selling more cars was because of the interest shown by an Austrian-born car dealer, Max Hoffmann, in America. He took delivery of three 1100 cc Porsches in the autumn of 1950 (one for himself and two for the great racing enthusiast Briggs Cunningham). He sold 32 in 1951, despite the car costing as much as a Cadillac in the United States. By 1954, he was taking a third of Porsche's production and, later, American sales built up to 70 per cent.

Sales were boosted by competition successes in relatively standard 356 cars as well as the achievements of the special machines covered in the section on the early racing Porsches (see page 173).

During the winter of 1951–2 many changes were made to improve the Type 356. The most dramatic was the introduction

The distinctive lines of the 356 Speedster, introduced in 1954 and built until 1957. Aimed decisively at the American market, hence its transatlantic name, it sold well in California, was a light, lively performer and relatively cheap by Porsche standards. Provided by Ray Wright.

of an optional 1500 cc engine. The bore of the 1300 cc unit was at its limit, so Porsche increased the stroke by using a roller-bearing crankshaft that enabled the crank's throw to be increased within the restrictions of the Volkswagen-based crankcase. These roller-bearing cranks were an intricate puzzle of 13 major parts, made by a Stuttgart firm, Hirth. They needed careful treatment and necessitated far more frequent engine rebuilding than with a conventional crankshaft and bearings, but they did endow the car with a much superior performance and made it far more pleasant to drive. One of the most noticeable changes was the substitution of a one-piece windscreen for the earlier split screen made from two panes of glass: the cost of tooling for a one-piece screen had been too high until production had built up sufficiently.

Despite his success in selling standard Porsches, Hoffmann was of the opinion that the styling was all wrong. Therefore he persuaded Porsche to build him a special-bodied Type 356 roadster that he thought would be more attractive to Americans, who were more accustomed to the clearly defined wing lines of British sports cars such as the MG TC and the Jaguar XK 120. As it happened, the Porsche design office had already drawn up such a body for a young enthusiast called Heinrich Sauter in 1950. This had a normal Porsche nose with abbreviated tail and lower-cut doors. This was to be the design that became the America Roadster supplied to Hoffmann. The bodies were made from aluminium because it was expected

that most of them would be used for racing. Hoffmann achieved his objective in that this design sold quite well in America from April 1952.

With more design work flowing in and an ever-increasing demand for the Type 356, the company expanded its premises behind Reutter's works in 1952, despairing of ever getting the old Porsche factory back. Fewer cars were being ordered with the 1100 and 1300 cc engines, so the 1500 cc unit was offered in two stages of tune: the standard engine and the higher-powered 1500 Super. A plain-bearing version of the 1500 engine was also developed, although the sometimes troublesome roller-bearing engine continued in production because of Hirth's heavy investment in it, and because it was more reliable for racing.

The constant increases in power proved too much for the standard Volkswagen gearboxes, so Porsche designed a new one. This had synchromesh on all four gears and originated from a design rejected by Volkswagen. The operation of the Porsche synchromesh was so good that it has been adopted by many car manufacturers and has brought in handsome royalties to Porsche since its inception in 1952.

Larger brakes were also fitted to help cope with the extra power. Minor alterations continued to be made in matters such as lighting, but the next major change in the Type 356 was the option of a roller-bearing version of the 1300 cc engine for competition, from 1953: this was called the 1300 Super.

By 1954, Hoffmann was taking only 1500 cc Porsches, so he called the lower-powered version the 1500 America and sold it as cheaply as possible with most of the normal luxury fittings as extras. This name was changed to the Continental for 1955, but had to be dropped within the year because of legal objections by Ford, then about to re-introduce the Lincoln Continental.

In September 1954 all engines received a three-piece crankcase and the 1100 cc unit was phased out. Until then

ABOVE *The 'office' of David Edelstein's 356A. Note the rubber floor mats; there were no creature comforts on this model which was aimed foursquare at the enthusiast.*

RIGHT *The 356B, introduced for 1960, was distinguished by higher bumpers and overriders. Also the rear seats were lowered to increase headroom. Provided by Gordon Bond.*

Porsche had continued to use the Volkswagen crankcase, although it had to be modified for 1500 cc engines.

The Speedster arrives in the USA

September 1954 was also an important date in Porsche history, for this was when the Speedster was introduced on the American market. This stark little machine became one of the world's best-loved cars and still symbolizes what Porsche motoring means to many thousands of people, especially Americans. There was no wasted space, and consequently weight, on the Speedster. It had a distinctive, and minimally low, windscreen and an almost ridiculously skimpy rag top. Equipment on this open car was kept to a minimum and it used either version of the 1500 cc engine for maximum performance. The Speedster became everybody's boy racer, as fast and manoeuvrable as a pair of roller skates and even more fun. Hoffmann's sales soared with such an attractive little beast to publicize Porsche and, by March 1955, production had reached 5000, an occasion for more factory celebrations.

Almost immediately there were wholesale small modifications to the cars! Porsche engineers could not resist changing things and some of their ideas were distinct innovations, sired of necessity. This is why Porsche became one of the first manufacturers to fit windscreen washers as standard. The aerodynamic nose of the Porsche Type 356 was so well shaped that it scooped mud and dirt straight on to the windscreen.

Porsche then went the best part of six months without changing anything, but wound up by completely revising the

Type 356 to produce the Type 356A in September 1955. The new crankcase enabled the engine capacity to be increased to 1600 cc, which not only improved performance and made the car easier to drive, but also took maximum advantage of the class capacity in Touring and Grand Touring car races.

This meant that the Type 356A could be specified with five different engines: the 1300 producing 44 bhp; the 1300S with 60 bhp; the 1600 also giving 60 bhp; the 1600S with 75 bhp; and a new leading model, the 1500GS Carrera—named after the marque's successes in the Carrera Panamericana road races—using a racing engine developing 100 bhp. The pushrod 1500 cc engines were dropped.

The 10,000th Porsche

The year 1956 was a milestone in Porsche history. The company was allowed to return to its old home, which eased production problems considerably, and the 10,000th Porsche, a Type 356A, was produced. It was an emotional occasion also, in that 12 March 1956 was the company's Silver Jubilee, a great occasion for celebration.

The Speedster may have been cheap by Porsche standards, but it was still expensive when compared to many other imported sports cars in America. Consequently, anyone who could afford a Speedster was probably able to buy a more luxurious car anyway. Also, because the Speedster's price was pared to a minimum in Porsche terms, it did not make the company much money. The Speedster was therefore replaced by the Speedster D, a more luxurious and expensive version with a higher profit margin. It was called the D because its body was made by the outside firm of Drauz, near Stuttgart, who had been called in to relieve the pressure of constant expansion on Reutter. It was then that the Californians suddenly began to confirm the old adage, 'you never really know what you've got till it's gone'. They howled in rage at the loss of their Speedsters and the factory promptly renamed the Speedster D the D-type Convertible, because it was much

PORSCHE
Carrera 2
EMD 932B
GB

nearer the convertible in character and style.

As production was increased, there were fewer changes in specification, apart from an improvement in the gearbox casing in 1956. In the old days, when production was much lower, components were ordered in smaller batches and as a result it was easier to change their specification. Now that Porsches were pouring off the lines in Zuffenhausen it was more difficult, so it was 1957 before any further significant changes were made to the Type 356A. The 1300 models were dropped, and a de luxe version of the Carrera was offered with a heater and a slightly 'softer' engine giving 10 bhp less, but making the car easier to drive. The 1600S went over to plain bearings, which were quieter, but retained its high power output because it still had a wilder camshaft than that on the normal 1600 engine. This latter engine was now fitted with cheaper iron cylinders, which also made it quieter.

Notable alterations in 1958 included further improvements to the gearbox's synchromesh, and an extra 5 bhp for the Carreras by increasing their capacity to 1600 cc; but the next big development was in September 1959 when the Type 356B was introduced. This had a thoroughly Americanized nose with higher headlamps and much stronger bumpers, also mounted higher front and rear. As is so often the case with a developing car, the Type 356B weighed more and its performance suffered a little, but at least its braking was better. The interior was enlarged at the back by more surgery in the floorpan, and a new engine was offered, the Super 90. This was a pushrod 1600 cc unit with nearly as much power as the Carrera engine. The Carrera 356 continued in production, although most cars with these engines used competition bodywork. The 1600 and 1600S remained, but the 1600S was uprated by using the Super 90's valve gear. The types of body available were the same, although the D-type Convertible was renamed the Roadster in deference to the Californians.

Production increased even further on completion of a third factory at Zuffenhausen. Reutter, on the point of being taken over by Porsche, continued to make as many bodies as possible, but various outside suppliers were used. They included the German Karmann company, who produced first the Roadster, then a hard-top coupé until 1961. Extensive revisions were made to the body at this time, with an enlarged rear window for the coupé, a larger engine cover and a modified front luggage compartment to give it more capacity. As ever, there were many detail changes in fittings.

Soon, the 75 bhp 1600S became known as the Super 75, and during 1962 it was fitted with the cast-iron cylinders used on the 1600. At the same time, the Carrera capacity went up to 2 litres and this model became known as the Carrera 2. Larger numbers were produced to qualify it for GT racing.

The body unit was carried over with minor alterations for the final version of the traditional Porsche, the Type 356C in 1963. This had a number of further refinements in the fittings, plus disc brakes all round from the Ate company. They were basically of Dunlop origin, although one of their special features was the incorporation of a drum in the rear disc to Porsche patents, which made the handbrake far more efficient than with normal disc applications. New 15 in disc wheels were fitted with these brakes and further improvements were made to the suspension. The 1600, 1600S and Super 90 engines were replaced by the 1600C (75 bhp) and 1600SC (95 bhp) units, with the 2000GS, or Carrera 2, remaining unchanged. In this way the Type 356 ran out its production life, being made in its final year, 1965, alongside the 911. In 17 years a total of 76,302 examples of the 356 series was produced. It was a model that bought world-wide fame to Porsche, establishing an air-cooled, rear-engined theme to be perpetuated in the 911.

PORSCHE 356C CARRERA
1963–5

ENGINE	
No. of cylinders	4
Bore/stroke mm	92 × 74
Displacement cc	1966
Valve operation	Two overhead camshafts per bank
Compression ratio	9.5:1
Induction	Twin carburettor
BHP	130 at 6200 rpm
Transmission	Four-speed
CHASSIS	
Frame	Platform
Wheelbase mm	2100
Track—front mm	1306
Track—rear mm	1272
Suspension—front	Independent, trailing arms, transverse torsion bars
Suspension—rear	Independent, swing axle, transverse torsion bars
Brakes	Hydraulic disc
PERFORMANCE	
Maximum speed	203 km/h (126 mph)

LEFT *The fabled Carrera version of the 356 arrived in 1955 and continued in production until 1965. The engine was a twin overhead camshaft conversion of the 356 pushrod unit, embodying no less than 14 bevel gears. This is a 356C model. Provided by John Piper.*

BELOW *Last model in the 356 line was the 356C which appeared in July 1963 for the 1964 model year and remained in production until 1965. The flat, rather than rounded hub caps, indicating the presence of disc brakes, identify it. Provided by Ivor Coverley.*

ARRIVAL OF THE 911

It took seven years to produce the first Porsche 911, but it was to be good for some 20 years with development. Although the 911 was a completely new car, Ferry Porsche had decided that it should stick to the principles established so successfully in the 356 series. In other words, it should be a grand tourer with an air-cooled engine and the same type of wind-cheating body. The designers used their seven years to good effect for the 911 turned out so well: it offered far superior interior and luggage accommodation within a wheelbase only 127 mm (5 in) longer than that of the Type 356, and its styling was even more attractive. This was the work of Ferry Porsche's son, Ferdinand, known as Butzi.

Torsion-bar suspension was retained all around to save space. The front torsion bars ran parallel with the frame and used a lower wishbone and MacPherson strut for wheel location because this system occupied the least space. Anything that could be saved in this area was reflected in a larger front luggage boot. This had to be big enough to carry a set of golf clubs, again chiefly to please the Americans, but there certainly would not be any objections from other markets. The rear torsion bars were housed across the frame with wheel location by trailing arms and a low-mounted bracket. In this way a maximum amount of room could be devoted to rear seats. The old engine position with the power unit and its tall cooling fan overhanging the rear axle was retained for the same reason. Rack-type steering was used with a twin universally jointed steering column linked to a central pinion.

The flat-four engine used in the Type 356C was at the end of its development and more power was needed to keep Porsche sports cars ahead of rapidly developing saloons such as Jaguars, Mercedes-Benz and Citroëns. A four-overhead-camshaft engine like the one used in the Carrera was considered too complicated and expensive for use across the range, so Dr Ferry Porsche opted for a single overhead camshaft on each bank of cylinders. These would be six in number for smooth running and because it was visualized that the engine would be 'stretched' to larger capacities as the car was developed over the years. After much discussion, it was decided to use chains to drive the camshafts, as alternative methods, such as shafts and gears, or belts, were either too noisy and expensive, or not sufficiently well tested for Porsche. A 2-litre capacity was selected to obtain the necessary performance.

At first the new car was called the 901, but this was changed almost immediately—and before any cars were delivered—to the 911 to avoid trouble with Peugeot, whose cars used type numbers with a zero in the middle. The range continued to be known as the 0-series, however, and was made alongside the Type 356C from September 1964 until production had built up

ABOVE *1973 911E with Targa roof; a snug interior resulted. Provided by Ron Shea.*

BELOW *1972 911E Sportomatic. The engine is a 2.3-litre fuel-injected flat-six. Provided by Barry Sumner.*

sufficiently to discontinue the 356 in March 1965. The following month this cheaper model was replaced by the Porsche 912, which amounted to a 911 with the 1600SC engine. This was more economical to produce and meant that the 912 could be sold for less than the 911.

The Targa

With the cessation of 356 production, the Porsche company was conscious of the gap left in the range for a convertible. This led to the introduction of the Targa variant of the 911 in September 1965. Its distinctive body style, said to have been inspired by the British Triumph sports car's 'Surrey' split hard top, featured a strong, permanent hoop following the roofline across the car. A metal panel above the front seats could be detached and a plastic rear window behind the hoop could be unzipped or left in place to prevent draughts swirling back on to the occupants' necks.

Once some initial carburation problems were out of the way, Porsche uprated the 1991 cc engine from 130 to 160 bhp by raising the compression ratio, changing the camshafts and valves, and fitting slightly different carburettors and a new heat exchanger. This is the engine that was introduced in July 1966 to power a new high-performance version of the 911, the 911S.

A new line of cars, designated the A series, was introduced in August 1967 for the 1968 model year. The standard 911 became the 911L (for luxe) and a new, cheaper, version called the 911T (for touring) was introduced. It had more spartan fittings like those on the 912 and an engine like that of the 911, except that it had cast-iron cylinders to save money and produced only 110 bhp. It did not matter very much, however, as the fittings weighed less. In this way, Porsche had four basic models: the 912 with 90 bhp; the 911T with 110 bhp; the more luxurious 911L with 130 bhp; and the 911S with 160 bhp. All models were available in Targa or fixed head coupé form, and the 912 could be bought with a four-speed manual transmission to keep costs down. At the same time the variations on the range were further increased by the introduction of optional Sportomatic transmission—a successful semi-automatic system of gear changing.

The entire range was overhauled for the 1969 model year with a dramatic improvement in handling as the greatest benefit in this B series. Reasonable understeer at normal speeds was achieved by moving the rear wheels backwards by 57 mm (2¼ in) while keeping the engine and transaxle in the same place. Magnesium casting further reduced the overhanging weight. The increased angle of driveshaft operation was taken up by new constant-velocity joints. Further improvements were effected by increasing the wheel widths to 152 mm (6 in), which meant slightly flared arches.

Mechanical fuel injection was fitted to the two top models to increase power by 10 bhp and help meet American exhaust-emission regulations. The 911L's designation was changed to 911E, the 'E' standing for *Einspritz*—'injection'. An optional 'comfort' kit was listed for the 911T, bringing its interior up to the 911E and 911S standards. Self-levelling hydro-pneumatic front suspension struts were fitted to the 911E as standard to improve the ride even further, and they became optional on the 911T and 911S. All models received larger rear brake callipers and the 911S also acquired bigger alloy callipers at the front. Ventilation and heating were improved on all

models and numerous fittings were uprated.

Handling and torque were further improved for the following year (August 1969 to July 1970) by the introduction of the C series cars with an engine bored out from 80 mm to 84 mm, giving a capacity of 2195 cc. In addition a larger clutch was fitted to all C series 911s, the 912 having been replaced by the mid-engined 914 (see page 171).

A lightweight version of the 911S was homologated for competition to replace the previous lightweights, which had been made in small quantities and known as the 911R. Few alterations were made for the D series cars built between August 1970 and July 1971. They centred chiefly around detail changes in the fuel-injection and ignition systems to meet changing exhaust-emission regulations.

The next series, however, was highly significant. These cars represented a distinct change of policy for Porsche in that their modifications, although still made with little regard to cost, were aimed far more at improving the car for road use than for competition. In this way the company recognized how far competition cars were diverging from anything that could be used on the road. The engine stroke was increased for the E series (from August 1971 to July 1972) from 66 mm to 70.4 mm to enlarge the capacity to 2341 cc—rather than boring out yet again, which would have been more logical for competition. A bigger bore generally denotes a high-speed competition application; a longer stroke offers more flexibility on the road and, more important, in heavy traffic.

In Europe, the 911T retained its Zenith carburettors and gave 130 bhp; in the United States it was fitted with mechanical fuel injection, which produced 140 bhp. The 911E produced 165 bhp in 2.4-litre form (this designation was used rather than the more accurate 2.3 litres to link the model with Porsche racing successes) and the 911S 190 bhp. Also, the compression ratio of the 2.4-litre's engine had been reduced to enable it to be run on lead-free petrol.

The increased power and torque of the 2.4-litre led to the fitting of a new, stronger, transmission with four speeds as standard and a fifth as an option, although the majority of cars were fitted with five-speed gearboxes anyway. The F series 911, from August 1972 to July 1973, had its oil tank moved back to its pre-E series position.

The 2.7-litre Carrera

The year 1973 was also significant in Porsche history in that the Carrera was re-introduced. Until then the factory had not devoted much time to racing the 911, concentrating instead on more specialized vehicles. With an eye to success with standard-shaped cars in the future, Porsche brought out a 2.7-litre lightweight version of the 911S and named it the Carrera to emphasize its high performance. The combination of 210 bhp from a bored-out 2687 cc engine and lightweight bodywork produced what is still one of the fastest 911 production cars, despite subsequent development.

Initially, the production run of 500 of these cars was planned for homologation into the Group 4 (modified GT cars) racing category, but there was such a demand for the Carrera that more than 1000 were made to qualify it for the Group 3 class for standard GT cars.

The Carrera, with its distinctive 'duck-tail' rear spoiler to reduce lift at high speeds at that end of the car, was produced in three versions: the RS (for *Rennsport*, or sports racing) with basic road trim; the RST with luxury touring equipment more like the 911S; and the RSR, an ultra lightweight with few creature comforts. The capacity increase to 2.7 litres also

allowed the factory to produce a 2992 cc version with bore enlarged from 90 mm to 95 mm to take full advantage of the international 3-litre capacity classes.

The 911S had been lightened to form the Carrera RS by dispensing with the rear seats, using plastic bucket seats for the driver and passenger, a thin-gauge windscreen, and thinner metal bodywork with aluminium or plastic used wherever possible. Later versions of the first batch of Carreras also featured modified rear suspension geometry to cope with 279 mm (11 in) wide rear tyres that were fitted to many of them. These modifications were not carried out throughout the range because there was no need for them with normal-width tyres.

The G series Porsche 911 for the 1974 model year was the car that many people said could never be produced. Fresh regulations in the United States demanded that new cars should be able to withstand a 8 km/h (5 mph) impact without damage to any important parts, such as lighting—and Porsche bumpers had never been renowned for their durability, particularly in the hurly-burly of American parking.

RIGHT *When a turbocharged version of the 911 appeared for 1974, it incorporated so many modifications that it was re-designated the 930. Capacity began at 3 litres and rose to 3.3 in 1978. Brakes from the 917 racers were also introduced. This 1979 model includes these modifications.*

BELOW *In 1973 the Carrera name was introduced on the 911 line with the RS, for* Rennsport *(Race Sport). The engine was a 2.7-litre unit but there was no sound insulation in order to save weight and lighter body panels were used for the same reason. The engine cover and rear spoiler were made of glass fibre. Provided by John Blatter.*

The engineers and designers of Zuffenhausen had coped with worse problems, however, such as keeping the 917 racing cars on the ground! They simply redesigned the G series bumpers in aluminium to absorb such impacts from an extra depth on steel mountings; hydraulic dampers to return the bumpers to their original position were available as an option, soon to become mandatory in America.

Meanwhile, the 2.7-litre capacity had proved so successful that it was adopted for all G series cars, except the Carrera RSR, which went up to 3 litres. The 911T was dropped from the range, the cheapest model now being called simply the 911, with 150 bhp. The 911S with 175 bhp became the middle model, with the standard Carrera producing 210 bhp as before. This became available with far more roadgoing options, however, but kept its Bosch mechanical fuel injection in the interests of top-end performance.

The turbocharged Porsches

By 1974 it was becoming apparent that turbocharging was to be the best way of boosting an engine's performance without falling foul of exhaust-emission regulations and without increasing its capacity dramatically. The worldwide oil crisis during the winter of 1973–4 also indicated that very large engines had seen their heyday. Therefore the works ran a turbocharged Carrera RSR of 2.1 litres capacity in international racing in 1974. Its capacity was dictated by regulations which said that turbocharged engine capacities must be multiplied by 1.4 to give them an equivalent for competition against normally aspirated cars: thus the 2.1-litre Carrera competed in the 3-litre class. This model proved to be an invaluable test bed for the dramatic new H series car to come in August 1974. This was to be what amounted to a 3-litre Carrera RSR chassis with a turbocharger that had been under development since 1969, particularly on Can-Am racing cars and on the 2.1-litre Carrera prototype. The changes were so extensive that this model was christened the 930, although it remained a 911 at heart.

In fact, the season's development with the 2.1-litre car proved beneficial in that the Porsche engineers managed to adapt the 3-litre production engine quite successfully. They did this by controlling intake pressure with a 'waste gate', or flap valve, allowing the turbocharger to pick up speed quicker without inlet pressure to oppose it. The engine of the 930 was also modified so that its torque curve suited the turbocharger (to avoid 'turbo-lag'), and the K-Jetronic fuel injection worked especially well in this application.

The range of production cars was juggled, with the 912 designation returning on cars imported into the United States during 1976. The 912E, as it was called, was a short-lived car intended as a stop-gap between the cessation of 914 production early in 1976 and the arrival of the 924 (see page 187) in the United States in 1977. This variant of the 911 had the four-cylinder 1971 cc Volkswagen-based engine used in the 914 (see page 171), fitted with L-Jetronic fuel injection to give 86 bhp.

The 911 was the only model in the 1976 range (I series) to use the 2.7-litre engine, which had been uprated to 165 bhp, very much like the previous year's 911S. The four-speed gearbox was fitted as standard with the option of a new three-speed Sportomatic or the five-speed transmission. The 3-litre Carrera was retained at 200 bhp and the Turbo (as it was called, rather than Type 930) at 260 bhp.

The Carrera inherited the same style of wheels as the Turbo with optional rim widths of between 178 and 229 mm (7 and 9 in) and had a lavish standard of equipment. Cast-iron front-brake callipers similar to the alloy units fitted to the Turbo were used and the rear wing was increased in size in conjunction with the bigger tyres and wheels.

Numerous detail improvements were made on the J series 911S for the 1977 model year, but nothing significant. New colour schemes enhanced the Turbo's exclusive air, and 16 in wheels were fitted with ultra-low-profile tyres.

Important changes were afoot for 1978 with the K series. A new basic model, the 911SC, replaced both the Carrera and the 911. It was similar to the Carrera, except that it had 180 bhp, with more torque.

For the first time, the Turbo could be driven on the road (where legal!) at somewhere near its limits when new brake discs were eventually cleared for production. These were both ventilated and perforated and had been developed from those

1977 Carrera with Targa top. It was in 1975 that the Carrera version of the 911 was increased from 2.7 to 3 litres capacity and was produced in this form until 1977. It was an unusually well-equipped model which included an electrically operated and heated external mirror as well as headlamp washers, also electrically powered. There were no less than three gearbox options available at no extra cost: a four-speed unit, a five-speed one or a three-speed Sportomatic. Provided by Ken Scott.

PORSCHE 911 CARRERA 3.0
1975–7

ENGINE	
No. of cylinders	6
Bore/stroke mm	95 × 70
Displacement cc	2994
Valve operation	Single overhead camshaft per bank
Compression ratio	8.5:1
Induction	Bosch K-Jetronic fuel injection
BHP	200 at 6000 rpm
Transmission	Five-speed
CHASSIS	
Frame	Unitary construction
Wheelbase mm	2270
Track—front mm	1370
Track—rear mm	1350
Suspension—front	Independent, MacPherson struts, longitudinal torsion bars
Suspension—rear	Independent, semi-trailing arms, torsion bars
Brakes	Hydraulic disc
PERFORMANCE	
Maximum speed	230 km/h (143 mph)

used on racing 911s which had inherited them from the 917 (see page 180). In keeping with this new-found braking ability, the Turbo's engine was increased in both bore and stroke (97 mm × 74.4 mm) to enlarge the capacity to 3.3 litres, with a subsequent rise in power to 300 bhp with yet more torque. An intercooler was fitted to the intake system to improve turbo-charger efficiency, which meant redesigning the spoiler. The 911SC was also listed with Turbo running gear.

The future of the 911 seemed uncertain when Dr Ernst Fuhrmann, who had risen to become Porsche's chairman, said the company would concentrate on the new 928. In January 1981 he was succeeded by a new chairman, Peter Schutz, a German who had spent much of his life in America. Schutz promptly gave the go-ahead for a new bout of 911 development with the famous flat six-cylinder engine being made even more powerful and economical and a fully open spyder body being shown at the Frankfurt Motor Show in September 1981, with a new four-wheel drive system to improve handling.

The four-wheel drive system, with power variable between front and rear wheels, did not go into production immediately, being promised for a stunning competition 911, to be homologated for the international Group B when 200 had been built in 1985. But, in belated recognition of the appeal of the 911 as a purist driving car rather than a boulevard cruiser, all 1984 models, other than the Turbo, were called Carreras ... and given a longer-stroke, 3164 cc, 231 bhp engine that was also ten per cent more economical. The Turbo and the Cabriolet, introduced in 1982, continued virtually unchanged.

RIGHT *1972 914/6. This is the Porsche version of the 914, a joint Porsche/Volkswagen model. It was powered with the 1991 cc six-cylinder 911T engine and mid-mounted. A Porsche five-speed gearbox was employed. Maybe not the happiest of models, it was introduced for 1970 and lasted until 1975. It was sold as a Porsche in America and as a VW-Porsche in the rest of the world. Provided by John Cleave.*

BELOW *The Volkswagen-powered 914, instantly distinguished by its four-stud wheels rather than the five-stud ones of its Porsche-powered opposite number. The engine was the 1.7-litre Volkswagen unit from the VW 411, fitted with Bosch fuel injection. There were two increases in engine capacity, to 1971 cc in 1973, which replaced the original unit, and an optional 1795 cc to 1976: the 914/6 had ceased production in 1975.*

A VOLKSWAGEN-PORSCHE MODEL

All seemed to be set fair for the future when Volkswagen and Porsche agreed to build the 'Fourteener' in 1967. The Porsche company wanted to produce a cheaper car to protect itself in that end of the sports-car market. Volkswagen wanted to go upmarket with a sporty image. Mid-engined cars had been outstandingly successful in competition, particularly those made by Porsche; and Porsche did not have the capacity to make a cheap mid-engined sports car, such was the success of the 911 range. Volkswagen did, and that company had historic links with Porsche, not the least in that they marketed each other's cars. So it only needed a handshake between Ferry Porsche and Volkswagen chief Heinz Nordhoff for them to agree to build the 914.

It would come in two versions, one with cheap Volkswagen running gear, the other with more expensive Porsche parts. Porsche would design the new car, Volkswagen would have the body made. Ferry and Heinz were old friends; Professor Porsche knew that Nordhoff would build so many 914 bodies that the cost would be lower than anything he could achieve, and he would get them on the cheap for his version of the mid-engined car. But it did not work out quite like that and the 914 died a few years later, a relative failure. Why?

Basic layout of the 914

The layout went back to Porsche's roots in its very first prototype. A Volkswagen engine was turned round 'backwards' for better weight distribution at the expense of interior accommodation. But this did not seem to matter: the 914 was intended as a two-seater all along, and careful design ensured that it had plenty of room in the cabin and for luggage in two boots. The shape was based on a design exercise by the German firm of Gugelot and was functional, if not pretty. The engine on the cheaper 914/4 came from the Volkswagen 411E, a fuel-injected four-cylinder producing 80 bhp; the 110 bhp

Porsche 911T 2-litre unit was substituted on the more expensive 914/6. Both models used the Porsche five-speed transmission in modified form with the option of a Sportomatic gearbox. The suspension and steering followed those on the 911 except that coil springs were used at the rear to make room for the engine.

Volkswagen wheels, hubs and disc brakes were used at the front with special disc brakes adapted at the back on the 914/4; Porsche hubs, wheels and brakes were used all round on the 914/6.

The 914 was intended as a cheap sports car and it was unveiled to an intrigued world in 1969. But by then Heinz Nordhoff had died and Volkswagen's new chief, Kurt Lotz, had bigger problems on his mind. He also had a different method of pricing: Porsche would have to pay the going rate for the Karmann-built body, which worked out at even more than that of a 911 unit! This meant that, no matter how Zuffenhausen pared away the costs, the Porsche 914/6 cost nearly as much as a 911 and customers could not see that it was anything like as attractive.

All 914s were called Porsches in America and the 914/4 a VW-Porsche elsewhere. No right-hand-drive cars were built by the factory—Volkswagen was anxious to retrieve tooling costs as quickly as possible and Porsche could not afford it—so right-hand-drive conversions by dealers made the 914 very expensive in the United Kingdom and Japan.

None of this would have mattered very much had it been demonstrable that the 914 was far superior to the 911; but it was never more than on a par in terms of performance and handling. At the time Volkswagen was simply not a sporty name in Europe, and, to the Americans, Porsche meant something quite different, a true GT car.

Detail improvements were made in the 1971 model year with some modifications to meet European exhaust-emission laws. The 914/6 engine stayed at 2 litres as the 911T went up in capacity, to keep a clearly defined demarcation zone between the models, and such was the lack of demand and low profit margins on the car that it was dropped in 1972. The 914 continued in its Volkswagen form with further improvements to the engine and fittings. With the ending of the Porsche 2-litre version of the 914, Volkswagen decided to fit its own 2-litre engine for 1973. This was a more powerful development of the existing Volkswagen 1.7-litre fuel-injected four-cylinder to be sold alongside the smaller and more economical unit. Sound and heat insulation was improved at the same time and the ride softened for comfort. De luxe fittings became available as an optional package with a sport kit, offering alloy wheels, anti-roll bars and quartz lighting, for the enthusiastic driver. This was to be the 914's most successful year, with production reaching within ten per cent of the original target of 30,000 units a year.

The 1.7-litre engine was bored out to 1.8 litres in 1974 with carburettors for extra power in Europe and fuel injection in America to meet emission regulations. Stronger bumpers were fitted in 1975 to cope with ever-changing United States Federal standards and more detail changes were made, including bright new colour schemes. But sales still flagged and the 914 faded away in the spring of 1976. It was a pity, for the 914 had so much potential.

RIGHT *356s in action at the International Classic Car Weekend at Donington in 1979. The cars are Tony Standen's 356B roadster (number 35) and the 356 coupé of John Lucas.*

BELOW *A rare bird. It was in 1972 that Porsche built 11 prototypes based on the 914. The engine was a potent 2.4-litre 911S unit, while suspension was also uprated to S standards and the wheel arches extended to cope with wider wheels. This 916 was, however, deemed by the Porsche costing department as too expensive to produce. Provided by Ken Scott.*

PORSCHE 916
1972

ENGINE	
No. of cylinders	6
Bore/stroke mm	84 × 70
Displacement cc	2341
Valve operation	Single overhead camshaft per bank
Compression ratio	8.5:1
Induction	Bosch fuel injection
BHP	190 at 6500 rpm
Transmission	Five-speed
CHASSIS	
Frame	Unitary construction
Wheelbase mm	2450
Track—front mm	1391
Track—rear mm	1445
Suspension—front	Independent, MacPherson struts, longitudinal torsion bars
Suspension—rear	Independent, semi-trailing arms, coil springs
Brakes	Hydraulic disc
PERFORMANCE	
Maximum speed	233 km/h (145 mph)

PORSCHE IN COMPETITION

The factory was too busy trying to produce the Type 356 at Gmünd to compete in racing officially until 1951, but private owners raced their cars from the start, and they won. The very first victory for a Porsche has been recorded as that of Kaes in Porsche number 1, who took his class in the Innsbruck races in 1948, before Prince Joachim zu Fürstenberg and Count Konstantin Berckheim drove their 1100 cc coupé to victory in the Swedish Midnight Sun Rally in 1950. The one-armed Austrian, Otto Mäthe, was also prominent in circuit racing and the Alpine Rally with an 1100 cc coupé at this time; and Walter Glöckler, a Volkswagen dealer from Frankfurt, had considerable success with a Porsche special of similar construction to the first Type 356 prototype. He called his car a 'spyder', a designation that dated back to the days when gentlemen raced the lightest possible horse-drawn carriages, whose progress resembled that of a scuttling spider.

For the 1951 Le Mans 24-hour endurance race, two of the Gmünd coupés were prepared because they were 90 kg (200 lb) lighter than the Stuttgart steel coupés. With slightly tuned engines and enclosed wheels, they were good for 160 km/h (100 mph). However, only one made the race; the other car, and a reserve, were involved in accidents. But that one car won its class in the hands of French Porsche concessionnaire Auguste Veuillet and Edmond Mouche.

The arrival of the Type 550

The 550 was to be the first Porsche designed specifically for racing, with its ladder-type frame and alloy Komenda body in open or closed form. The coupés were faster because of their superior aerodynamics, but the open versions with their better visibility and lighter weight were used on circuits where top speed was less important. The Type 550s had independent torsion-bar and trailing-arm suspension with swing axles at the back and massive drum brakes to cope with speeds up to 225 km/h (140 mph). At first they were fitted with 1500 cc pushrod engines boosted to 98 bhp (the very limit of development for that unit) to tide them over during the lengthy gestation period of the new four-cam engine. Glöckler gave the new car, appropriately a spyder, its début by winning at the Nürburgring in May 1953. A sister car was built for Le Mans and both were fitted with 78 bhp versions of the pushrod engine for reliability and went so well that Richard von Frankenberg and Paul Frère led in von Hanstein and Wilhelm Hild to first and second places in their class. These cars were fitted with coupé tops for this ultra-fast race, but shed them again by the time the Nürburgring came round again in August. Lined up alongside them for practice was a third Type 550, which made a very different noise. It was the first to be fitted with the far more complex flat-four engine with its dry-sumping, twin coils, distributor and plugs, and its 110 bhp conveyed through the distinctive Hirth roller-bearing crank. It was first raced into third place in the Freiburg hill climb in August 1953 with Hans Stuck at the wheel. Meanwhile the works prepared the earlier Type 550s for a Guatemalan team headed by Jaroslav Juhan to race in the Carrera Panamericana. Juhan's car was fastest on four of the eight stages spread over five days before retiring to leave its class win to team mate José Herrarte, with Fernando Segura second in a Type 356 coupé.

The works was then concentrating on developing the Type 550/1500RS with four-cam engine for 1954. These late Type 550 cars were easily distinguished by their finned coachwork, although the actual lines of the body varied from car to car. One of the early 1954 Type 550s, called the *Buckelwagen* because of its 'hunch-backed' body style, also featured an underslung frame that was to be adopted on later Type 550s. These works Spyders enjoyed a great deal of success in the next 18 months: Herrmann won his class in the Mille Miglia in 1954 after a hair-raising incident that involved driving under a crossing gate as a train approached; and the Belgians Stasse and Frère outlasted the OSCAs to win their class at Le Mans.

The works then tried a lowered version of the RS, a lightened 550, called the RSK, after its K-shaped front suspension frame. The design of this car used a lot of lessons learned from an ill-fated RS with a special low-frontal-area body called the Mickey Mouse. It suffered from instability and was written off by von Frankenberg at the AVUS in 1956, and the RSK had similar problems during its first competition outings in 1957, despite the addition of small fins on the rear wings.

However, modifications were carried out, and in world championship sports-car racing in 1958 Porsche piled up the points to finish second to Ferrari, before another great win in the Targa Florio in 1959 for Barth with Wolfgang Seidel.

Porsche's preparations for a new 1.5-litre Formula 1 in 1961 continued throughout 1960, with Formula 2 cars alongside improved versions of the RSK called RS60 Spyders. The works loaned Stirling Moss's sponsor, Rob Walker, a Formula 2 car for the 1960 season, but the brilliant British driver did not have much chance to drive it, spending several months out of action following a crash in a Lotus. Bonnier and von Trips finished first and second in the German Grand Prix, however, and Bonnier won the Targa Florio with Herrmann in an RS60. Herrmann also won at Sebring in a similar car shared with Olivier Gendebien, and numerous class wins were recorded in all manner of events from endurance racing to rallying.

Porsche in Formula 1

During the winter of 1960–1, Porsche spent much time on the new, more powerful, flat-eight engine for Formula 1, and on developing disc brakes, although the existing drum brakes had always proved perfectly adequate. An experimental chassis

PORSCHE TYPE 804
1962

ENGINE	
No. of cylinders	8
Bore/stroke mm	66 × 54
Displacement cc	1494
Valve operation	Two overhead camshafts per bank
Compression ratio	10:1
Induction	Four carburettors
BHP	180 at 9200 rpm
Transmission	Six-speed
CHASSIS	
Frame	Tubular
Wheelbase mm	2300
Track—front mm	1300
Track—rear mm	1330
Suspension—front	Independent, wishbone and longitudinal torsion bars
Suspension—rear	Independent, wishbone and longitudinal torsion bars
Brakes	Hydraulic disc
PERFORMANCE	
Maximum speed	Approx 273 km/h (170 mph)

RIGHT *Porsche's Formula 1 car in its final 1962 form, powered by a 1.5-litre flat eight-cylinder engine; note air intake for cooling fan. Suspension was by all-round torsion bars, and Porsche-designed disc brakes were used. Provided by the Donington Collection.*

BELOW *The 550, introduced in 1953, has the distinction of being the first Porsche to be designed specially for racing, and was available in Spyder (open) and coupé forms. The engine was a 1498 cc unit, although the 550A of 1956 produced 135 rather than 110 bhp. Provided by Peter Jackson.*

30

LEFT *A favourite Porsche stamping ground: the Sicilian Targa Florio race. In 1964 Porsche 904s came first and second; this is the latter-placed car driven by Balzarini and Linge.*

RIGHT *The 906 was a successful racing Porsche with tubular spaceframe chassis and gullwing doors. Introduced in 1966, it was powered by the Carrera six engine and won the Targa Florio and Daytona 24-hour races. Provided by Martin Hone.*

BELOW RIGHT *A 908/2, driven by Vic Elford and Richard Attwood, takes second place in the BOAC 500-mile race at Brands Hatch in 1969.*

OVERLEAF *Herbert Muller in a 908/4 at Spa in 1975 before retiring with gearbox trouble while in third place.*

with wishbone and coil suspension all round was also built for Formula 1. Four-speed gearboxes were developed because the existing six-speed units fitted to Formula 2 cars had proved to be too difficult for many drivers.

As the new eight was not ready for 1961 the less powerful but reliable four sufficed. But for 1962 the eight-cylinder engine was sleeved down to 1.5 litres for Formula 1 (the Type 804) for Gurney and Bonnier to use at Zandvoort in May. The latest chassis used wishbones with the more familiar torsion bars. However, Porsche's new engine had come too late, for Coventry-Climax (in Lotus and Cooper cars), BRM and Ferrari engines were now developing at least as much as its 180 bhp. Gurney managed one victory in the French Grand Prix when faster cars dropped out, but usually the Formula 1 Porsches were outclassed by Lotus with its new monocoque 25, BRM with its reliable engines, or the durable Ferraris. Despite being regarded as the fastest driver of 1962 with Lotus's Jim Clark, Gurney could only finish fifth in the world championship, and Bonnier was 15th. Porsche, who had spent a fortune on development, realized that at least another 10 per cent power was needed, which could not be justified on cost, so they quit grand prix racing at the end of the season and concentrated again on sports-car and GT events.

Porsche competition activities continued on three planes from 1964: the 904 and 911 were in racing and rallying; various hill-climbing cars were developed as circuit racers up to 3 litres; and the 917 was in the top classes (see page 178). The 904 represented a complete breakaway from established Porsche tradition in that it used a hefty box-frame chassis with a glass-fibre body bonded to it. This beautiful new car, the work of Butzi Porsche, was at first intended to have the production six-cylinder engine that was to go into the 911 model, ahead of its rear axle. Most early examples had the existing four-cylinder engine, however, although works cars were fitted with either the new six-cylinder unit or the eight-cylinder racing engine. Sufficient were built bearing the Carrera GTS label to qualify for GT racing and they won their second race—the Targa Florio—when the front-line 1963 model Spyders fell by the wayside in 1964. Colin Davis and Antonio Pucci were first with Linge and Balzarini second in another 904. From then on, the 904 was to prove outstandingly reliable, dominating the 2-litre classes in endurance racing.

The 911 continued to be successful in rallying, leading to the development of the 911S in 1966 and the start of a big rally programme for 1967, spearheaded by the crack British team of Vic Elford and David Stone. This pairing won their class in the 1967 Monte Carlo Rally, with outright victories in the German Rally, the Tulip Rally and the Geneva Rally, and Sobieslaw Zasada won his home Polish Rally in a 911S. These cars were also raced successfully in Sportomatic form to win the Marathon de la Route, an 84-hour successor to the Liège–Rome–Liège Rally at the Nürburgring. Elford combined with Herrmann and Jochen Neerpasch for this event.

The great rallying successes

The next three years were golden for Porsche in international rallying. Elford and Stone started by winning the Monte Carlo in 1968 from team mates Pauli Toivonen and Marti Tiukkanen. This year also saw Björn Waldegård emerge as a major force in Porsche rallying with a victory in the Swedish Rally. Numerous other top events fell to the 911S, and 911Rs driven by Erwin Kremer/Helmut Kelleners and Willi Kauhsen won the Spa 24-hour, and Glemser and Kauhsen took the Marathon de la Route.

No sooner had Elford won the Monte Carlo Rally than he was off to Daytona for the 24-hour race, which he won in a 907, a 904 derivative, with Neerpasch. Siffert, Herrmann and Stommelen were second in a 907, with Buzzetta and Jo Schlesser third in another 907. Siffert and Herrmann, followed by Elford and Neerpasch, repeated the success at Sebring, and all looked well for the 1968 World Sports Car Championship. But then everything started to go wrong and John Wyer's team of Gulf Ford GT40s beat the 907s by 22 seconds at Brands Hatch. A new car, called the 908, was introduced with a 3-litre version of the 2.2-litre 'production' six-cylinder unit in a similar chassis to the 907, but it proved to be no faster. It was, however, the first time that Porsche had produced a car to take advantage of the full capacity limit for international sports-car racing: at that time 3 litres for prototypes and 5 litres for 'stock block' cars.

P
55
SHELL
DUNLOP
PORSCHE

MARTINI RACING
Turbolader KKK
GOODYEAR
BOSCH
COLT
MARTINI INTERNATIONAL CLUB
MARTINI
Ate Bremsen
BILSTEIN
GOODYEAR

SUPRA
MULLER
4
Shell

The 917 (opposite) made its début at Spa in 1969, but it was far from fully developed, so the 908 remained as Porsche's front-line car. Siffert had put the 917 on pole position, but decided to race the 908 with Redman, in long-tailed form. A revised spyder body with flatter profile, nicknamed the Sole, appeared next at the Nürburgring, with Siffert and Redman taking it to victory. By then this wonderfully successful combination had done enough to win the World Sports Car Championship for Porsche, so all eyes were turned on Le Mans to see if they could win there. This time the leading Porsches ran into trouble and a Wyer GT40 driven by Jacky Ickx and Jackie Oliver scraped home 200 metres ahead of Herrmann and Larrousse's 908 after a thrilling battle.

The Porsche hierarchy was shocked at having been drubbed by a relatively old Ford GT40, so promptly gave up and arranged for Wyer to run the team the next year! In the meantime, the works Porsche 908s were handed over to the private Porsche Salzburg team to complete the season; Siffert and Redman won in one of these cars at Watkins Glen.

There seemed to be no stopping the 911s, either. Waldegård and Helmer won the Monte Carlo Rally again in 1970—the second consecutive win for them and the third for Porsche—and repeated this feat in the Swedish Rally.

Meanwhile, Wyer took over the big sports cars for 1970, with the 917 as a front runner. It was felt, however, that a 908, or an even lighter version of it, would be at an advantage on tricky circuits such as that used for the Targa Florio. The works, therefore, developed the 908/3. It had an alloy tube frame, but the 3-litre power train's differential was mounted behind the gearbox to make the car more manoeuvrable on tight corners. To compensate for this extra swinging weight, the driver was moved forward. Three of these cars were sent to Sicily for Wyer's team with a fourth for Porsche Salzburg, and Siffert and Redman led in Wyer team mates Rodriguez and Kinnunen.

The mighty 917

There is no doubt that the 917 was the greatest racing Porsche ever, and one of the most spectacular cars the world has seen. From the moment that Ferry Porsche gave the 12-cylinder project the go-ahead in 1968, world dominance of sports-car racing, with lap times faster than Formula 1 cars, was feasible. In essence, the 917 started as a 908/3 with half as much power again from the 4.5-litre engine and continued in its ultimate turbocharged form virtually to double that output to more than 1000 bhp. After problems in actually keeping the projectile on the ground in its first year of racing in 1969, it powered Porsche to a hat-trick of World Sports Car Championships under the inspired guidance of the Wyer team, and went on to achieve total dominance in the lucrative Can-Am racing in the United States and Canada in 1972 and 1973 in turbocharged form. Porsche was also lucky in having three of the greatest sports-car drivers of this era when these unrestricted giants were let loose on a track: Josef 'Seppi' Siffert, Pedro Rodriguez and Mark Donohue.

The 917 was born of a decision by the Commission Sportive Internationale to outlaw the massive 7-litre Fords and Chaparrals from the World Sports Car Championship in 1968: in future the series would be contested only by 3-litre cars with a minimum weight of 650 kg (1433 lb) or homologated 5-litre cars with a minimum weight of 800 kg (1764 lb) of which at least 25 had been built. By framing the regulations in this way, the CSI was sure that the pure racing cars, with GP-style 3-litre engines, would have an advantage over the 'monsters' with stock-block engines. Surely nobody, not even Ferrari, Ford, Chevrolet (via Chaparral) or Porsche, had the resources to build more than 25 identical outright racing cars, such was the cost of construction and development? It was a challenge that Ferry Porsche accepted so that he could steal a march on his rivals, and one that was to cost Porsche millions of marks,

RIGHT *A long-tail 917 leading the Le Mans 24-hour race in 1969 driven by Stommelen, but, after this first-lap triumph, it fell back and retired with oil loss. Elford took over the lead in another 917 but dropped out after 21 hours with mechanical trouble.*

BELOW LEFT *1968 Monte Carlo Rally and the winning 911T of Vic Elford fitted with 911S rally gear. It was a car that was to give Porsche scores of rallying successes.*

BELOW *1970 Spa 1000 kilometres. The Siffert/Redman Gulf 917 leads team mates Rodriguez and Kinnunen, the former duo winning at 241 km/h (150 mph).*

PORSCHE 917-30 1973	
ENGINE	
No. of cylinders	12
Bore/stroke mm	90 × 70
Displacement cc	5374
Valve operation	Four overhead camshaft
Compression ratio	6.5:1
Induction	Bosch fuel injection with twin turbochargers
BHP	1100 at 7800 rpm
Transmission	Four-speed
CHASSIS	
Frame	Alloy tubular
Wheelbase mm	2500
Track—front mm	1670
Track—rear mm	1564
Suspension—front	Independent, coil springs and wishbones
Suspension—rear	Independent, coil springs and wishbones, longitudinal links
Brakes	Hydraulic ventilated disc
PERFORMANCE	
Maximum speed	Approx 370 km/h (230 mph)

LEFT *Monza 1971: the 917 of Rodriguez and Oliver won the event with another 917 in second place.*

BELOW *The fastest Porsche ever built, the 917-30. Mark Donohue, who dominated the Can-Am racing series in 1973, at the wheel.*

The 934 Porsche was produced in 1976 in Group 4 trim for GT racing. Provided by Mark Niblett/Charles Ivey racing.

although much of this expenditure was recouped from selling the cars to customers and from an untold amount of invaluable development experience and publicity gained from such an exercise.

The main problem with the 917 in 1969 was the aerodynamics: despite suspension-operated flaps like those used on the 908/3 and later banned, the 917 was notoriously unstable with its great power (around 560 bhp) and highly efficient streamlining.

This difficulty was resolved when a brilliant English engineer, John Horsman, who ran the development and preparation side of Wyer's Gulf-sponsored team, got to work on the 917. He rejected the efforts of the Porsche technicians, led by Piech, who tended to concentrate on reducing drag, leaving the drivers to worry about keeping the car on the road. Horsman, who was quite capable of driving the cars himself, although he did not race personally, approached the problem with a fresh mind. He chopped off the 917's tail and built it up in shorter wedge-shaped form; this increased drag but saved weight and, more important, increased downthrust, which worked wonders for the car's stability. In one fell swoop, Siffert was far faster in the revised 917 despite its extra drag. The Porsche factory, which was providing technical support for the Wyer and Salzburg teams, promptly followed this line of thought with great success.

It was just as well, because frantic efforts at Modena had resulted in a formidable big Ferrari lining up with the Porsches for the 1970 season. Rodriguez and Kinnunen, in the first Gulf Porsche, won the Daytona 24 hours with team mates Siffert and Redman second just in front of the Mario Andretti/Arturo Merzario/Jacky Ickx Ferrari 512S. Then Ferrari won at Sebring from Peter Revson and film star Steve McQueen in a 908 when the Gulf and Salzburg Porsches were eliminated by hub trouble or accidents. After that, the Porsches really got into their stride, winning most World Sports Car Championship races in the 917. Pedro Rodriguez, younger brother of Ricardo who had started racing in an RS, began the Porsche domination with one of his typically brilliant drives in soaking wet conditions at Brands Hatch. He simply drove away from the rest of the field, even though the Ferraris of Amon and Ickx and the Salzburg 917 of Elford had been faster in practice.

The 917's engine was increased in capacity to 4.9 litres with 600 bhp for the next round of the championship at Monza, but Rodriguez still won in a 4.5-litre after problems with the new engine, and accidents. The 908/3 won the Targa, but it was back to the big Porsches for the very fast Spa circuit, where Rodriguez lapped at more than 258 km/h (160 mph), before retiring with a broken gearbox. Siffert was only fractionally slower and won with Redman, who had shared the winning Porsche in 1969.

The next event for the 917s, after the 908/3s had been used again at the Nürburgring, was Le Mans, with no fewer than eight Porsches disputing the overall lead with 11 Ferraris. In a race of attrition, Herrmann and Attwood lasted longest to win in a Salzburg short-tail 4.5-litre 917: and Herrmann promptly retired from racing after 20 years at the top. Siffert and Rodriguez left everybody else standing at Watkins Glen in the next round, duelling in the Gulf 917s, and Rodriguez won after Siffert's car had a puncture.

Not surprisingly, the magnificient 917 helped Porsche win the world championship in 1970 and again in 1971. Such was the dominance of the 917 that the CSI decided to reframe the regulations in favour of the 3-litre cars, and, after successes in the North American Can-Am series, the 917 was retired. It was the end of an era.

The 934, 935 and 936

It was later, during 1974, that the works used the 908/3 and 917 as the basis for development of its new prototype racer, the 936. The Type 930 roadgoing Turbo was homologated as the 934 for Group 4 racing and extensively modified as the 935 for Group 5 events, which were to qualify for a revised World Championship of Makes. All these cars used turbocharged engines in 1976, and Jöst continued to race his 908/3 with Can-Am bodywork to win at the Nürburgring.

The Loos-entered 934, with a 480 bhp 3-litre engine classed as 4.2 litres, and with 917 brakes, won the European Touring Car Championship GT class for Toine Hezemans in 1976, as the works Type 935 disputed the World Championship of Makes. Its 590 bhp turbocharged engine was kept to a nominal 4 litres which worked out best in terms of minimum weight regulations. Despite fierce opposition from 700 bhp BMW 3.5 CSLs, the 935s took their world championship, winning every race except that captured by Jöst's 908/3.

The Type 936, which shared similar success in the World Sports Car Championship, had what amounted to a 908/3 frame with the 2.1-litre turbocharged engine and 917 brakes, gearbox and titanium driveshafts. Only one car was entered in each event, but, boosted by Jöst's 20 points for his victory in the 908/3, took the title, as the more ambitious effort by Renault with the Alpine failed through unreliability or poor pitwork.

Ickx and van Lennep completed a virtual clean sweep for the year by winning at Le Mans in a 936 that led all the way except for the first few laps. Stommelen and Manfred Schurti finished fourth in a 935.

Porsche's chief rival in 1977, the French Renault team, concentrated on Le Mans, leaving the World Championship of Makes to the Germans. BMW put in only a token effort, however, and the Porsche people were among the first to admit that their clean sweep in the championship brought them little satisfaction. The Porsche works team, backed by Martini, ran 2.8-litre 935-77 cars with 630 bhp gained from twin turbochargers, which also almost eliminated the throttle lag problem.

Renault was bent on revenge, and got it with a new 1978 A443 prototype. This was the fastest car down the Mulsanne

ABOVE *Silverstone 1976. Jacky Ickx's clutch failed on the line and he lost 1¾ hours replacing it. But he then broke the lap record with his 935 placed, eventually, in second-to-last position!*

ABOVE RIGHT *A pair of 936s of the type that won at Le Mans in 1976 and 1977, and ran again in 1979 until they withdrew with electrical troubles. The engine was a 2142 cc turbocharged flat-six which developed 520 bhp. Modifications for 1977 included a reduced frontal area and twin turbochargers.*

RIGHT *1976 Le Mans. Porsche's 936 was driven by two former Le Mans winners, Jacky Ickx and Gijs van Lennep, and led throughout the race. The only problem occurred when an exhaust system required replacement just before midday on Sunday. It took 33 minutes to replace it which reduced the 936's lead from 16 to 8 laps but it was still enough. A 935 was placed fourth.*

12
14
DUNLOP
Shell
PORSCHE
MOTORSPORT

MARTINI
MARTINI
RACING
SPRECHFUNK
Turbolader
20
BILSTEIN
GOODYEAR
GOODYEAR
1976
Gr 6

LEFT *Niki Lauda is pictured in the warm up for the 1983 South African Grand Prix, his McLaren powered by a 1.5-litre Porsche 'customer' engine. He was later to retire in the event proper.*

BELOW LEFT *Jacky Ickx and Derek Bell snatch a sensational victory at the 1982 Brands Hatch 1000 km in their 956, which clinched Porsche the World Sports Car Championship of Makes and Ickx the driver's title.*

BELOW *1973 Targa Florio: Porsche Carrera RSR 3-litre prototypes took first and third places in the event. Here the Leo Kinnunen/Claude Haldi car, which was placed third, is seen rounding one of the hundreds of corners on the tortuous Piccolo Madonie circuit.*

Under all this equipment is the Porsche 924 engine, a 2-litre overhead camshaft unit which was also used in the classic Audi 100.

PORSCHE 924 1975 to date	
ENGINE	
No. of cylinders	4
Bore/stroke mm	86 × 84
Displacement cc	1984
Valve operation	Single overhead camshaft
Compression ratio	9.3:1
Induction	Bosch K-Jetronic fuel injection
BHP	125 at 5800 rpm
Transmission	Five-speed
CHASSIS	
Frame	Unitary construction
Wheelbase mm	2400
Track—front mm	1420
Track—rear mm	1370
Suspension—front	Independent, MacPherson strut
Suspension—rear	Independent, semi-trailing arms, transverse torsion bars
Brakes	Hydraulic front disc, drum rear
PERFORMANCE	
Maximum speed	196 km/h (122 mph)

Straight—at 367 km/h (228 mph)—since the 917s had touched 386 (240). The Porsche team was never able to contest the lead with the Renault-Alpines, and had to be content with second and third places for Bob Wollek, Barth and Ickx in a 936-78 and Haywood, Gregg and José Dolhem in a 936-77, behind the Alpine of Pironi and Jaussaud.

In 1979, Le Mans was very much a case of Porsche against the rest; no fewer than 19 of the 55 starters were Porsches, with no Renaults. The two front runners were the Essex Petroleum-sponsored 936s for Ickx and Redman, Wollek and Haywood, with tremendous publicity for a private 935 driven by its owner, Dick Barbour, Stommelen and film star Paul Newman. The most interesting Porsche, however, was a very special 935 built by the Kremers, with bodywork modified to give a 'ground effect' like Formula 1 cars. This was called the 935K3 and was driven by Klaus Ludwig and the American brothers Don and Bill Whittington. The prototypes succumbed to tyre or mechanical troubles, leaving the 935K3 in the lead, which it held to the end, despite losing 14 laps with a broken fuel injection pump belt.

Porsche left a host of 935 customers to pick up the challenge in the World Championship of Makes in 1980 and 1981. As a result, Lancia won the title both years, with its 1.4-litre turbocharged Monte Carlos collecting maximum points in the smaller classes. Porsche 935K3s won numerous races, however, and Jöst rebuilt his 908 again with 936 bodywork as a 908/80 and nearly won Le Mans in 1980! Fuel pump and gearbox trouble delayed the car, driven by Jöst, Ickx and Michel Leclère, and they were narrowly beaten into second place by a French Rondeau.

When it was realized that Porsche could still win at Le Mans, the factory fitted the 2.65-litre turbocharged engine from an abortive Indianapolis project to a 936/81 with a 917 Can-Am gearbox for Ickx to try for his fifth victory, in 1981. The engine was retained for a new monocoque car, the 956, with which Ickx and Bell duly won at Le Mans in 1982, before the works 956s took the World Endurance Championship that year. Following a sensational drive at Brands Hatch in October, the 956 went on to win the championship again in 1983.

In the meantime, Porsche returned to Formula 1, when they provided engines for the McLaren team in 1983. The car proved very reliable and McLaren won the championship comfortably in 1984 in the hands of Niki Lauda and Alain Prost. So much for competition, but what of the road cars?

FRONT ENGINES TAKE OVER

Superficially, the latest Porsches look alike: the 924 and the 928 are both wedge-shaped coupés of relatively conventional layout with a water-cooled engine at the front and rear-wheel drive. In reality, they are poles apart, with the cheaper 924 using as many proprietary Volkswagen and Audi parts as possible and the 928 being pure Porsche, owing little to anybody else. This is because they were conceived together in the early 1970s as two separate sports cars with the 924 intended as a Volkswagen and the 928 as a Porsche. As it worked out, the 924 only became a Porsche by accident.

The layout was decided for the new Porsche 928, intended as a replacement for the 911 series, before work started in earnest on the 914. It was used also for the 924 following marketing reports from Volkswagen, who had ordered a cheap, new sports car from Porsche to replace the 914 and said that the new car should bear some family resemblance to the projected Porsche. Other requirements for the new Volkswagen sports car were that it should use an absolute maximum number of parts from the Wolfsburg range, not just some as in the case of the 914. This would keep down the cost. Price was all-important with the 924, as it was becoming apparent, from queues of up to a dozen customers for every used 911, that there was a big market for a cheaper German sports car. Porsche was happy at the thought of one of Zuffenhausen's designs, rather than somebody else's, meeting this need. It had also been decided that the 924 should have more room inside and be more comfortable than the 914 to make it more popular for potential customers. All these factors influenced the Porsche designers as they worked on the 924 and 928 projects. They entered production in 1975 and 1978.

Although work had started first on the 928, the need for a new cheap sports car was more pressing, particularly as the 911 series had shown itself to be capable of being updated satisfactorily. The 2.7 Carrera and Turbo projects were ample evidence of this. Therefore, with 914 sales never really reaching target, the 924 was introduced first. Volkswagen

928 TTE

LEFT *The Porsche 924 (foreground) and 928 are superficially similar but the former was originally conceived by Porsche as a sports car project for Volkswagen and employs a variety of Audi/VW parts. By contrast, the 928 is a purpose-built GT and is V8 powered.*

BELOW *The 928 in all its glory in its original 4.4-litre form. The gearbox is rear-axle mounted, while the exposed pop-up headlamps are a distinctive feature. The absence of bumpers is illusory; they are contained within flexible front and rear body panels.*

PORSCHE 928/928S
1978 to date

ENGINE	
No. of cylinders	8
Bore/stroke mm	95 × 78; from 1983 97 × 78
Displacement cc	4474, 4664
Valve operation	Single overhead camshaft per bank
Compression ratio	8.5:1, 10:1
Induction	Bosch K-Jetronic fuel injection
BHP	230 at 5250 rpm, 310 at 5900 rpm
Transmission	Five-speed, four-speed automatic option
CHASSIS	
Frame	Unitary construction
Wheelbase mm	2500
Track—front mm	1552
Track—rear mm	1530
Suspension—front	Independent, coil springs and wishbones
Suspension—rear	Independent, coil springs and semi-trailing wishbones
Brakes	Ventilated disc
PERFORMANCE	
Maximum speed	228 km/h (142 mph), 249 km/h (155 mph)

originally commissioned its design, but dropped the idea during a political upheaval. However, the company contracted to build the car for Porsche at the NSU plant at Ingolstadt, near Stuttgart. The 924 still showed considerable evidence of its links with Volkswagen, however, because that was the way it had been designed.

The 1993 cc engine was essentially the unit Volkswagen developed from the Audi 100 powerplant for its range of LT commercial vehicles. The chief difference between the four-cylinder water-cooled Audi and Volkswagen units was in the single belt-driven overhead camshaft in place of the Audi's pushrod valve operation. Porsche improved the engine further by raising the compression ratio to 9.3:1 and by fitting Bosch K-Jetronic fuel injection. The result gave 125 bhp, which, although not startling, was good enough for a small car with low drag and especially miserly fuel consumption. This unit was mounted well back in the engine bay, and canted over to the right to allow a low bonnet line.

The transaxle, which used an Audi four-speed cluster, was connected to the power unit by a long torque tube, which also provided mountings for the gear linkage and exhaust system. The transaxle layout had the additional advantages of spreading the load in the event of an accident severely affecting either end of the car, and allowing itself to be mounted relatively softly because of the distance between front and rear mountings. The main disadvantage was that it infringed on luggage space, but this had to be accepted.

The torsion-bar and trailing-link rear suspension was very ingenious in its use of existing components from the Volkswagen range. It was basically the same as the 911's, except that it used parts from the Volkswagen Super Beetle! The driveshaft joints came from the Volkswagen utility vehicle. The Beetle's coil-spring struts were used at the front, and were linked to wishbone arms from the Volkswagen Scirocco. The steering was also Scirocco-based, and the brakes, disc front and drum rear, came from the Volkswagen K70 saloon. The use of drums at the back ensured that the 924 had a good handbrake at reasonable cost. To complete the puzzle, many of the smaller parts and interior fittings came from Volkswagen or Audi cars.

The introduction of the 928

The Porsche 928, introduced just over a year after the 924, was a different car altogether. It readily adopted the intended supercar image despite being more of a touring machine than an outright sports car. As such it complemented the 911 range rather than competed with it. Porsche chose a V8 engine because of the need to have a large power unit mounted in the front of the car. A low bonnet line was also necessary, but a flat-eight would have been too wide to give room for the front wheels to be swung round satisfactorily. The ideal compromise for a compact engine in terms of length, width and height was a 90-degree V8, so that was what Porsche designed. It was a brand-new all-alloy unit with considerably oversquare dimensions. A 95 mm bore and 78.9 mm stroke gave a capacity of 4474 cc with the bore dictating the other measurements. It was fixed at 95 mm to enable development to proceed in common with the 3-litre flat-six engines, which shared the same bore. Like the rest of Porsche designs for the 1970s and 1980s, it was intended to cope with any conceivable legislation, so it had a relatively low compression ratio of 8.5:1 to allow it to be run on lead-free petrol. Ironically, the cheaper 924 demanded higher-grade fuel because of its Audi ancestry! The new unit had a single overhead camshaft for each bank of cylinders in the interests of efficiency and to keep down the overall width and production costs. Twin overhead camshafts on each bank of a 90-degree V8 would have been impossibly wide, or the engine would have been too tall had the angle been narrowed. Hydraulic tappet adjusters were fitted to ease maintenance and promote quieter running, and camshafts were driven, in company with the water pump, by a cogged belt now that this form of propulsion had been proved reliable. The well-tried Bosch K-Jetronic fuel injection was used.

The clutch was fitted at the engine end of the torque tube in the same manner as on the 924, except that it was a twin-plate affair—which was very unusual at the time. This meant that the clutch was well able to absorb a lot of torque, but at the same time, by careful attention to its controls, was light in operation.

Although the 928 was fitted with a transaxle like that of the 924, it was fundamentally different in that the gearbox was ahead of the rear axle instead of behind it. The 924 had to compromise with its gearbox position because of availability of components, but no such compromise was necessary for the 928, so it had the gear clusters within the wheelbase for the best weight distribution. This also saved weight in that the propeller shaft and torque tube were shorter. In this way it was

more like the established transaxles used by Ferrari than those of Alfa Romeo or Lancia. Direct drive was chosen for top gear, with Porsche synchromesh of course, rather than indirect as before, to keep down noise. The gear change reverted to the old Zuffenhausen layout with first away to the left and back, and fourth and fifth gears in a direct plane. The reasoning behind this was that the V8 engine had so much torque that first gear would only rarely be needed, whereas it had to be used more often with the flat-six engine.

The Daimler-Benz three-speed automatic transmission was offered as an option from the start, in view of the car's touring appeal. Apart from being of German origin, the Daimler-Benz transmission was attractive to Porsche because it was of great mechanical efficiency, even if it was not quite as smooth as some American automatic gearboxes. This meant that the 928 automatic lost very little in performance compared to the manual edition. There was no question of the company building its own automatic gearbox; it was not big enough for that yet.

The 928 fitted with automatic transmission had the torque converter mounted at the gearbox end of the power train in the interests of efficiency, so a different body section was needed. The engine retained the same bell housing as on the manual version, but with only a ring gear for the starter to occupy it.

Anti-dive geometry was built into the front suspension and an ingenious layout called the Weissach system (after Porsche's development ground largely set up for the 914 near Stuttgart) was fitted at the rear. This was an unconventional trailing-arm system that actually 'steered' to produce toe-in as the car slowed down. Normally trailing-arm systems produce toe-out under such conditions, which leads to instability. And it was all done with rubber bushes!

Rubber, in the form of Pirelli P7 tyres, played a large part in the 928's development. These tyres really came into their own, with wonderful grip and handling, when the suspension's

A turbocharged version of the 924 was offered in 1979 and is identifiable by the intake grilles above the front bumper, the intake duct on the right of the bonnet and the alloy wheels.

characteristics were developed around them. It was the painstaking sort of process at which Porsche engineers excelled. The steering received equally dedicated attention. A Porsche rack-and-pinion system was developed around a special ZF pump, with the result that its power assistance decreased with speed to produce the best of both worlds: lots of power at low engine revolutions with plenty of feel as the power assistance decreased with the increase in the car's speed.

The 928's body was typically frugal in appearance, with no apparent bumpers. There are many people who appreciate this simplicity of line, but an equal number inquire, quite rightly, what would happen if something bumped into their precious Porsche? As ever, Porsche engineers had an answer: the 928's bumpers are hidden within the body and meet all stringent crash regulations. The actual body panels over them are one-piece plastic mouldings with 'elastic paint' which simply pop in and pop out with the bumpers!

It was the wheels that really set off the 928, though. They were beautifully sculptured from alloy to a futuristic pattern that complemented the simple lines of the body.

Automatic transmission became available for the 924 as an option nearly a year after its introduction, in October 1976. In addition, instrumentation was improved and rubbing strips added to the body sides, and soon after that, in January 1977, a special edition was produced. These cars had anti-roll bars front and rear, alloy wheels, and a leather-covered steering wheel, with Porsche-Martini factory racing colours of white, red and blue to commemorate the double world championship victories in 1976.

The 924 Turbo, 924 Carrera GT, 928S and 944

Far more dramatic changes were afoot for 1979. Porsche capitalized on experience with the 930 to turbocharge the 924 and give it a 928-style performance at roughly two-thirds the price, or half the price of a 930. Cost-consciousness aside, the 924 Turbo had more than a hotted-up engine: the running gear was changed in keeping with its power output, rising from 125 bhp to 170. A KKK turbocharger was tucked well down beside the engine, which had a special lower compression head and retained its Bosch K-Jetronic fuel injection. The bottom end of the engine was already strong enough to take the extra boost, but a new 911-style clutch had to be fitted with a stronger propeller shaft and torque tube, and revised gearing. The 924 Turbo was also given attractive new alloy wheels of 16 in diameter to take Pirelli's low-profile P7 tyres.

An additional benefit that sprang from using these bigger wheels was that larger brakes could be fitted, with discs at the back to cope with the extra performance. Dampers were uprated, and steering ratio reduced.

Functional changes were made to the body with new grilles, four air inlets in the nose, and a NACA duct (named after the style of low-drag air intake used on American space probes) on the right-hand front wing. A spoiler was fitted at the back and, altogether, the 924 Turbo turned out to be a much more sophisticated car than the standard model.

Later in the year a Carrera GT version of the 924 was produced to test potential customers' reactions to proposed production in the 1980s. This was a development of the 924 Turbo with much weight saved by the removal of interior trim and the use of plastic and aluminium panels in place of steel in the bodywork. Power was increased to 210 bhp and the body shape modified to improve aerodynamics; alloy was used for the wider 15 in wheels, 178 mm (7 in) wide at the front and 203 mm (8 in) at the rear. Firmer suspension, a limited-slip differential and larger, ventilated, competition brakes were fitted to this sporting machine.

Meanwhile, development continued on the 928 following its introduction early in 1977. The first major change was in the launching of the 928S model in 1979 to put this Porsche firmly in the world's supercar class with a performance almost as good as that of the 930. To achieve this, the 4.4-litre engine's liners were removed to give 4664 cc from a 97 mm bore. As a result the power was increased from 240 to 300 bhp. Outwardly, there was little to distinguish the two 928 Porsches other than the fitting of very restricted spoilers at the front and rear of the S type, and a new style of alloy wheel. The automatic gearbox was standard and the five-speed manual unit was optional as it was evident that the 928 was going to appeal mainly to the touring customers.

The culmination of all this development was revealed in the 944 introduced in September 1981. This was essentially a 924 Turbo with steel panels to give a lasting finish and a new 2.5-litre in-line four-cylinder engine based on one bank of the 928's. A prototype was impressive at Le Mans in 1981, finishing seventh. The 944 was expected to sell well in countries like the United States, where low-speed pulling power is more important than top speed, and the 924 Turbo in areas where taxation is severe on engines above 2 litres. The Carrera continued to be developed for competition as the 924GTR, with a 375 bhp turbo engine for circuit racing, and for rallying as the Carrera GTS with 280 bhp and revised suspension, with all-alloy

The Porsche 928S, introduced in 1979, with 4664 cc engine and distinctive road wheels and rear spoiler. The increase in capacity was achieved by increasing the bore size by 2 mm and the engine also boasted improved breathing, 10:1 compression ratio and twin exhaust pipes.

bodywork. Further developments included anti-lock braking, a phase two 928S in 1983, and a 924 turbo diesel engine for ultimate economy and performance.

Improvements in the 944 for 1985 include wider wheels and re-styled dashboard, and there is talk of a 924 replacement in 1986.

With Porsche having expanded from a one-model to a four-model company in the 1980s, the Stuttgart firm is doing better than at any time in its history. The old professor would indeed have been proud of the cars that today bear his name.

BELOW *Introduced for 1982, the 944 has a 2479 cc four-cylinder overhead camshaft engine of Porsche design. The body was based on the 924 and 924 turbo.*

BOTTOM *The evergreen 911 is now available in cabriolet form, a long-established Porsche tradition.*

BELOW RIGHT *The Porsche 959 is a four-wheel-drive model for Group B racing. The engine is a 2.8-litre air-cooled flat-six with water-cooled cylinder heads. Top speed is 299 km/h (186 mph).*

RIGHT INSET *Four-wheel-drive Porsches made an impact in the 1984 Paris–Dakar rally.*

Gruppe B
177
Rothmans
PORSCHE

VOLKSWAGEN

The distinctive air-cooled, rear-engined car that Adolf Hitler initiated and Ferdinand Porsche designed was completed by 1938, but this *Volkswagen*, or People's Car, never went into production because of the outbreak of the Second World War. It was not until 1945 that output began, under the auspices of the British army, but by 1949 the Volkswagen works was back in German hands. The car, soon to be named the Beetle, was skilfully improved and refined under the direction of Heinz Nordhoff so that in 1973 it overtook the Model T Ford as the most popular car in the history of the automobile. It is still in production, with more than 20 million built, and made by VW's overseas subsidiaries. However, it was in 1974, with the arrival of the Golf, that the ubiquitous Beetle was finally replaced as Volkswagen's best-selling model. With a new generation of front-wheel-drive cars now being produced, the Wolfsburg-based company, today one of Europe's largest automobile manufacturers, can look forward with confidence to the 21st century.

WOB·SP 39

Although Volkswagen came to fruition in the post-war world, the firm is, in truth, a child of the 1930s; for the company's extraordinary growth—certainly for the first 16 years of its life—was based on just one model, the designs of which were completed in 1938. Yet the air-cooled, rear-engined Beetle that today looks and sounds like no other is the most popular model in the history of the motor car with over 20 million examples built.

Volkswagen eventually accomplished the difficult task of finding the right model to replace this automotive phenomenon. It was not until 1974 that the front-wheel-drive transverse-engine Golf, which had nothing in common with its distinguished predecessor other than its wheelbase, finally made the breakthrough that Volkswagen, and Germany, were waiting for. Enriched by the take-over of Audi in 1965, VW has gone on to produce a new generation of models, yet the archaic Beetle continues to be built in Brazil and Mexico by the firm's overseas subsidiaries.

The Volkswagen story starts not in northern Germany at the Wolfsburg headquarters, but far away in the south at Stuttgart, in pre-war days the capital of Germany's motor industry. It was for this reason that 55-year-old Ferdinand Porsche had established, in December 1930, a design office there to service the needs of the motor manufacturers. At this time Porsche was one of Germany's best known car designers, yet, ironically, he was Austrian—born in 1875 into the final flickering years of the old Austro-Hungarian empire. The third son of a tinsmith from the village of Maffersdorf, Porsche found a natural affinity with metals and mechanics, though it was the new power of electricity that first captured his imagination. He combined these two commitments in his first car, the Lohner Porsche of 1900, with its front wheels driven by hub-mounted electric motors.

It was late in 1905 that Porsche became technical director of Austro-Daimler where his most famous model was the 1910 5.6-litre Prince Henry. While at Wiener-Neustadt he met Karl Rabe, a Czech-German draughtsman, and mathematician Josef Mickl, both of whom were to play important roles in the creation of the Volkswagen. Porsche remained at Austro-Daimler for 18 years and left in 1923 after a stormy board meeting.

Ferdinand Porsche was not without a job for long and by April 1923 he had moved to Germany and the Stuttgart-based Daimler company, though characteristically he began work before his contracted starting date. He was to remain at Daimler-Benz, as the company became following its merger with Benz in 1926, until 1928 when he departed following another boardroom disagreement. However, at the beginning of 1929 he was back in his native Austria as technical director of the Steyr company. It was there that he designed the 2.1-litre six-cylinder Type 30, while the 5.3-litre eight-cylinder Austria was a prestigious model intended for announcement at the 1929 Paris Salon.

Cruelly this year's event coincided with the Wall Street stock market crash and one of the first casualties was Steyr's bankers, the Austrian Bodenkreditanstalt, so its industrial assets were taken over by the Kreditstalt Am Hof bank which, ironically, had a controlling interest in Austro-Daimler, Porsche's old enemies. This financial liaison was to lead to the creation of Steyr-Daimler-Puch in 1935, the last two firms having joined forces in 1928.

Realizing that he would again be up against his former adversaries, Porsche resigned from Steyr in 1930 and found himself again without a job. Although he had plenty of offers of work, his reputation as a champion of workers' rights (he always arrived at work at the same time as they did, ahead of his co-directors) made firms reluctant to grant him managerial status. So his only option was to enter business on his own account and offer his design services to firms within the motor industry. Financial support came from Adolf Rosenberger, a businessman/racing driver whom he had known during his Daimler-Benz days. Porsche realized that his design bureau would have to be within easy reach of the very heart of the motor industry and that meant Stuttgart and a trip back to Germany. His team would have to be a small one, exclusively Austrian and mostly recruited from Steyr. There he had met up again with Karl Rabe, by then the firm's chief engineer, who left the Austrian company to become Porsche's 'right hand'. Then there was aero-engine designer Josef Kales, engineer Karl Fröhlich who was a gearbox expert, and axle and steering specialist Josef Zahradnik. Yet another old associate of Porsche, mathematician Josef Mickl, joined the team which was completed by his son Ferry, then 21 years old.

Ferdinand Porsche (1875–1951), father of the Volkswagen, the world's most popular car.

Difficult times

Offices were established at 24 Kronenstrasse, Stuttgart, but Porsche could not have chosen a worse time to set up in business. Germany, which had attracted much American capital in the 1920s, suffered a terrible financial collapse in the wake of the Wall Street Crash and by 1931 four and a half million Germans were unemployed. However, Rosenberger managed to obtain a commission from the Wanderer company and, although it was the firm's first assignment, the design was diplomatically titled Type 7 in the Porsche design register. Next followed a 3.5-litre straight-eight model for the same firm (Type 8), although it was stillborn following the creation, in 1932, of Auto Union, of which Wanderer was a part, which allocated large-car production to Horch. The big Wanderer does have a significant role in the Volkswagen story, however, because of its two-door saloon body with distinctive sloping back and integral headlamps. The design was the work of former Daimler-Benz stylist Erwin Komenda, who had recently been recruited to Porsche's Kronenstrasse team.

But one bright spot in an otherwise gloomy 1931 was Porsche being granted, that August, a patent for 'Spring Suspension of Independent Car Wheels, especially for Motor Vehicles'. This was the now famous, simple but ingenious torsion-bar suspension system, and Porsche's income was gradually augmented in the 1930s as manufacturers began to take up the idea.

Type 10 in Porsche's design register was for a swing-axle suspension system for Horch, completed in April 1931, but then there were no more orders. Although the torsion-bar work absorbed a certain amount of time, Porsche realized that he would have to initiate a project to keep the talented Austrian engineers occupied. So in September 1931 he began talks with Karl Rabe with a view to designing a small car, purely as a speculative venture and well suited to those austere times. The assignment was given the type number 12 and drawings were completed by the end of the year.

It was soon after work had begun on the project that Porsche had a customer in the shape of Dr Fritz Neumeyer of motorcycle manufacturers Zundapp. He was keen to diversify into cars but insisted that the vehicle be fitted with a rear-mounted water-cooled 1200 cc five-cylinder radial engine. Porsche was hardly in a position to argue and the cars—there were three built—were completed at Zundapp's works in the spring of 1932. As this concept represents the starting point of the Volkswagen project, its design is of considerable interest and relevance to the Beetle story.

The Type 12 was built up around a backbone chassis with all independent suspension: a transverse leaf front and swing axle rear, inspired by the 1923 Type 11 Tatra. Zundapp's prototype had a body styled by Erwin Komenda and was a scaled-down version of that used on the big Type 8 Wanderer saloon, which by this time Porsche was using as his personal transport. The rear-mounted power unit meant that louvres were introduced behind the side windows and the front, which of course lacked a radiator, had a rather Tatra-like appearance. It also displayed a degree of aerodynamic awareness with its sloping windscreen, integral headlamps and spatted rear wheels. This scientific discipline was already well established in Germany and had its origins in Zeppelin airship technology.

Therefore, although the Zundapp prototype, representing as it does the starting point for the Volkswagen project, might appear unusual to British or American eyes, it can be seen as an accurate representation of central European car design of its day. However, the Type 12 was not a success, largely because its unusual rear-mounted engine overheated, so Neumeyer decided not to proceed with the idea but to concentrate on the business that he knew best: that of motorcycle production.

Origin of the Beetle's shape: 1932 3.5-litre Type 8 Wanderer prototype, designed by the Porsche Bureau; used daily by Porsche.

Komenda's Wanderer bodywork was scaled down for the 1932 Type 12 Zundapp with rear-mounted 1.2-litre five-cylinder engine.

The 1933 Type 32 for NSU outside Porsche's offices at 24 Kronenstrasse, Stuttgart. This is one of two fabric-bodied examples.

Nineteen thirty-two turned out to be worse for Porsche than the previous year, but matters improved in 1933 when the bureau received a visit from Baron Fritz von Falkenhayn, who was head of NSU—Germany's largest motorcycle manufacturer. The firm had produced cars between 1905 and 1931 but had given up automobile production to concentrate on two-wheelers, and Fiat took over its automobile manufacturing facility at Heilbronn. Von Falkenhayn was thinking in terms of a cheap car and Porsche came up with a similar concept to the aborted Zundapp prototype, though it was a rather larger vehicle of 1.5 rather than 1.2 litres. The assignment was given the Porsche Type 32 number and work on the project began in August 1933, with the drawings completed by December. Again three examples were built and Komenda was once more responsible for the styling. The principal difference between these and the earlier Type 12 was that the front of the car doubled as a boot lid that hinged at the bulkhead. Again a backbone chassis was employed although on this occasion the suspension medium was Porsche's own patented torsion bars. This time the bureau was responsible for the vehicle's engine with Josef Kales designing a 1.5-litre air-cooled four-cylinder horizontally opposed engine (or *boxermotor* as it is called in Germany). But again the vehicle never went into production because the Type 32's creation came to the attention of Fiat, who reminded NSU of their contractual obligations.

ABOVE *A sketch by Adolf Hitler showing improvements that he wanted to make to the front of the Beetle which were subsequently adopted.*

BELOW *Porsche Bureau drawing of the 1935 V3 prototype series. Note bonnet-mounted headlights and cut-off boot lid.*

The rise of Hitler

Nineteen thirty-three, however, was to prove a momentous year for Germany because, on 30 January, Adolf Hitler was elected the country's chancellor. It was to pave the way to a Nazi dictatorship and, with the the death of the aged Marshal Hindenburg the following year, Hitler was proclaimed Führer (leader) of the Third Reich. He had come to office determined that Germany should once again become a world power and was also intent on producing a network of purpose-built motor roads called *Autobahnen*. But, significantly, he was also determined that the government should initiate the manufacture of a *Volkswagen* or 'People's Car' for use on the new highways. These ideas had been exercizing Hitler's thoughts for at least ten years, and to see how this came about we must briefly retrace our steps to Braunau, a small town on the Austro/Bavarian border.

It was there, in 1889, that Hitler, the son of a customs official, was born. He attended various schools and finally left the High School at Steyr at the age of 16. Always a voracious reader, his choice of books embraced the fields of art, architecture, military history and, significantly, technology. After serving with the German infantry in the First World War, Hitler joined the small right-wing German Workers Party in Munich. It was re-named the National Socialist German Workers or Nazi, party, which spoke out against the recently signed Treaty of Versailles and communism as well as embracing a virulent anti-Semitism which was a deep-rooted Hitlerian prejudice. As ever, Hitler had read widely to reinforce this obsession, and one of the books he had devoured on the subject was titled *The International Jew*, published under the name of Henry Ford. At this time Ford's Model T was the most famous and popular car in production. Indeed it was estimated that in 1920 every other car in the world was one of these spidery, tough Fords.

In 1923 Hitler was involved in an abortive *putsch* against the Weimar government and the Munich authorities sentenced him to five years' imprisonment, later commuted to one year. While incarcerated in Landsberg castle, about 80 km (50 miles) west of Munich, Hitler read Henry Ford's *My Life and Work*, a ghosted autobiography which told the story of the conception, manufacture and success of the Model T. During a visit in early 1924 from Hans Frank, a young Munich lawyer, Hitler informed him of a way he had conceived of dealing with the nation's unemployed. They would be put to work building a network of roads specially designed for the needs of the motor car. Then the government would initiate the mass production of a small car which would be cheap enough to be bought by the man in the street. The inspiration for the latter was clearly Ford's Model T, while the idea for the motor road would have come from the Italian *autostrade*.

Hitler completed his prison sentence at the end of 1924 and maintained his interest in cars (although he never drove himself), read motoring magazines, and attended race meetings and hill climbs. However, his political ambitions only came to fruition with the arrival of the economic blizzard that swept across Germany between 1929 and 1933. Immediately after coming to power in 1933, at his first cabinet meeting, Hitler raised the matter of the *Autobahnen*. The scheme was announced in February 1933 and the first section to be built

Looking very Beetle-like, the 1933 Type 32 Porsche project for NSU. A four-cylinder air-cooled boxermotor *was employed.*

was between Frankfurt and Mannheim, with Hitler digging the first ceremonial shovelful of earth in September. Work continued for close on a decade and by 1943 there were 3827 km (2380 miles) of *Autobahnen* in Germany.

The next item on Hitler's agenda was his idea for a People's Car. He had already had a meeting with Ferdinand Porsche on the subject of the Auto Union racing car (see Audi section, page 22), and in the autumn of 1933 Porsche met him at Berlin's Hotel Kaiserhof to discuss the project. The designer found himself constrained by a number of inviolate parameters relating to the design. Hitler was insistent that the car should have a top speed of 100 km/h (62 mph), a fuel consumption of seven litres per 100 km (about 42 mpg) and should be able to carry two adults and three children. Not only this, he was emphatic that the car be air-cooled and, above all, should cost no more than RM (Reichsmarks) 1000 (£86).

Although Porsche's first reaction was to turn the idea down, he nevertheless accepted the commission using the aborted NSU Type 32 as his starting point. The Volkswagen project was allotted the Type 60 number in Porsche's design register and the first drawing was dated 17 April 1934. The following month Hitler had the opportunity of commenting on the first sketches but he disliked the Type 32-inspired front end and sketched a new one which was subsequently adopted. It was on this, or a later occasion that he drew a comparison between the Volkswagen and a beetle when he commented: 'It should look like a beetle, you've only got to look to nature to find out what streamlining is.'

Porsche signed a contract for the Type 60's development in June 1934, when the car's price was fixed at RM 990 (£85). The project was placed in the hands of the German Automobile Industry Association and at the Berlin motor show, held in February 1935, Hitler announced: 'The first model will be finally tested by the middle of this year.' This was far from the truth because Porsche was experiencing great difficulties with the design. The backbone chassis (originally with a wooden floor, but it subsequently evolved into a proper metal platform), torsion bar suspension and general body profile were resolved relatively quickly. The problem lay with designing a cheap, satisfactory power unit. Porsche had discounted the 1.5-litre engine from the Type 32 on the grounds of weight, cost and fuel consumption.

He then concentrated on trying to evolve a simple air-cooled engine. The first (Type A) was a vertical four with each set of pistons rising and falling with its neighbour; but its crankshaft broke. Then there was a sleeve valve two-cylinder *boxermotor* (Type C), while the D Motor had a similar layout with conventional overhead valves; but this proved to be excessively noisy. However, at least one example was built and fitted to a car.

The design that was standardized came from a new recruit to the Porsche bureau. Franz Xavier Reimspiess, a 33-year-old Austrian, had joined the team in September 1934 and, like some of his colleagues, had previously worked for Austro-Daimler. It was not long before he had convinced Porsche of the wisdom of adopting a four- rather than a two-cylinder engine for the Type 60. Within 48 hours he had come up with a sketch of a four-cylinder *boxermotor* which was immediately costed by estimator Oswald Kux and found to be appreciably simpler than the engines then under development. Designated the E Motor, the 'over-square' four, initially of 984 cc, has since gone on to power over 20 million Volkswagens. Reimspiess later designed the famous VW monogram, although initially it was embodied in the German Labour Front's cog wheel motif—the GLF later took the project over.

LEFT *One of the VW 30 prototypes of 1937 built by Daimler-Benz and exhaustively tested by the SS after the German government had effectively taken over the Type 60 project.*

BELOW *'It should look like a beetle . . .' said Hitler, and the VW 30 prototypes did. These examples are shown during the rigorous test schedule.*

Two prototypes had been built in the double garage of Porsche's home at 48–50 Feuerbacherweg, Stuttgart, because there were no workshop facilities at Kronenstrasse. These 1935 cars were joined by three further experimental ones in 1936 and this trio, powered by Reimspiess's new engine, was handed over to the German Automobile Manufacturers Association for a punishing 30,000 km (18,000 mile) test programme. This meant covering 750 km (466 miles) every day, with the varied route including parts of the Black Forest, the Alps and a long stretch of the new *Autobahn* between Stuttgart and Bad Neuheim. All three cars were fitted with Kienzle tachographs to record their average and maximum speeds and observers were present from the Berlin and Stuttgart technical institutes. This demanding schedule soon revealed some shortcomings in the design. The most serious occurred when the cast iron crankshafts, adopted on cost grounds, continually fractured. The originals cast by Sulzer broke and were then replaced by harder stronger ones from Krupp; but the same fate befell them. It was then decided to dispense with the feature, and conventional forged crankshafts were ordered from Daimler-Benz. Less seriously, some gear levers broke and there were problems with electric fuel pumps, so a mechanical one was later standardized.

The state takes over

In January 1937 the Manufacturers Association issued a report which generally favoured the Volkswagen design, although it was felt that the car could not be manufactured for the projected RM 990. The association was, however, quite prepared to take the concept over. Hitler had other ideas, and from May 1937 the Volkswagen became a state-funded project. It became the responsibility of the German Labour Front, a state organization which took the place of the abolished trade unions. The Front immediately made available RM 500,000 (£42,918) for the project and Daimler-Benz was commissioned to produce a further batch of 30 cars. With state participation now assured, the second series of tests—which followed a similar route to the first—were undertaken by members of the SS who were barracked at nearby Kornwestheim.

Once these had been successfully completed, Erwin Komenda finally refined and simplified the car's styling. On cost grounds a rear window had not been included in the original design but this was incorporated in a mock-up undertaken by the Reutter coachbuilding firm in the winter of 1937/8. Then a divided window was introduced and, with the output of the engine's cooling fan boosted, the number and size of louvres were reduced and located below the new window. At the front a one-piece boot cover, rather like the one introduced on the Type 32, was installed after experiments had been undertaken with shortened lids. Also, for the first time, small running boards were featured. Here, at last, was the Volkswagen in its completed form, which would have been easily identifiable today. Yet another batch of 44 cars produced to this final specification was ordered from Daimler-Benz, and at the same time the engine's capacity was increased by 1 cc to 985 cc.

With the design at last finalized, by 1938 the location of the car's manufacturing facility had also been agreed. As most of the German car industry was located in the south of the country this seemed the logical place for the Volkswagen factory, but Berlin thought otherwise. Aware of the fact that Henry Ford built his factories close to the sea, canals or rivers to give ease of access for materials and exports, Hitler was no doubt responsible for choosing a site on the banks of the Mitteland Canal (which joins the River Rhine to the Elbe) in the north of Germany near the village of Fallersleben, about 80 km (50 miles) east of Hanover. As the intention was to ape the giants of Detroit, Porsche and a small entourage had visited America in 1936 and 1937 to study production techniques and to woo back skilled German personnel who had emigrated to the New World. In addition, orders for machine tools and manfacturing equipment were placed with American companies.

The KdF-Wagen

In May 1938 Adolf Hitler ceremonially laid the foundation stone at the factory site where examples of the pre-production prototypes had been put on display. This was when he announced that the new car was to be called, much to Porsche's horror, the KdF-Wagen. KdF stood for *Kraft durch Freude* (Strength through Joy) which was the Labour Front's leisure section. Not only this but the planned town to house the factory's workers was to be named *Stadt des KdF-Wagens* (Town of the Strength through Joy Cars).

Just over two months later, in August 1938, Labour Front

BELOW *Probably the first of the 1935 V3 prototypes, pictured in the garden of Porsche's Stuttgart house; it was built in the double garage there.*

RIGHT *The VW's shape resolved on this 1938 VW 38 with split rear window and running boards. It is shown at the 1938 works foundation-stone laying.*

chief Robert Ley announced the unique method by which the public could acquire one of the new, rigorously tested cars. The KdF could only be bought on a hire purchase system but the car would be sold when the final—rather than the first—payment had been made. A savings book would be issued on receipt of a RM 1 fee and this would be considered the equivalent of placing an order for a car. The basic saloon would cost the projected RM 990 (£85), while a version with a roll-back sun roof would cost RM 60 (£5) more. There was only one colour scheme on offer: blue-grey. In addition there would be a RM 200 (£17) fee to cover two years' third party and part comprehensive insurance. The idea was that there would be no agents or middlemen, and customers would have to travel to the factory to collect their cars. However, if this was not possible there would be an additional RM 50 (£4) delivery charge. By the end of 1938 the Labour Front had received no less than 169,741 applications, a figure that was eventually to rise to 336,668.

With work progressing on the KdF-Wagen factory, the first stage of which was completed in the spring of 1939, in Stuttgart Porsche was pressing ahead with an exciting sports version of the design. By this time he had more room and workshop facilities following a move to the Zuffenhausen area of the city in 1938. It was in late 1937 that Porsche raised the matter of producing a competition version of the KdF-Wagen with the Labour Front, who initially turned the idea down as not being quite in the spirit of a utilitarian People's Car. So the bureau pushed ahead with the design of a coupé with a mid-positioned water-cooled V10 engine which incorporated no KdF-Wagen parts. Then the authorities had a change of heart and recognized that a sports design based on the new car would provide good publicity. Porsche was given the go-ahead to proceed with the concept with a view to running the car in the projected Berlin-Rome-Berlin road race destined for September 1939.

Three examples of this Type 64 were built, closely following KdF-Wagen chassis and engine layout. The power unit, however, was boosted from 22 to 50 bhp with larger valves, twin carburettors and higher compression ratio. Although the race was cancelled because of the outbreak of the Second World War, Porsche had one for his personal transport and used it on those deserted wartime *Autobahnen*. More significantly, the Type 64 represented the first stirrings of the Porsche marque destined to blossom in the post-war years as the 356 model of 1949.

Plans to put the KdF-Wagen into production at the end of 1939 were completely blown off course by the Führer's decision to invade Poland on 1 September. Two days later Britain and France, honouring their treaty obligations, declared war on Germany and the Second World War had begun. The intention had been to produce 150,000 KdF-Wagens in

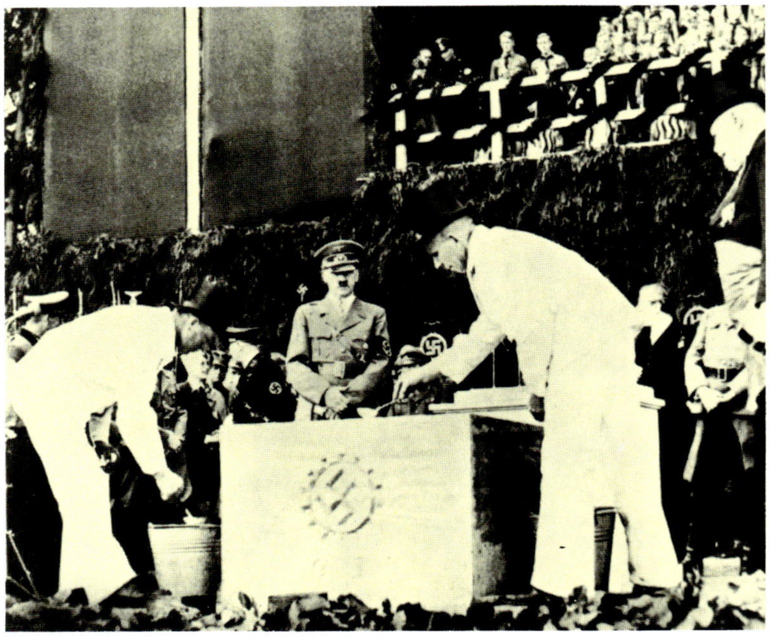

ABOVE *Adolf Hitler officiates at the foundation-stone laying of the Volkswagen factory held on 26 May 1938, when he announced the VW would be known as the KdF-Wagen (Strength through Joy car). It was then that Hitler was driven in an example to nearby Fallersleben railway station by young Ferry Porsche.*

LEFT *The first stirrings of the post-war Porsche marque can be seen in the Type 64 version of the KdF-Wagen built for the aborted 1939 Berlin–Rome–Berlin race. Only three were made: one was used by Porsche, another by Jacob Werlin, Hitler's motoring adviser, and the third by Bodo Lafferentz, who saw the Beetle into production.*

1940, with the figure rising to 1.5 million by 1943. This would have meant that the KdF-Stadt plant would have become Europe's largest car factory by far, with an output challenging the giants of the American motor industry. Nevertheless, the costly body dies had been delivered to the plant and, on 15 August 1940, the first KdF-Wagen left the production line. At this stage the Porsche Type 60 designation was dispensed with and the car was retitled the VW Type 1. A few cars were manufactured up until 1944, but wartime output totalled a mere 640 examples. They were mostly distributed among the higher echelons of the Nazi party, from Hitler downwards.

Wartime derivative

Despite this, in February 1940, a vehicle far more suited to the state of war, but based on the KdF-Wagen chassis, entered production. The Kübelwagen (or bucket car, named after its seats) had its origins back in 1934 when the German Automobile Manufacturers Association, in a document ostensibly relating to the Type 60's carrying capacity, added as a postscript that it should have sufficient room for three men, a machine gun and ammunition... In 1937 a spare VW 30 chassis was crudely modified to take three seats and a machine gun. The following year a more refined version with canvas doors was undergoing tests in the Stuttgart area. This was considerably re-thought in 1939 and a far more angular product with steel bodywork was constructed. A number of these Type 62s were built and saw action in Poland, the first theatre of war. It was found that the Kübel's lowest speed was 8 km/h (5 mph)—about twice the desired one which was geared to

ABOVE *One of the few surviving examples of the VW 38 series (chassis number 3803), owned by Volkswagen and used by Ferdinand Porsche until 1945.*

BELOW *The Kübelwagen, the military version of the KdF-Wagen, introduced in 1940 and manufactured throughout the war years.*

ABOVE *The Kübelwagen was largely the work of Ferdinand Porsche's son Ferry. High ground-clearance was made possible by the use of reduction gearing.*

LEFT *A few* Holzbrenner *(wood-burning) KdF-Wagens were made during the war to counter petrol shortages.*

the pace of a soldier walking with a full pack. This shortcoming was cleverly remedied by a solution from Porsche which allowed them to retain the KdF-Wagen's gearbox intact by introducing reduction gears in the rear hubs, while the front suspension was also modified by lowering the position of the stub axle. This reduced the Kübel's speed to an acceptable pace and also raised the ground clearance.

The extension of the war to North Africa saw the air-cooled Kübelwagens performing well there, and for the same reasons coping with the sub-zero temperatures of the Russian front. In the former instance Rommel, as head of the Afrika Korps, ordered 500 Kübelwagens specially modified for desert conditions with a protected ignition system and a larger than standard air filter. But, due to an administrative error, the consignment was sent to Russia and Rommel had to content himself with the standard product. These were fitted with smooth tyres of the type used on aircraft undercarriages which helped the Kübels to perform well in the North African sands. Production was relatively modest, however, with output around the 10,000-a-year mark and most were built in 1944. In all, 50,435 Kübelwagens were made during hostilities which is modest compared with the production of the Jeep, the Allied equivalent, which was mass manufactured in huge quantities totalling 639,245. Derivatives of the Kübelwagen followed, including the amphibious Schwimmwagen which was produced in relatively small numbers.

In addition to KdF-Wagen-related production, the VW factory produced wings and fuselages for the Junkers Ju 88 bomber along with spares for BMW aero engines. Large quantities of stoves for troops bogged down in the Russian winter were also manufactured. In March 1943 the works began production of a pilotless aircraft with Volkswagenwerk receiving about £125 for every V1 it produced, although a projected monthly target of 500 examples was never reached.

However, it was due to Allied awareness of the aircraft contracts being undertaken that, on 8 April 1944, the American Eighth Air Force undertook the first of six bombing raids on the factory. The massive plant was particularly vulnerable to attack, being totally exposed and easily pinpointed on the banks of the Mitteland Canal. As a result of these raids over three quarters of the works was completely destroyed.

It was on 10 April 1945 that the Allies reached the nearby village of Fallersleben but the troops did not enter KdF-Stadt because it was not marked on their maps. However, a German army chaplain made an appeal to the US forces and later a few American soldiers entered the town; despite this the factory fell within the British military zone. The plant was in ruins and production was halted. Could anything be salvaged from the chaos?

VOLKSWAGEN REBORN

Germany's unconditional surrender was signed on 7 May 1945 and later that month KdF-Stadt's British-nominated town council changed the community's name, with its Nazi taint, to Wolfsburg, taken from the nearby 14th-century castle. (Ironically the Nazis had contemplated calling the town Wolfsburg, as Hitler occasionally used Wolf as a pseudonym.) Consequently Volkswagenwerk became for a time the Wolfsburg Motor Works. It was in July that the 30 Workshop Control Unit of the Royal and Mechanical Engineers was based at the plant and, in August, Major Ivan Hirst arrived to take charge of the factory, his immediate superior being Minden-based Colonel Charles Radclyffe.

Production, incredibly, had started up in June when 138 Kübelwagens were assembled from spare parts, and for a time bodies in desert khaki continued to arrive by train at Wolfsburg from the Ambi-Budd body plant in Berlin. The other vehicle to be built in reasonable numbers was the Type 51 (Porsche Type 82E) which combined the KdF-Wagen body with the Kübelwagen chassis, and by the end of the year 703 had been produced, compared with a total of 522 Kübels built in 1945.

As transport was at an enormous premium in a devastated post-war Germany, the factory was patched up and Ivan Hirst received an important order for 10,000 Volkswagen saloons for the British army. Then there were 50 blue-painted examples for the RAF, while the Russians also ordered a batch coloured, appropriately, maroon. In 1946 output began to rise and in March the 1000-vehicle-a-month barrier was broken for the first time. Kübelwagen output had all but ceased and it was the Volkswagen saloon that moved centre stage. Of the 7787 vehicles produced at the works during 1946, 7677 were saloons.

The real risk to the plant, however, was that it might be taken as reparations booty. The French had even contemplated moving the whole manufacturing facility to France, but opposition from their own industry put paid to the idea. Early in 1947 Henry Ford II visited Wolfsburg, drove a Volkswagen and even looked into the possibility of buying the plant. However, the complex legal ramifications relating to the firm's ownership were a sufficient deterrent for Ford to drop the idea. Also the American industry favoured cars with large, water-cooled front-mounted engines and regular body changes; the Beetle broke virtually every rule of that particular design philosophy.

As the British were running Volkswagenwerk at the time, it was inevitable that they would also take a close look at the design. During 1945 the works had been visited by a team from the Society of Motor Manufacturers and Traders who were investigating the activities of the German motor industry during hostilities. They were impressed by what they saw at Wolfsburg, so the Beetle became the subject of a separate report published in 1946, by the British Intelligence Objectives Sub-Committee. During the war, in 1943, the British Humber company had been given a Kübelwagen for evaluation and analysis; it had been captured in North Africa having run out of petrol following Rommel's retreat from El Alamein. The Kübel was completely dismantled and about 45 kg (100 lb) of sand was removed from the interior in the process! However, the 64-page document completely failed to appreciate the ingenuity and sophistication of the Porsche design and one of its particular paragraphs has echoed down the years. It reads: 'We do not consider that the design represents any special brilliance, apart from certain detail points, and it is suggested that it is not to be regarded as an example of a first class modern design to be copied by the British industry.' Inevitably history has had the last word. Humber, along with the rest of the Rootes Group, have ceased to exist, while Volkswagen has grown to become one of Europe's largest car manufacturers and the Beetle the most popular model in automobile history.

RIGHT *Major Ivan Hirst of the Royal Electrical and Mechanical Engineers who, in the early post-war years, did so much to get the Volkswagen into production.*

BELOW *An amphibious version of the KdF-Wagen, the Schwimmwagen, was produced from 1942. Only 14,283 were built.*

But the report set a tone that was to be perpetuated in the 1946 appraisal, which incorporated a reprint of the Humber Kübelwagen analysis. The evaluation was again undertaken by Rootes, a firm not renowned for its design innovation, but this time their engineers had the opportunity of studying a Volkswagen car, finished in army green livery, which had reached them early in 1946. Having been given the chance of closely examining it they did concede that, 'from the body engineering point of view, the design of this vehicle is exceptionally good and shows a great advance on previous construction methods'. However, the air-cooled engine came in for less favourable comment and, when the Volkswagen was road tested against a cart-sprung Hillman Minx Mark III with side-valve, water-cooled, front-mounted engine, the latter was found to be a good 10 km/h (6 mph) faster than the German car, covering the timed quarter mile at 98.9 km/h (61.5 mph). The resulting report was made available to the British motor manufacturers but there is little evidence to suggest that any of its findings was taken up.

It was in the autumn of 1947 that Major Hirst, along with his immediate superior Colonel Radclyffe, appointed a German to take over the running of the Volkswagen factory. It was an appointment of crucial significance to the firm's future, for Heinz Nordhoff was supremely well qualified for the task. He was the third of a trio of personalities who dominate the Volkswagen story; Adolf Hitler, who initiated the project,

VOLKSWAGEN BEETLE 1131 cc
1943–53

ENGINE	
No. of cylinders	4
Bore/stroke mm	75 × 64
Displacement cc	1131
Valve operation	Pushrod
Compression ratio	5.8:1
Induction	Single carburettor
BHP	25 at 3300 rpm
Transmission	Four-speed

CHASSIS	
Frame	Platform
Wheelbase mm	2400
Track—front mm	1295
Track—rear mm	1250
Suspension—front	Independent, trailing arm and torsion bar
Suspension—rear	Independent, swing axle and torsion bar
Brakes	Mechanical drum to 1950, thereafter hydraulic

PERFORMANCE	
Maximum speed	99 km/h (62 mph)

ABOVE *A 1947 Beetle under evaluation by the British Ministry of Supply. The nipple-type hub caps were discontinued at the end of the year, while the horn was relegated beneath the front wing in 1949.*

BELOW *The two-seater factory-approved Hebmüller Cabriolet, introduced in 1949, was produced until 1953. Offered in dual colours, black and ivory was the most popular option.*

Ferdinand Porsche who masterminded its design, and Nordhoff who turned the dream into a reality and created a crucial industrial cog in the mechanism of the German Federal Republic, which was established in 1948.

Born in 1899, Nordhoff qualified from the Berlin Charlottenburg technical university with a degree in mechanical engineering in 1927 and two years later joined Opel. In the 1930s he visited America, as Opel had been absorbed by General Motors in 1929. The outbreak of the Second World War had seen Nordhoff take over the running of Opel's Brandenburg factory—Europe's largest lorry plant. Nordhoff became Volkswagen's general manager on 1 January 1948 although it was not until September 1949 that Britain's military control came to an end. The ownership of the firm and factory was transferred to the German Federal Republic, who ceded it to the State of Lower Saxony where Wolfsburg is located.

Once Nordhoff was in control he took two decisions which were to ensure the Beetle's outstanding success. His first was to pursue, just as Henry Ford had done with his famous Model T, a one-model policy. Secondly, he decided not to change the car's appearance but to refine it so that it would evolve organically from the inside outwards. As he later remarked: 'Professor Porsche had worked something into it that made this diamond very much worth our while polishing.'

By 1949 Volkswagen was by far and away Germany's largest manufacturer with 45 per cent of the country's total output and Nordhoff's priorities were twofold. He had to improve the car's quality and, above all, produce an export model. This was introduced in July 1949, along with a four-seater cabriolet by the Karmann company of Osnabrück that was produced right up until 1980 and, indeed, outlasted the German-built saloon by two years. There was an open two-seater by Hebmüller of Wülfrath, but this lasted only until 1953.

ABOVE *A Standard Beetle (the Export cars are distinguished by chrome plate) of 1952. Note split rear window, discontinued in 1953, while an optional horn ring can just be seen.*

RIGHT *Heinz Nordhoff (1899–1968), architect of Volkswagen's astounding post-war success.*

The Beetle abroad

Even when Porsche had the Volkswagen under development, during the days of the Third Reich, it had been intended to market an export version. Type 66 in the bureau design register was for a right-hand-drive example, although it is unlikely that any were built. Exports began unofficially with British and American ex-servicemen bringing Beetles back with them from Germany. In August 1947, a Dutchman, Ben Pon, signed a contract with the factory to become Volkswagen's first overseas agent. He sold the cars in his native Holland and in January 1949, at Nordhoff's bidding, he took a Volkswagen to America to try to generate some enthusiasm there for the model. But he was unable to raise much interest so he sold his one car for $950 and headed for home. Nordhoff, himself no stranger to the New World, made the same trip but took photographs with him rather than a car, and Max Hoffmann's New York agency agreed to represent VW. However, despite this, only 601 Beetles were registered in the United States in 1952. Hoffmann's franchise was cancelled in late 1953 and two years later, in 1955, Volkswagen of America was established. That year 32,662 Beetles were sold but, close on a decade later in 1964, Beetle sales stood at a massive 276,187. It had become the country's top selling imported car with the Bug, as it is known there, becoming an integral part of American folklore. Beetle sales in America peaked in 1968 when 423,008 cars were sold, so Wolfsburg closely geared the model's evolution to the all-important US market, Volkswagen's largest outside West Germany.

Although there were thoughts about building the Beetle in America these were not pursued. However, manufacturing facilities followed on from the establishment of subsidiaries in Brazil in 1953, Australia four years later and Mexico in 1964. With these moves the Beetle effectively became an international car, following in the wheel tracks of the Model T Ford, the vehicle that had inspired its creation.

In the booming 1950s Beetle production soared. The 100,000th example was built in 1950 with the millionth car leaving the Wolfsburg production line only five years later, in 1955. With this increased demand more factory space was necessary, even though Wolfsburg was to expand to be the largest car factory under one roof in the world. Nordhoff had introduced a Beetle-based Transporter model in 1950, but its manufacture was transferred to a new plant at Hanover, opened in 1956. Two years later all engine production was concentrated there. Volkswagen also had a factory at Brunswick, opened in 1938, which was responsible for front-axle production and transmissions were manufactured at yet another plant at Kassel, opened in 1958. With the American market booming, Volkswagen established yet another manufacturing facility at the North Sea port of Emden geared specifically for the transatlantic market, and this became operational at the end of 1964.

Throughout the 1950s Nordhoff pursued his policy of mechanical refinement, though at the same time retaining the Beetle's unique character. In 1953 the distinctive split rear window was dispensed with to improve visibility, and in 1954 the car's engine capacity was increased from 1131 to 1192 cc, achieved by enlarging the bore size from 75 to 77 mm. Although this had little effect on the car's top speed of 99 km/h (62 mph), acceleration perked up somewhat. From 1955 VW introduced its model year at the beginning of August, lasting until the end of the following July. All subsequent references to model changes therefore relate to this new procedure. The next significant alteration to the Beetle's appearance came in 1958 when the window size was increased both front and rear, and for 1961 the engine underwent a major redesign, the first since 1938, although the capacity remained the same.

Far more radical was a new model, based on the Export Beetle chassis, that appeared for 1956. It was a coupé built by Karmann to a design by the Italian Ghia styling house. This provided a car of sporting appearance but without the attendant cost or complication as the mechanics were pure Beetle. A convertible version arrived in 1959 and the Karmann Ghia continued to benefit from Beetle updates until the models were discontinued in 1974.

It was not until 1961 that Volkswagen announced a model that could have been the Beetle's successor. This was the 1500, known by the factory as the Type 3 (the Beetle was Type 1 and the Transporter Type 2) and was available at the time of its appearance in saloon and Karmann Ghia forms. Almost

RIGHT *The Type 1 Karmann Ghia, based on the Export Beetle chassis, was introduced for 1956, while the cabriolet arrived in 1958. The models remained in production until 1974 and received all engine updates and refinements.*

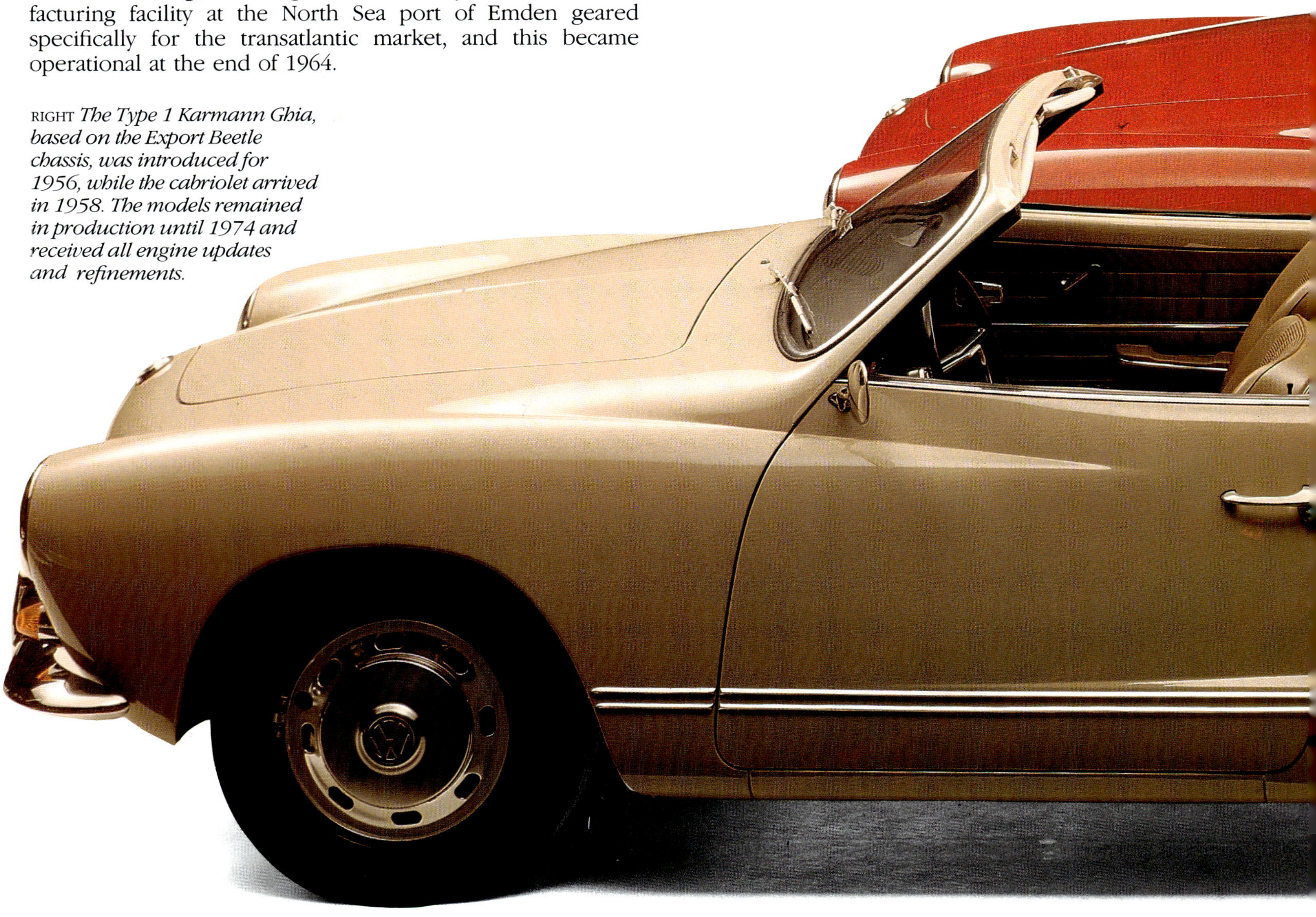

TOP *The Type 3 was also produced in Karmann Ghia form and first appeared as a 1500 in 1962. It was produced only as a coupé and lasted until 1969.*

VOLKSWAGEN 1500/1600 (TYPE 3) 1961–73	
ENGINE	
No. of cylinders	4
Bore/stroke mm	83 × 69; from 1966 85 × 69
Displacement cc	1493, 1584
Valve operation	Pushrod
Compression ratio	7.5:1, 7.7:1
Induction	Single carburettor, 1600TL twin
BHP	54 at 4200 rpm, 65 at 4600 rpm
Transmission	Four-speed
CHASSIS	
Frame	Backbone platform
Wheelbase mm	2400
Track—front mm	1310
Track—rear mm	1346
Suspension—front	Independent, trailing arms, longitudinal torsion bars
Suspension—rear	Independent, swing axle, transverse torsion bars
Brakes	Hydraulic front disc, drum rear
PERFORMANCE	
Maximum speed	125 km/h (78 mph), 135 km/h (84 mph)

TOP *The Type 3 Volkswagen, introduced in 1961, with its Beetle-inspired backbone chassis and air-cooled rear-mounted engine.*

LEFT *The Type 4 model, the 411, was introduced for 1969, with this Variant estate car version arriving in 1970. Again an air-cooled rear engine featured.*

inevitably it followed the proven formula of backbone chassis, torsion-bar suspension and rear-mounted air-cooled engine. This was of 1493 cc with an 83 × 69 mm bore and stroke, a four-cylinder *boxermotor* which differed in some respects from the Types 1 and 2 engines. Instead of the power unit's cooling fan being located at the rear of the engine it was driven off the end of the crankshaft, while the all-important oil cooler was placed on its side. This meant that the height of the engine was drastically reduced so that it was only 406 mm (16 in) high. Consequently, the car's carrying capacity was increased by the introduction of a rear boot. The 1500's styling was therefore far more up to date than the Beetle's, and in 1962 a Variant station-wagon joined the range. In 1965 came the fastback TL saloon with engine capacity increased to 1584 cc (85 × 69 mm) across the board. The slow-selling Karmann Ghia version was discontinued in 1969, although Type 3 output lasted until 1973. By this time 2.3 million examples had been built, a respectable enough figure, but the Beetle's successor had yet to be found.

Yet the 1960s were boom years for Volkswagen. It was Europe's largest manufacturer and in 1965 came the first million-Beetle year for the firm. There were also some corporate stirrings to broaden the model's appeal. For 1966 there was an increase in engine capacity to 1285 cc (77 × 69 mm) for a supplementary 1300 Beetle capable of 120 km/h (75 mph). In 1967 yet another variation appeared, a 128 km/h (80 mph) 1500 model of 1493 cc (83 × 69 mm). In 1968 came a semi-automatic option on the 1500 with the swing-axle rear suspension replaced by semi-trailing arm.

Then, in April 1968, Volkswagenwerk received a body blow with the death of Heinz Nordhoff, architect of the firm's astounding post-war expansion, at the age of 69. Tools were downed in a minute's silent tribute to the man who had steered Volkswagen through the most crucial phase of its existence. He was replaced by Dr Kurt Lotz, who had joined Volkswagen in 1967 as Nordhoff's heir apparent. He had an impressive business career, having become managing director of the Swiss-based electrical engineering giant of Brown Bouverie et Cie. He was to witness the arrival that August of yet another model with its roots firmly planted in the Beetle's by then unorthodox mechanics. The 411 was Wolfsburg's Type 4, powered by a 1679 cc (90 × 66 mm) air-cooled flat-four engine, the rear-mounted unit following the Type 3's compact layout. Suspension was by coil spring, however, with MacPherson struts at the front and semi-trailing arms at the rear. It was Volkswagen's first four-door car, but it was also offered in two-door and Variant station-wagon forms. Although capacity was increased to 1795 cc (93 × 66 mm) in 1973 along with the option of an E fuel injection version, the ungainly model never really caught on and a mere 400,000 were produced.

VOLKSWAGEN 411/412 (TYPE 4)
1968–74

ENGINE	
No. of cylinders	4
Bore/stroke mm	90 × 66, 93 × 66
Displacement cc	1679, 1795
Valve operation	Pushrod
Compression ratio	8.6:1
Induction	Single carburettor, from 1969 Bosch electronic fuel injection
BHP	80 at 4900 rpm
Transmission	Four-speed
CHASSIS	
Frame	Unitary construction
Wheelbase mm	2500
Track—front mm	1380
Track—rear mm	1350
Suspension—front	Independent, MacPherson strut
Suspension—rear	Independent, semi-trailing arms, coil springs
Brakes	Hydraulic front disc, drum rear
PERFORMANCE	
Maximum speed	152 km/h (94 mph)

ABOVE *The ungainly Type 4 was Wolfsburg's first four-door model. It was redesignated the 412 for 1973 with more streamlined bonnet and improvements to braking, suspension and gearbox.*

BELOW LEFT *Yet another attempt to replace the ageing Beetle was by the 1970 K70, a front-wheel-drive model from the recently absorbed NSU company. It lasted only until 1975, as Golf sales forged ahead.*

BELOW *The Type 3 went fastback for 1966 with a new 1584 cc engine, while front disc brakes were also introduced. Designated the 1600TL, it was to remain in production until 1973.*

The Audi and NSU take-overs

On the face of it Kurt Lotz had an unenviable job. Although these were million-Beetle years (1968–71), the model was clearly not going to go on for ever, but a successor continued to elude the automotive giant. There was a ray of light on the horizon, however, for in 1965 Volkswagenwerk AG (it had become a public company in 1960) had purchased Auto Union from Daimler-Benz. The Audi name was re-introduced and the 70 model of 1965 was the first of a new generation of front-wheel-drive cars from Ingolstadt. Then four years later, in 1969, Auto Union merged with NSU which gave Volkswagen a 60 per cent share in the new combine. It was NSU which gave Volkswagen the opportunity for its next attempt to rid itself of the Beetle albatross, and in 1970 came the front-wheel-drive K70, a rather conventional four-door saloon with 1605 cc (82 × 76 mm) four-cylinder engine and all-independent MacPherson strut suspension. It went into production at a new plant at Salzgitter but the K70 proved to be more of a flop than the Type 4. There was an increase in engine capacity to 1807 cc (87 × 76 mm) in 1973, but only 211,151 were sold before it was quietly discontinued in 1975.

VOLKSWAGEN K70
1970–5

ENGINE	
No. of cylinders	4
Bore/stroke mm	82 × 76; from 1972 87 × 76
Displacement cc	1605, 1807
Valve operation	Single overhead camshaft
Compression ratio	8:1, 9.5:1
Induction	Single carburettor
BHP	75 at 5200 rpm, 100 at 5300 rpm
Transmission	Four-speed
CHASSIS	
Frame	Unitary construction
Wheelbase mm	2690
Track—front mm	1390
Track—rear mm	1420
Suspension—front	Independent, MacPherson strut
Suspension—rear	Independent, semi-trailing arms, coil springs
Brakes	Hydraulic front disc, drum rear
PERFORMANCE	
Maximum speed	144 km/h (89 mph), 160 km/h (99 mph)

The Beetle in the meantime was continuing to evolve. In 1970 there came an additional 1302 model for 1971 specifically aimed at the all-important American market. It also represented the first radical departure from the original Porsche design through the introduction of front MacPherson struts in place of the intrusive transverse torsion bars, permitting a larger boot space. At the rear, semi-trailing arms replaced the swing axle as pioneered on the semi-automatic 1500, although torsion bars continued as the suspension medium. Also, a new 1584 cc (85 × 69 mm) engine replaced the 1500 unit and this was offered in the 1302 along with the 1300 engine. In addition there was the torsion bar suspension 1300 as well as the faithful 1200, virtually unchanged since 1961. It was also for 1971 that L and S suffixes were introduced on the Beetle range which were perpetuated until the type was finally discontinued. L indicated that factory-fitted extras had been incorporated in the model, all intended to increase the Beetle's appeal, while S denoted that the most powerful engine in that year's model range was employed. Thus the 1600-engined new MacPherson-strut Beetle was the 1302S and the 1300 version the 1302.

Kurt Lotz had turned to Porsche, who were design consultants to Volkswagenwerk, for their ideas for a Beetle replacement and the result was a saloon, coded EA 266, conceived by Ferry Porsche's nephew Ferdinand Piech. It was powered by a transversely mounted four-cylinder water-cooled engine lying flat under the rear seat. An example was spotted in Lapland with Super Beetles as guardians, thus confirming the parentage. Although EA 266 was not destined to enter production, a further Volkswagen-Porsche liaison resulted in the 914 sports car arriving in 1969. The 914/4 was powered by the Type 4's 1679 cc fuel-injected engine and assembled by Karmann, while the 914/6 used the Porsche 911 2-litre flat six which was completed at Stuttgart. This mid-engined car, with MacPherson strut front suspension and semi-trailing arm rear, was sold as a VW-Porsche in Europe and as a Porsche in America, but sales were unspectacular. A mere 3360 Porsche-engined examples were sold, although the VW-powered version went somewhat better with 114,103 produced. Output ceased in 1976.

LEFT *Beetles competing in Rallycross at Lydden Hill, 1974.*

ABOVE *The VW Porsche 914 Volkswagen-engined sports car.*

In October 1971 Kurt Lotz stepped down from the Volkswagen chairmanship to be replaced by Rudolph Leiding. He had joined VW just after the war and had served with distinction in Brazil and with Audi-NSU. One of his first actions was to cancel the complex EA 266 project, although he did initiate a sporty two-plus-two from Porsche making the maximum use of Audi and Volkswagen components. It was

ABOVE *Mexican Beetle. Since European saloon production ceased in 1978, the model has been imported from Mexico.*

BELOW *A 1972 1300 Beetle, but fitted with the more powerful 1600 engine denoted by the 'S' suffix.*

Leiding who witnessed, in February 1972, a significant anniversary as the Beetle set a new record for the world's most successful car when the 15,007,034th example left the Wolfsburg production line, overhauling Ford's figure set by the Model T in 1927. (Subsequently Ford 'discovered' an additional million and a half Model Ts and the figure was revised to approximately 16,561,850, but in any event this total was also overtaken by Volkswagen in 1973.)

The new 1302 model was only destined for a two-year production life, and for 1973 the 1302 range was replaced by the 1303 model which shared the same mechanics. There were obvious body changes with a new higher, curved windscreen while the rear wings were redesigned to accommodate new circular light clusters. It was 1973 that witnessed the most complex range of Beetle specifications ever offered when it was possible to have practically any engine size and body combination with any type of trim. However, the first of a new generation of Volkswagens had appeared in May 1973. This was the Passat, based on the in-house front-wheel-drive Audi 80, with a new hatchback body section. Available in two-, four-door and Variant forms it was offered with 1296 cc (75 × 73 mm) or 1471 cc (76 × 80 mm) engines. Suspension was by MacPherson struts at the front with semi-trailing arms and dead axle at the rear.

Then, in 1974, in a world feeling the effects of the previous year's Arab/Israeli war and spiralling oil prices, Volkswagen made a loss, the first in its history. The deficit was DM 807,000,000 (£142.5 million) and it was a year that saw Beetle production slump to 451,800 units, around half the 1971 figure. However, in May the German press had been shown yet another new model on which so many of Volkswagen's hopes were based: the front-wheel-drive Golf that had nothing in common with the Beetle apart from its 2400 mm wheelbase.

It had been in 1969, while visiting the Turin motor show, that Kurt Lotz had picked out six cars which particularly attracted his attention. On investigation they proved to be the work of a former Bertone stylist Giorgetto Giugiaro, who the previous year had established Ital Design in Turin. Therefore Giugiaro was given the assignment of styling the Beetle's replacement, and there was remarkably little difference between the mock-up which Ital Design produced and the finished product. No doubt impressed by the progress being made on the Golf design, VW commissioned a two-door sporting car from Giugiaro. The Golf-based Scirroco was offered in 1093 cc (69 × 72 mm) and 1471 cc forms.

VOLKSWAGEN BEETLE 1303S

1972–5 (Cabriolet to 1980)

ENGINE	
No. of cylinders	4
Bore/stroke mm	85 × 69
Displacement cc	1584
Valve operation	Pushrod
Compression ratio	7.5:1
Induction	Single carburettor
BHP	50 at 4000 rpm
Transmission	Four-speed

CHASSIS	
Frame	Platform
Wheelbase mm	2420
Track—front mm	1375
Track—rear mm	1350
Suspension—front	Independent, MacPherson struts
Suspension—rear	Independent, semi-trailing arms
Brakes	Hydraulic drum
PERFORMANCE	
Maximum speed	131 km/h (82 mph)

The Karmann-built Cabriolet Beetle, manufactured from 1949 to 1980. This 1978 example is fitted with optional sports-type wheels. Provided by The Patrick Collection.

AT LAST, THE GOLF

The front-wheel-drive hatchback Golf was offered with a choice of two- or four-door bodies and 1093 cc and 1471 cc four-cylinder overhead camshaft Audi engine options. Suspension was all independent with MacPherson struts at the front and rear trailing arms. It was the Golf that moved centre stage at Wolfsburg and, with the first million examples produced in 31 months, the Beetle had, at last, to make way for this front-wheel-drive compact. The last Beetle left Wolfsburg in July 1974 with output continuing at VW's Emden and Brussels factories. Demand kept up and the the 18,000,000th example left Emden in October with world-wide production still running at 2600 units a day. The range was being continually simplified, however. The 1600 cc-engined 1303 was dropped

ABOVE *The Polo, a VW version of the Audi 50, introduced in 1975.*

LEFT *The Golf, introduced in 1974.*

BELOW *The Golf GTI for 1976 with fuel-injected 1588 cc engine. Top speed was 182 km/h (113 mph). A 1780 cc unit arrived for 1983.*

VOLKSWAGEN GOLF GTI
1975–83 (first series)

ENGINE	
No. of cylinders	4
Bore/stroke mm	79 × 80; from 1982 81 × 86
Displacement cc	1588, 1780
Valve operation	Overhead camshaft
Compression ratio	9.5:1, 10:1
Induction	Bosch K-Jetronic electronic fuel injection
BHP	110 at 6100 rpm, 112 at 5500 rpm
Transmission	Four-speed

CHASSIS	
Frame	Unitary construction
Wheelbase mm	2400
Track—front mm	1390
Track—rear mm	1360
Suspension—front	Independent, MacPherson strut
Suspension—rear	Independent, trailing arm
Brakes	Hydraulic front disc, drum rear

PERFORMANCE	
Maximum speed	180 km/h (112 mph), 190 km/h (118 mph)

in 1975 and the model, along with the 1300 engine, was discontinued in the following year. Despite this the 1600 engine and MacPherson strut/semi-trailing arm rear layout soldiered on with the low-production Cabriolet. This just left the torsion bar 1200 model continuing to uphold Beetle saloon honours. In 1976 Volkswagen moved decisively into profit with the new generation of front-wheel-drive cars.

These had been joined in 1975 by the Polo, introduced at Wolfsburg the previous year as the Audi 50 and the smallest of the model range, a two-door hatchback with 895 cc (69 × 59 mm) and 1092 cc engine options. The Golf series was also continuing to expand. At the 1975 Frankfurt show Volkswagen announced its zippy GTI version of the model with new fuel-injected 1588 cc (79 × 80 mm) engine and a top speed of 182 km/h (113 mph). The 1600 engine, in carburettored form, was also available for the Golf, Passat and Scirocco.

BELOW *The Passat, a VW version of the Audi 80, appeared in 1973. This is diesel-engined.*

BOTTOM *The Golf-based Scirocco. This 1977 example had 1093, 1471 and 1588 cc options.*

VOLKSWAGEN SCIROCCO
1974–82 (first series)

ENGINE	
No. of cylinders	4
Bore/stroke mm	69 × 72, 76 × 80; from 1975 79 × 80
Displacement cc	1093, 1471, 1588
Valve operation	Single overhead camshaft
Compression ratio	8:1, 8.2:1, 9.5:1
Induction	Single carburettor; Bosch K-Jetronic fuel injection (1588)
BHP	50 at 6000 rpm, 70 at 5600 rpm, 110 at 6100 rpm
Transmission	Four-speed

CHASSIS	
Frame	Unitary construction
Wheelbase mm	2400
Track—front mm	1390
Track—rear mm	1360
Suspension—front	Independent, MacPherson strut
Suspension—rear	Independent, trailing arm
Brakes	Hydraulic front disc, drum rear

PERFORMANCE	
Maximum speed	143 km/h (89 mph), 162 km/h (101 mph), 185 km/h (115 mph)

For 1977 came a diesel version of the Golf, the first mass-produced small car in the world to be so powered and offered in 1471 and 1588 cc forms.

By this time Volkswagen had a new chairman. In January 1975 Rudolph Leiding had resigned and his place was taken by Toni Schmücker a month later. Schmücker was a former Ford executive who had shown his mettle in sectors of the ailing German steel industry. One of his first actions was to sell the Porsche-designed sporting two-plus-two coupé back to its creators who then contracted Volkswagen to build the model for them at the NSU plant at Neckarsulm, which was facing closure. The result was the Porsche 924, introduced in late 1975 and the most popular model that the Stuttgart company has ever marketed.

The Beetle was still continuing to be manufactured at Emden, but only 33,239 examples were built in Germany in 1977. Then, on 19 January 1978, the last Beetle saloon was produced—although the model was still on sale in Europe, being imported by VW from its Mexican subsidiary. This arrangement is still in force at the time of writing and the model is also being built in Brazil, with total production having exceeded the 20 million mark. Despite the demise of the German-built saloon, the Cabriolet remained in production at Karmann's Osnabrück plant and the last open version was built there on 10 January 1980. After close on 40 years of manufacture the German-built Beetle was no more.

Yet another new front-wheel-drive model, the Derby (effectively a Polo with a boot), arrived in 1977, available in 1093 and 1272 cc forms. For 1978 the Passat received a facelift, the car was lengthened, and a diesel-powered version followed in 1980. In 1979 Karmann had unveiled its Golf Cabriolet with

BELOW *The Derby was, in effect, a Polo with a boot. It was introduced in 1978.*

BOTTOM *A Golf with a boot, the Jetta arrived in 1981, and was updated in 1984.*

ABOVE *The Cabriolet version of the Golf, a spiritual successor to the Karmann-built open Beetle and also developed by the Osnabrück company, was introduced in 1979 and has been in production ever since. Initially 1588 cc powered, a 1780 cc engine arrived in 1982. The simplicity and effectiveness of the hood mechanism means that it can be lowered in a mere five seconds. The built-in roll-over bar is a distinctive feature.*

LEFT *The Santana, a booted version of the Passat, arrived in 1982. At the time of its announcement it was available with two four-cylinder engines, of 1595 and 1781 cc, while there was also a 1921 cc five-cylinder option available. The model is also assembled in China.*

1457 and 1588 cc engine options, a spiritual successor to the open Beetle which was on the point of being withdrawn from production. Later, in September, the 3,000,000th Golf came off the Wolfsburg production line, underlining its achievement as the undisputed Beetle successor.

The Golf was also making plenty of friends abroad and, up until March 1978, versions of the Golf sold in America, where it is called the Rabbit (the Passat is the Dasher), had been built at VW's Emden factory. But from then on the Rabbit was manufactured at Volkswagen's own assembly plant at Westmoreland, Pennsylvania. Although the Rabbit initially sold well, it never attained the popularity of the Beetle, and Rabbit production ceased there in June 1984. It was subsequently re-started with the re-styled Golf being produced.

Yet another 1978 introduction for Volkswagen was the four-wheel-drive cross-country 1.7-litre Iltris for the German army. Built at the Audi plant at Ingolstadt, by 1980 it was also being produced for civilian use but, more significantly, it was to form the basis of the illustrious Audi Quattro (see page 33).

Having put a boot on the Polo and called it the Derby, for 1980 Volkswagen did the same with the Golf and came up with the Jetta. Both the Passat and Scirocco were re-styled for 1982 with the former receiving the option of the 1.9-litre Audi five-cylinder unit. There was also another new model in 1982: a notchback (a booted hatchback) version of the Passat called the Santana (Quantum in America). The same year the GTI engine was uprated to 1781 (81 × 86 mm) and a turbocharged version of the 1588 cc Golf diesel was introduced. For 1984 the Golf received a long awaited facelift with a re-styled front as well as being longer and wider than its predecessor, to provide additional leg room for rear seat passengers. There is now a total of six engine options: four petrol and two diesel.

Today Volkswagen's truly international status is underlined by the Santana being assembled in China and made by Datsun in Japan. The Golf is built in Mexico, Yugoslavia and, of course, Germany. Yet Volkswagen, now running under the direction of Carl Hahn, who took over from Schmücker in 1982, is the youngest of Europe's major car makers, with this phenomenal growth achieved in a little under 40 years: a truly astounding achievement.

ABOVE *The Scirocco was re-styled for 1982 with more leg and head room for passengers. This is a 1984 GL version with 1781 cc engine.*

LEFT *The Golf, re-styled for 1984, is similar to but larger than its predecessor, with more passenger space, larger fuel tank and four petrol engine options, ranging from a 1043 cc standard model to 1781 cc fuel-injected GTI. There is also a 1588 cc diesel version.*

Index

Italic figures refer to captions to illustrations

Acknowledgements

The publishers wish to thank the following organizations and individuals for their kind permission to reproduce the photographs in this book:
Autopress, Germany 29 below, 30; Autosport 72 above; BMW (GB) Ltd 66, 68 above, 70; Neill Bruce Photographic 28 above, 212 below, 213 below left; Daimler-Benz AG 124 above, 125; Formula One Photographic/Michael Keppel 4 below left, 83 below; Geoff Goddard 4 above right, 15 centre right and below, 20 above, 21 below, 23, 24–5, 37 above inset, 101 above right, 131 above, 134 above and centre, 176, 181, 182 above, 195, 204 above; Chris Harvey 2 centre left, 2–3, 35 below, 36–7, 146 above, 186 centre; LAT 34, 71 below, 77 below, 80 left, 80–1 below, 127 centre and bottom left, 147 bottom, 150 below, 180, 182 below, 184–5, 186 above, 214 below; Roger Manku 185 above; Mercedes-Benz 122 below; George Monkhouse 102–3, 112; Don Morley 1 centre left, 2 above, 35 above; National Motor Museum, Beaulieu 3 below, 4 top and bottom, 15 above, 19 above, 26, 27, 28 below, 33 below, 38, 127 centre and bottom right, 131 below, 135, 146 below, 214 above, 218 below, 219 above and below right, 212 above; Adam Opel AG 127 top, 129–130, 132–3, 136–8, 139 below, 140 below, 141–4, 145 above centre and bottom, 151 above and below; Porsche Cars (GB) Ltd 155 above and centre, 7, 194; Cyril Posthumus 22, 25 above left, 34 below; Peter Roberts 2 below, 17 centre, 19 centre, 20 below, 25 above right, 83 top, 85 above left, 87 above, 93 top right, 101 below left, 104–5 above, 113, 128, 131 centre, 139 above, 140 above, 199 centre and below, 202 above and below, 204 below, 206 below, 207 below; Rothmans International 195 inset; Rainer Schlegelmilch 4 below right, 41 below, 64 below left, 78 above, 79 above, 81 above, 145 top and below centre, 147 top and below centre, 150 above, 151 centre, 220 above; Halwart Schrader (Wieslaw Fusaro) 15 centre left, 18–19; Nigel Snowdon and Associates 3 above, 177 below, 178–9, 184 above, 186 below; VAG (UK) Ltd 17 below, 29 above and centre, 31, 32 below, 33 above, 37 below inset, 39 below, 203 below, 205 above, 206 above and centre, 207 above, 210–11, 213 above, 218 above left and right, 219 above left; Vauxhall Motors 147 above centre, 148 inset; Volkswagenwerke AG and Audi NSU Auto Union AG 18 inset, 21 above, 32 above, 39 above, 197, 198, 200 right, 201, 208 below, 209, 212 above, 213 below right, 215, 219 below left, 220, 221; Andrew Whyte 16, 17, above, 48 top; Jonathan Wood 197 bottom, 199 above, 200 left, 203 above, 205 below, (Imperial War Museum) 208 above, 211 above.

Special photography: Laurie Caddell 97 below, 118–9 below, 119 above, 122–3 above; Ian Dawson 4 above left, 50, 55 above, 56, 57–60, 62–3, 64 top, 66–7, 78–9, 148–9, 153–5, 156–175, 177 above, 183, 187, 188–193, 216–7; Andrew Morland 97 above, 100, 116–7, 118 above, 120 above, 120–121 below; Rainer Schlegelmilch 42, 43 above, 44–7, 48 centre right, 49, 51–4, 55 below, 61, 63 right, 64–5, 68–9 below, 71 above, 72 below, 72–3, 73 below, 74–6, 77 above, 83 above left and right, 84, 85 above right and below, 86, 87 below, 88–91, 92–3, 93 inset, 94–6, 98–9, 104–5 below, 107–111, 114–5, 121 above, 124–5 below.

In addition, the publishers would also like to thank the owners who allowed their cars to be photographed (see captions). Also they would like to thank Professor Dr. Ferdinand Porsche for providing the foreword, and the following for their assistance: Laura Warren and Beverley Gale of VAG (UK) Ltd, Ken Moyes and Miriam Carroll of Vauxhall-Opel Cars, and the press offices and archives of Adam Opel AG, Audi NSU Auto Union AG, BMW AG, BMW (GB) Ltd, Daimler-Benz AG, Mercedes-Benz (UK) Ltd, Dr. Ing. h.c.F. Porsche AG, Porsche Cars (GB) Ltd, and Volkswagenwerke AG.

Audi

BMW

PORSCHE

STUTTGART